U0117236

闽

THE RIVER MIN

江

大型影像文化创作工程全纪录

THE FULL RECORD OF
THE LARGE-SCALE IMAGE CULTURAL CREATION PROJECT

主 编　崔建楠

海峡出版发行集团 | 海峡书局
THE STRAITS PUBLISHING & DIBLISHING GROUP

目录
CONTENTS

序

三个世纪的闽江

涧南

在一百多年前，有一位名叫汤姆逊的苏格兰人，从广东、台湾辗转来到福建。当他从闽江口坐船向福州城进发的时候，他看到了闽江沿岸高山上葱茏的树木植被和裸露的岩石，还有偶尔显露出来的白墙红瓦的庙宇。后来他又看见了著名的罗星塔，也看见了远远的福州城里的镇海楼。他彻底被福州的美丽迷住了，他住了下来，流连在福州城里城外。作为一位游历了中国许多地方的西方摄影家，汤姆逊赞叹闽江两岸的风光风物，他甚至认为闽江可以与欧洲的泰晤士河等几条著名河流相媲美。在常驻福州的美国传教士（茶叶商人）卢公明（著有《中国人的社会生活》一书，福建人民出版社2009年出版）的陪同下，汤姆逊曾经坐船经过水口、樟湖坂等地到达南平。作为西方纪实摄影的先驱者之一，汤姆逊回到欧洲出版了《福州与闽江》、《中国和中国人影像》等在西方世界十分著名的出版物。他的作品真实生动地再现了闽江沿岸的风景、人物、建筑、家居生活等等，让今天的人们看起来仍然十分亲切，并且极具历史价值。虽然历经百年，但这些老照片在图像质量、内容的深刻性、广泛性和艺术性方面都堪称杰作。

一百多年之后的2014年至2015年，又有一群人，一群痴迷于闽江的摄影人，用地面行走、水上漂流、空中俯瞰的方式，往返于闽江上下，从春走到了夏，又从秋走到了冬。他们比汤姆逊走得更远，他们几乎走遍了闽江上游的干流沙溪、富屯溪和建溪，以及这些干流末端的许多源头。他们还走过了闽江南平至福州的主流，以及主流上的支流古田溪、尤溪、梅溪和大樟溪。

他们拍摄了闽江全流域的河流以及消失中的古道隘口码头；拍摄了诸多清澈的源头和源头那些安静的小村。他们拍摄了河流周边优美的风景和良好的植被生态；拍摄了尚存的传统农耕方式和演变中的新农耕。他们拍摄了闽江流域复杂的民间信仰和多彩的传统民俗；拍摄了正在变化中的村庄和逐渐坍塌的传统民居。他们拍摄了深深根植于民间的美味佳肴和多姿多彩的传统手工艺；拍摄了闽江两岸各种各样的人物和他们极具时代特征的普通生活。

八千里路云和月，他们的行走已经比汤姆逊的时代要快捷方便得多，他们的记录手段也比汤姆逊时代丰富现代得多！

子在川上曰：逝者如斯夫！向汤姆逊致敬，是实施"闽江"大型影像文化工程的起因，也是出版这本大型画册《闽江》的起因。

涛涛闽江，流逝千年。从汤姆逊的闽江到今天的闽江，岁月变迁。幸好一百多年前有汤姆逊，为我们留下了那个时代闽江的许多影像，让今天的我们乃至今后的人们可以从这些珍贵影像中去探索那个时代的中国、那个时代的福建。

而如今的中国，是一个剧烈变化的时代，是一个进步巨大的时代，福建亦然。

历史需要用影像将这样的巨变和进步保留下来，为历史留下一份纪录、一份档案、一份真实。

再过一个百年，这些记录都将成为历史，就像我们今天看汤姆逊，一百年后的人们也会看我们这些关于闽江的影像纪录。

Preface

The River Min, with a
history of three centuries

Jian Nan

Over a hundred years ago, a Scottish named Thomson came to Fujian through Guangdong and Taiwan. When he set out for Fuzhou by boat, he saw the verdant vegetation and bare rocks as well as some partly visible temples on the mountain along the bank of the River Min. Later when he saw the well-known Luoxing Tower and Zhenhai Tower in Fuzhou, he was fascinated by the beautiful scenes of Fuzhou and decided to stay there. As a western photographer who visited many places in China, Thomson highly praised the scenery of the River Min and believed it could be compared with the Thames in Europe. Accompanied by the American missionary Justus Doolittle, Thomson traveled to Shuikou, Zhanghuban and Pingnan. As one of the western documentary photography pioneers, Thomson published "Fuzhou and the River Min" and "China and the Chinese Image" in Europe. His works vividly recorded the scenery, people, buildings and home life along the River Min, which of great historical value. Although the pictures were taken a hundred years ago, they remain classical with high quality image, insightful contents and artistic value.

One hundred years later, in 2014 and 2015, a group of photographers who are also fascinated by the River Min, walked around the river all through the year. They went further than Thomson. They went to the main streams of upper Mingjiang River, such as the Shaxi River, the Futunxi River and the Jianxi River and the sources of these rivers. They also went to the main stream from Nanping to Fuzhou as well as the branches along the main streams.

They photographed the whole basin of the River Min and the disappearing ancient passes and docks, the clear river sources and the quiet village along the rivers as well as the ecological vegetation. They also photographed the traditional farming and the new farming, various folk religions and traditional folk customs and the changing village and the falling traditional residence. They also photographed the traditional folk cuisine and crafts as well as ordinary daily life of various people.

They can walk faster than Thomson and have more modern means for recording.

Confucius said: "Thus things flow away". To honor Thomson is the motive for the image culture project "The River Min" and this picture album.

Time has changed since the age of Thomson. It is fortunate to have Thomson to keep the images of the River Min over a hundred years' ago, which enable us to explore China and Fuzhou at that time through these precious pictures.

Today's China is undergoing a dramatic change. Great progress is made in China as well in Fujiang.

The changes and progresses in history need to be kept through images as documents, records and realities.

Another hundred years later, all these records will become history, just like what we see Thomson today. People a hundred years' later will see what we keep today.

二十世纪初，福州万寿桥边停泊着的连家船 ／ 汤姆·希拉摄于1900年（影易时代提供）
The picture of Wanshou Bridge in 1900 by Tom Hira.

【福州台江万寿桥】

十

Wanshou Bridge, Fuzhou

横跨于闽江之上的万寿桥建于元代，元之前的北宋元祐八年（1093年）为福州太守王祖道建的浮桥。北宋崇宁二年（1103年），又将浮桥改为石墩桥。元大德七年（1303年），万寿寺僧王法助得到元成宗铁木耳的嘉许，募集了数百万贯资金，奉旨把万寿桥改建成简支石梁石板桥。

万寿桥前后建造共花了19年时间，到1322年（元至治二年）才竣工，桥长391米，宽4.5米，共87孔。后人为了纪念万寿寺和尚王法助的功绩，便把这条大桥命名为万寿桥。

万寿桥的建造是世界桥梁史上的奇迹，在当时的技术条件下，桥墩如何在激流中矗立；长九米，重逾40吨的大石梁怎样搭建，都成为后人未知的谜。撰写《中国科学技术史》的李约瑟先生通过调查得知人们采用的是"浮运法"。闽江万寿桥近海，潮水每天变化，工匠等到涨潮时，把巨石用木排运到桥墩跟前，借用涨潮的浮力，把石块放置在石墩上便可造成。这是1053年建造泉州洛阳桥时人们发明的，约百年之后万寿桥也采用此法建造。

1930年，万寿桥改为公路桥，在原有桥墩上用混凝土加高两米，路面和桥栏均采用钢筋混凝土，工程由日商"大和工业合资会社"承建。

1949年以后，因福州解放，此桥改名为"解放大桥"。1970年，解放大桥采取桥上架桥的形式，加高四米、加宽桥面两米。

1994年，因闽江洪水的冲击，解放大桥下万寿桥桥墩崩离原位。1995年拆除万寿桥，重建解放大桥，一代名桥就此消失。

万寿桥建成近六百年后，1900年汤姆·希拉给万寿桥留下了这帧珍贵的影像。

2014 年的解放大桥以及台江和仓前（烟台山）的夜景　/　阮任艺 摄

Liberation Bridge in 2014 and the night scene of Taijiang River and Yantai Mountain (by Ruan Renyi)

Wanshou Bridge was built across the River Min in Yuan Dynasty. Before Yuan Dynasty, it was originally built as a raft bridge in the Northern Song Dynasty (1093) and renovated as a stone bridge in 1103. In 1303, Wanshou Temple rebuilt it on the imperial orders into a slab bridge with a funding of several millions cash.

It took a total of 19 years to build the bridge, which was completed in 1322. The bridge was 391 meters long, 4.5 meters wide and had 87 openings. It is named later as Wanshou Bridge in honor of the monk in Wanshou Temple.

The building of Wanshou Bridge is a wonder of world's bridge history. How the piers could stand in torrent and how the 40-ton stone bean could be set up were mysteries to people. Later it is known as "floating transportation" from the book "The History of Chinese Science and Technology". Giant stone was transported to the piers by the force of rising tide. This method was invented when building Luoyang Bridge in 1053 and used again for Wanshou Bridge around a hundred years later.

In 1930, Wanshou Bridge was renovated as highway bridge. Two meters' concrete was added on the original piers. Road surface and bridge railings were built in concrete. It was constructed by a Japanese company.

After 1949, Fuzhou was liberated and therefore the bridge was named as "Liberation Bridge". In 1970, it was heightened by four meters and widened by two meters.

In 1994, the piers were moved away due to the flood and Wanshou Bridge was torn down in 1995.

The picture of Wanshou Bridge in 1900 by Tom Hira, 600 years after it was completed.

汤姆逊 1870 年前后拍摄的闽江金山寺（影易时代提供）   Jinshan Temple (by Thomson in 1870)

【金山寺】
＋
Jinshan Temple

2014 年的金山寺 / 那兴海 摄
Jinshan Temple in 2014 (by Na Xinghai)

福州金山寺，坐落在洪塘镇乌龙江中一块石阜上，始建于宋朝绍兴年间。据《洪塘志》载："金山江心矗起，形象印浮水面，似江南镇江，故曰小金山。有塔七级，故曰金山塔寺。"金山寺虽然面积很小，却"五脏俱全"，除了"殿宇"之外还有一座七级石塔。金山寺虽然在 1934 年重建，但石塔仍是宋代遗存。

金山寺又被汤姆逊称为"塔锚地"（Pagoda Anchorage），在照片中，汤姆逊有意营造出的空白，以及早期摄影术造成的长时间曝光形成水面的静止，让小小寺庙看起来彷佛与世隔绝。这种空灵又带来一种近乎完美的宁静感。

Jinshan Temple of Fuzhou, located in the Wulongjiang River of Hongtang Town, was built in Song Dynasty. According to Hongtang Annals, the temple got its name from the image reflected in the river. Although Jinshan temple covers a small area, it has all functions. Besides temple, there is also a seven-stage stone pagoda, which remains after Jinshan Temple was rebuilt in 1934.

Jinshan Temple is also called as "Pagoda Anchorage" by Thomson. In the picture, the white space and the stillness of water created an isolation and perfect calmness of the temple.

【永泰方广岩（永福寺）】

+

Fangguangyan Temple (Yongfu Temple)

据《三山志》载，北宋建隆二年（961年），有僧人垒石为台，叠石为阶，在洞内建方广岩院，以该洞方正宽广，遂取佛经第十部类"方广"命名，寓意深长，又称方广岩、方广洞天。现洞内保留有古石阶，垂带石上镌刻"宋淳熙丙午（1186年）谨题"。

同治十年（1871年），汤姆逊在朋友的推荐下，顺闽江入大樟溪，来到方广岩寺。令汤姆逊印象深刻的有寺庙的建筑风格："那宽广的屋檐、雕花的屋顶和鲜艳的花栏杆，眼前的一切，是我从未见过，也从未梦到过的。"回忆在方广岩的那段时间，他说每天早上，他都在僧侣念经的声音或者撞钟的声音里醒来。汤姆逊为方广岩拍下了多张图片，成为他闽江影像里最精彩的作品。由于语言的原因，他将其中敲钟一幅标记为"元福寺"，又有后人译为"元府寺"。因为永泰县曾经为永福县，所以历史上也有人称方广岩为永福寺，以致后人在考据上多费了一些周折。

汤姆逊的方广岩图片最有价值的是，一百多年前的影像里的一些细节，至今保留。如柱子上的木质对联等，时光浓缩，令人唏嘘。

2015年仲夏，我们来到方广岩，将汤姆逊的作品和如今的寺庙一一对比。地面改变了，铺了红色的斗底砖；庙的门扇没有了，汤姆逊喜爱的"精美的雕花"没有了。经过常仁师傅指点，那钟也不是原来的了，因为钟上面的铭文变化了。挂钟的位置也改变了。

我们让常仁师傅模仿汤姆逊的作品拍摄，发现师傅敲钟的姿势和汤姆逊拍摄的敲钟师傅的姿势对不上了，因为钟挂得更高了。

汤姆逊拍摄的永福寺（影易时代提供）
Yongfu Temple (by Thomson)

永泰方广岩常仁师傅 / 涧南 摄
Master Changren at Fangguangyan Temple (by Jian Nan)

According to historical records, a monk built the temple in a spacious cave in 961. "Fangguang" in Chinese means broad and spacious. The original stone steps in the cave remains till today.

In 1871, Thomson visited Fangguangyan Temple, which impressed him very much by its architectural style. "The broad eave, carved roof and colorful handrail have never been seen and dreamed before", said Thomson. He took a lot of pictures of the temple, which become the masterpiece of his works. Due to the language obstacle, he named one of the picture of bell tolling as "Yuanfu Temple". As Yongtai county was called "Yongfu" county, the temple is also called "Yongfu Temple".

The most valuable is the details of the pictures, such as the wooden couplets on the pillar, which remind us the past time.

When we visited Fangguanyan Temple in the summer of 2015, there are many changes from the picture by Thomson. The floor has been changed into red; there is no more temple door; and the beloved carving is gone; the bell is no longer the original one.

We asked Master Changren to imitate the position of the monk who tolled the bell in the picture of Thomson, but he couldn't make it as the bell is hung higher.

01

02

01　　1870 年的延平全景图 / 约翰·汤姆逊 摄
　　The panorama of Yanping district in 1870 (by John Thomson)

02　　建溪由画面右侧流向南平的延平区，在画面左侧与富屯溪汇合，为闽江始 / 阮任艺 摄
　　The Jianxi River joins the Futunxi River on the left and flows from the right into Yanping district, which is the beginning of the River Min. (by Ruan Renyi)

【延平】

+

Yanping

古延平初隶属闽越国，后属侯官地。三国时期，延平为东吴辖地，隶属建安郡，晋太元四年改为延平县，古延平至今已有1800余年的历史。

汤姆逊1870年在常驻福州的茶叶商人卢公明的陪同下，沿闽江前往延平，拍下了延平古城的旧影。汤姆逊本来是要深入闽北内地的，因为在延平的意外历险受伤（失足滑坠，险些掉入三十米的悬崖下面），中止了他的行程。

三个世纪之后，"闽江"大型影像文化创作工程的摄影家们运用现代航拍手段，拍摄下延平的新景象。

The ancient Yanping was under the jurisdiction of Minyue Kingdom. During the Three Kingdoms, Yanping was governed by Dongwu. It was named Yanping County in Jin Dynasty and has a history of over 1800 years.

Accompanied by the American tea trader Justus Doolittle, Thomson traveled to Yanping along the River Min and took pictures of the ancient city. He planned to go into the interior of Northern Fujian and had to cancelled his trip due to the injury in an accident.

Three centuries later, the photographers of the image cultural creation project "the River Min" took pictures of the new looks of Yanping through modern aerial photographing.

01

01   作为中国近代文明发源地之一的福州马尾，因为马尾船政的缘由，多次被西方摄影家拍摄。特别是被世界航海界称之为"中国塔"的罗星塔，总是如同主角一般出现在这些图片中。1918 年，西德尼·戴维·甘博摄（影易时代提供）

      Mawei in Fuzhou, as one of the places where Chinese modern civilization originated, has been photographed by many western photographers for its shipping administration. Luoxing Tower, which is called "China Tower" in international navigation circle, appears as the main actor in these pictures. 1918 (by Sidney David Gamble)

02   三个世纪后，"闽江"摄影家再次以罗星塔为地标拍摄，人们可以看到，宝塔屹立、江水依旧，世间却发生了巨大变化 / 阮任艺 陈映辉 摄

      Three centuries later, the photographers of "the River Min" photograph Luoxing Tower as the landmark again. People can still see the unchanged tower and river though the whole world has been greatly changed. (by Ruan Renyi and Chen Yinghui)

金光普照福州城 / 那兴海 摄　Fuzhou city in sunshine (by Na Xinghai)

第一章 + 生生不息的千里闽江

闽江,从武夷山脉无数个沟壑山涧里走来,由滴水而成溪流,潺潺湲湲、跳跳荡荡、汇成大河一路奔腾向东海而去。

闽江有个正源,在建宁县张家山自然村的山坳里。和许多大江大河只有唯一的源头不同,闽江还有无数个源头。武夷山脉有多少棵大树,闽江就有多少个源头。去看地图你就会发现,闽江主流好像一棵大树的树干,而闽江干流沙溪建溪富屯溪以及这些干流上漫生着的那些溪流的"枝蔓",如同密集的树根,牢牢扎在武夷山脉那些山岭之间。

大地宏伟,闽山巍峨。北上的太平洋暖湿气流被武夷山脉阻挡,化为雨雾,浇灌山霖,汇为溪水、哺育子民。

由此,闽江被福建百姓尊为"母亲河"!

闽江是清澈的、是碧绿的,虽然一场暴雨就会让它浑浊,但是雨过天晴,那溪流江水转瞬又复澄澈。

闽江又是柔曼的:母亲之臂弯、母亲之明瞳、母亲之细语、母亲之胸怀;臂弯为之枕、明瞳是为灯、细语复叮咛、胸怀乃博大。

福建人有谁敢说,他不是喝着闽江水长大的呢?

The River Min

The River Min, running all the way from the ravines of Mount Wuyi to the East China Sea. The source of the river lies in the natural village of Zhangjiashan in Jianning County. Unlike other rivers, the River Min actually has numerous sources. Looking at a map, you can see that the mainstream of the River Min like a big tree trunk and its tributaries deeply root into Mount Wuyi with many streams growing along the Shaxi River, Jianxi River and Futunxi River.

Blocked by Mount Wuyi, the warm airflows from the Pacific Ocean turn into rains and fogs and form streams, nurturing the people of the land.

The River Min is called "the mother river" by the Fujian people. It is clear and green, though turns muddy after big storms. It is gentle, caring and great like a mother. None of the Fujianese dares to say he did not grow up by drinking the water from the river.

01　　沙溪从建宁县均口乡张家山自然村发源，由北至南经过宁化清流在永安再拐向东经过三明沙县汇入闽江 / 陈伟凯 摄
The Shaxi River, originating from the natural village of Zhangjiashan in Jianning County, runs south to Yong'an and then east to join the River Min in Sanming Sha County. (by Chen Weikai)

02　　闽江正源摩崖石刻 / 涧南 摄
Cliff inscription at the source of the River Min (by Jian Nan)

03　　从石缝中汩汩而出的源头之水 / 涧南 摄
The source of water (by Jian Nan)

02

03

闽江，中国福建省最大独流入海（东海）的河流，发源于福建省建宁县均口镇的张家山自然村，根据"唯远为源"的原则，闽江以沙溪为正源，全长 562 千米，以福州市连江县长门村江面为终点汇入东海。闽江正源就在画面中上部梯田尽头的山坳里，源头小溪在画面右边蜿蜒而下 / 阮任艺 陈映辉 摄

The River Min, the largest river in Fujian flowing into the sea (the East China Sea), originates from the natural village of Zhangjiashan in Jianning County. The total length of the River Min is 562 kilometers. The Shaxi River, its source river, comes from the hills at the end of the terraced fields in the middle of the picture and winds down to the right side of the picture. (by Ruan Renyi and Chen Yinghui)

闽江正源台田溪上闽江第一桥，远处山峰为九具石 / 那兴海 摄
The first bridge on the source river, with the peak Jiuxianshi in the distance (by Na Xinghai)

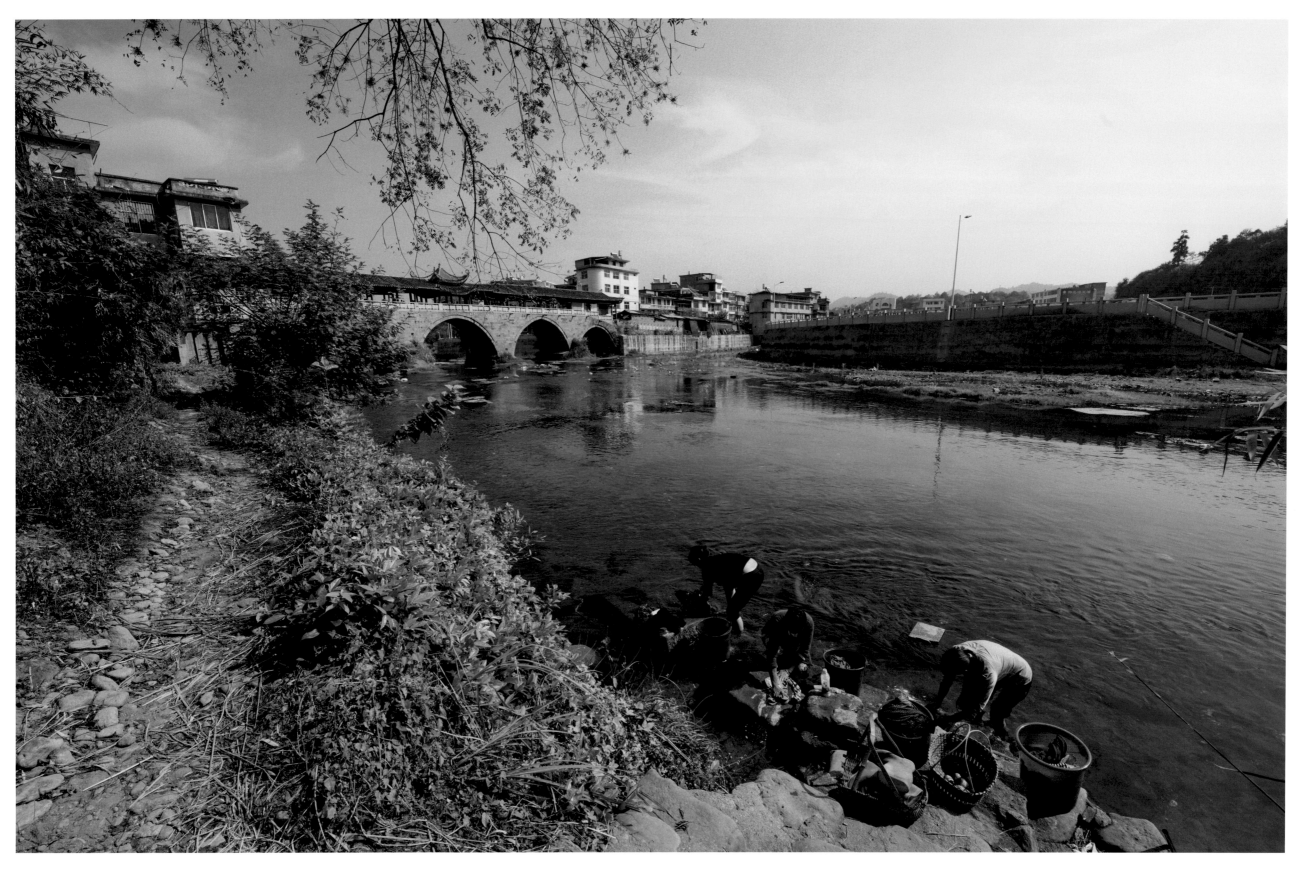

台田溪流经宁化县水茜乡进入水茜溪，水茜乡廊桥下当地妇女还保持在溪中浣衣的古老习惯 / 赖小兵 摄
The Taitianxi River joins the Shuixixi River, where the local women wash clothes as a tradition.（by Lai Xiaobing）

沙溪上游九龙溪沙芜乡洞口村河段是一个漂亮的大回旋，很像雅鲁藏布江大拐弯的缩小版，这片区域生态良好，而画面左侧公路的建设将打破其原始状态 / 阮任艺 陈映辉 摄

The big turn of the upstream of the Shaxi River in Dongkou village is like a scaled-down version of the Yarlung Zangbo River. This area maintains a good ecological environment. The construction of the road on the left side of the picture will destroy its initial conditions. (by Raun Renyi and Chen Yinghui)

安砂水库（又名九龙湖）地处闽江干流沙溪上游的九龙溪，是福建省安砂水力发电厂建坝截流汇堰而成的人工湖，湖面山清水秀，水质清冽，自然环境优良。安砂水库全景 / 阮任艺 陈映辉 摄

The Ansha Reservoir (also named as Jiulong Lake) lies in the Jiulongxi River. It is a man-made lake with clear and clean water. The panorama of the Ansha Reservoir (by Ruan Renyi and Chen Yinghui)

九龙溪水道水流平缓，客船在清流城关和嵩口码头每天往返一次 / 阮任艺 摄
On the gentle flow of the Jiulongxi River, passenger ship takes a return trip each day from Qingliu to Songgao dock. (by Ruan Renyi)

　　九龙溪上游翠江在客家祖地宁化由支流西溪与东溪（水茜溪）汇合而
成，东溪流过石壁的沃野良田 / 阮任艺　陈映辉 摄
　　The upper Jiulongxi River is joined by the Xixi River and the Dongxi
River, which flows across the farmland. (by Ruan Renyi and Chen Yinghui)

九龙溪在流经永安之后称为沙溪，永安桃源洞（画面右侧）及永安（画面左侧）全景 ／ 阮任艺 陈映辉 摄
The Jiulongxi River is called the Shaxi River after flowing through Yong' an. The panorama of Taoyuan Cave (right) and Yong' an (left) (by Ruan Renyi and Chen Yinghui)

01   九龙溪青州村河段的锦绣田园 / 阮任艺 陈映辉 摄
The farmland in Qingzhou Village by the Jiulongxi River (by Ruan Renyi and Chen Yinghui)

02   永安桃源洞全景 / 阮任艺 摄
The panorama of Taoyuan Cave of Yong'an (by Ruan Renyi)

沙溪流经三明市 / 阮任艺 陈映辉 摄

The Shaxi River flows across Sanming City (by Ruan Renyi and Chen Yinghui)

01

02

03

01   三明市沙溪河边步道 / 涧南 摄
      The footpath along the Shaxi River of Sanming City (by Jian Nan)

02   远眺沙溪口水电站 / 那兴海 摄
      Shaxi Hydropower Station in the distance (by Na Xinghai)

03   沙溪（图右上）从建宁县张家山自然村发源，流经宁化县、清流县、永安市、三明市、沙县后在南平延平区
      的王台乡与富屯溪（图右）合流，以西溪（图左）之名流向南平市区 / 阮任艺 陈映辉 摄
      Originating from Zhangjiashan in Jianning, the Shaxi River (upper right), after flowing through Ninghua, Qingliu,
      Yong'an, Sanming and Shaxian County, meets the Futunxi River (left) in Wangtai Village of Yanping District and forms
      the Xixi River (right) running towards Nanping City (by Ruan Renyi and Chen Yinghui)

01

01   富屯溪是闽江的中源，源出光泽县司前乡岱坪村，到延
      平区王台乡沙溪口汇合沙溪，是闽江上游的三大河系之一，
      由金溪、杭溪、杉岭溪、樵溪等五十多条溪流汇集而成。富
      屯溪邵武市拿口镇一带 / 陈伟凯 摄
      The Futunxi River is the middle source of the River Min
      and joins the Shaxi River at Yanping. It is one of the three river
      systems of the Mingjiang upriver, converged by over 50 steams.
      Nakou town of Shaowu City by the Futunxi River (by Chen
      Weikai)

02   富屯溪上游西溪发源自邵武桂林乡盖竹村巫山小组巫山
      北坡 / 阮任艺 摄
      The source of the Xixi River: Gaizhu village, Guilin town of
      Shaowu City (by Ruan Renyi)

光泽县崇仁乡富屯溪北溪流域，远处山峰为乌君山 / 阮任艺 陈映辉 摄　The north basin of the Futunxi River and Wujunshan Mountain in the distance (by Ruan Renyi and Chen Yinghui)

富屯溪邵武云灵山河段 / 阮任艺 陈映辉 摄　The Futunxi River at Yunlingshan Mountain of Shaowu City (by Ruan Renyi and Chen Yinghui)

01

01 富屯溪与金溪交汇处的顺昌县 / 陈伟凯 摄
Shunchang County, the conjunction of the Futunxi River and the Jinxi River (by Chen Weikai)

02 顺昌县富屯溪与金溪交汇处，一艘装了动力的渔舟划过水面 / 李世雄 摄
Shunchang County, the conjunction of the Futunxi River and the Jinxi River, with a fishboat passing by (by Li Shixiong)

金溪（画面左侧）与富屯溪（画面中上）在顺昌合流，在顺昌城关画了一个"S"形，流向南平 / 阮任艺 陈映辉 摄
The Jinxi River (left) and the Futunxi River (up middle) converge at Shunchang in a shape of "S" (by Ruan Renyi and Chen Yinghui)

01

01   福建第一高峰金铙山既是闽江正源沙溪的发源地，也是金溪的发源
      地，正源发源于南坡，金溪发源于北坡。金铙山飞霞 / 陈伟凯 摄
      Jinnaoshan Mountain, the highest mountain in Fujian, is the source
      for both the Shaxi River and the Jinxi River. Jinnaoshan Mountain (by Chen
      Weikai)

02   金溪上游建宁县均口乡的鸳鸯湖，白鹭蹁跹 / 吴寿华 摄
      Egrets at the Yuanyang Lake of the upper Jinxi River (by Wu Shouhua)

02

金溪河段建宁县高峰村的锦绣田园 / 阮任艺 陈映辉 摄

Farmland of Gaofeng Village of Jianning County by the Jinxi River (by Ruan Renyi and Chen Yinghui)

01

01   金溪在大田乡流域有一个美丽的长 "U" 形拐弯，那里人迹罕至，生态绝佳 / 阮任艺 陈映辉 摄
A beautiful U-turn of the Jinxi River at Datian Village (by Ruan Renyi and Chen Yinghui)

02   夕照大金湖 / 阮任艺 陈映辉 摄
Sunset glow at Dajin Lake (by Ruan Renyi and Chen Yinghui)

大金湖是金溪上的明珠，由池潭水库积水而成，大金湖碧水丹山，是福建省著名旅游区 / 阮任艺 陈映辉 摄
Dajin Lake, a well-known tourist spot in Fujian, is like a pearl on the Jinxi River. (by Ruan Renyi and Chen Yinghui)

大金湖旅游区包含了大金湖、上清溪、水上丹霞、罗汉山、泰宁古城，于 2005 年 2 月 11 日成为联合国教科文组织命名的世界地质公园的核心组成部分，成为继武夷山世界遗产之后又一个世界级的旅游胜地。大金湖三仙峰 / 阮任艺 陈英辉 摄

Dajin Lake tourist area, including Dajin Lake, the Shangqing River, Luohan Mountain and Taining ancient city, is a core component of Taining World Geopark recognized by UNESCO on Feb 11 2005. It is another world level tourist area in Fujian after Wuyishanis listed as World Natural Heritage and World Cultural Heritage. Sanjian Peak and Dajin Lake (by Ruan Renyi and Chen Yinghui)

金溪经过池潭水库大坝后，溪水流经池潭村，流向将乐县 / 阮任艺 陈映辉 摄

The Jinxi River goes through the Chitan Reservoir to Jiangle County (by Ruan Renyi and Chen Yinghui)

01   金溪将乐河段回头山，山地与河流形成了一个十分独特
的八卦形状 / 吴寿华 摄
      The Jinxi River at Huitoushan Mountain in Jiangle (by Wu
Shouhua)

02   金溪流经将乐后，与富屯溪合流，流向顺昌 / 涧南 摄
      The Jinxi River joins the Futunxi River after flowing
through Jiangle and flows to Shunchang. (by Jian Nan)

02

01   建溪与西溪交汇处的南平市延平区，右下为富屯溪下游西溪，左为建溪，右上为闽江 / 陈伟凯 摄
The Jianxi River and the Xixi River converge at Nanping City. The Xixi River (low right) The Jianxi River (left)
The River Min (upper right) (by Chen Weikai)

02   武夷山分水关既是与江西的分界，也是建溪众多溪流的发源之地，303 省道越过武夷山脉垭口通往福建
腹地。白色省道左边小溪是崇阳溪源头，画面中部远处小盆地是大安村黄连坑自然村 / 阮任艺 陈映辉 摄
Mount Wuyi is the dividing line of Jiangxi and Fujian and also the sources for many rivers. 303 provincial
road goes into Fujian through Mount Wuyi. The stream on the left side of the white provincial road is the source
of the Chongyangxi River. The little basin in the distance is the natural village of Da' an Village. (by Ruan Renyi
and Chen Yinghui)

01　　崇阳溪源头洋庄乡大安村黄连坑自然村源自闽赣交界武夷山分水关的清澈溪流，无名拱桥是古代出省驿道必经之路，也可称之为建溪第一桥 / 涧南 摄

The source of the Chongyangxi River lies in Da' an Village. The nameless arch bridge is the only way to ancient post road, and is also the first bridge on the Jianxi River (by Jian Nan)

02　　大安源位于武夷山市北部洋庄乡大安村，也是崇阳溪源头之一，大安源包括黄岗山大峡谷、龙归源、泰平洋水上广场等六大景区，景区内自然生态原始。大安源大金龙瀑布 / 袁荣祥 摄

Da' an source is located in Da' an Village and it is the source of the Chongyangxi River. The source include six scenic spots such as Huanggangshan gorge, Longgui source, Taipingyang water square. Dajinlong Waterfall (by Yuan Rongxiang)

　　桐木溪源于武夷山自然保护区的黄岗山，为九曲溪的源头之一，是建溪最清澈最纯净的水源 / 赖小兵 摄

The Tongmuxi River rises from Huanggangshan mountain, the natural conservation area of Mount Wuyi and is the most clean source of the Jianxi River. (by Lai Xiaobing)

　　梅溪，因发源于梅岭而称之为梅溪，是崇阳溪重要支流。梅溪上游叫上梅，下游叫下梅，下梅村因此得名。梅溪不仅养育过北宋著名词人柳永、南宋理学家朱熹，还是清代著名的茶市，"万里茶路"的起点。梅溪流经下梅村 / 阮任艺 陈映辉 摄

　　The Meixi River is an important tributary of the Chongyangxi River. The upstream is called "Shangmei" and the downstream is called "Xiamei", which gives the name "Xiamei" Village. Here was also the well-known "tea market" of Qing Dynasty. The Meixi River flows through Xiamei Village. (by Ruan Renyi and Chen Yinghui)

　　崇阳溪发源于武夷山脉崇安县岚谷乡铜钹山，源流上无数沟壑山涧汇成小溪汇入，经吴屯，武夷山市区（崇安）过武夷山景区（三姑）即为崇阳溪，九曲溪汇合其中 / 阮任艺 陈映辉 摄

　　The Chongyangxi River rises from Tongbo Mountain in Chong'an County. Many streams from ravines converge into the Chongyangxi River， after running through Wutun, Wuyishan City and Wuyishan scenic area (Sangu). The Jiuquxi River also joins them together. (by Ruan Renyi and Chen Yinghui)

　　九曲溪位于武夷山核心景区的峰岩幽谷之中，因它有三弯九曲之胜，故名为九曲溪。画面右面中部蓝色屋顶为天游峰，画面左侧溪水"U"左角处为玉女峰。画面上部远处为星村 / 阮任艺 陈映辉 摄

　　The Jiuquxi River winds around the mountains and rocks in Mount Wuyi. The blue roof in the middle of the right side picture is called Tianyou Peak, and Yunv Peak is on the left side corner of the U-turn. The distance is Xingcun Village. (by Ruan Renyi and Chen Yinghui)

　　九曲溪是发源于武夷山脉主峰黄岗山西南麓的溪流，位于武夷山核心景区的峰岩幽谷之中。武夷山有三十六峰，九十九岩，峰岩交错，溪流纵横，九曲溪贯穿其中，蜿蜒十五华里。

　　九曲溪山挟水转，水绕山行，每一曲都有不同景致的山水画意。"溪流九曲泻云液，山光倒浸清涟漪"形象地勾画出了九曲溪的秀丽轮廓 / 阮任艺 陈映辉 摄

The Jiuquxi River, rising from streams at the southwestern foot of Huanggang Mountain in Mount Wuyi, winds in the rocks and deep valleys of the core scenic area of Mount Wuyi, which has 36 peaks and 99 rocks. The Jiuquxi runs for about 15 li among these rocks and valleys and got its name "Jiuqu" meaning many bends. Each turns and bends of the Jiuquxi River elaborates different views and landscapes (by Ruan Renyi and Chen Yinghui)

武夷山星村远眺 / 阮任艺 陈映辉 摄
Mount Wuyi by Xingcun Village (by Ruan Renyi and Chen Yinghui)

01

01　　建溪主流南浦溪发源于武夷山脉和仙霞岭支脉处的浦城县忠信乡雁塘村苏州岭（柘岭），源流为柘溪，流经忠信、仙阳、万安至南浦溪　/　吴寿华 摄
　　　The Nanpuxi River, the mainstream of the Jianxi River, originates from Pucheng County. (By Wu Shouhua)

02　　观前是南浦溪上的重要码头，是古代闽江水路运输的最北端。由观前村上岸，经渔梁、九牧、枫岭关、仙霞关，一路北行，直到浙江江山的清湖镇，才走完出省的道路。观前古村俯瞰　/　阮任艺 摄
　　　Guanqian, an important wharf on the Nanpuxi River, located in the extreme north of ancient waterway along the River Min. Bird's-eye view of ancient Guanqian Village (by Ruan Renyi)

03　　南浦溪边观前村依然还保留着原始的生活状态　/　涧南 摄
　　　The original state of life in Guanqian Village by the Nanpuxi River. (by Jian Nan)

01

01   麻阳溪流经黄坑、麻沙、莒口等乡镇，由建阳汇入建溪 / 吴寿华 摄
The Mayangxi River meets the Jianxi River in Jianyang after flowing through Huangkeng, Masha and lvkou. (by Wu Shouhua)

02   汇集崇阳溪和麻阳溪后，建溪由建阳流向建瓯。建阳鲤鱼山上建于明万历三十年的多宝塔 / 吴寿华 摄
The Chongyangxi River and the Mayangxi River converge into the Jianxi River, which flows from Jianyang to Jian'ou. Pagoda Duobao was built on Liyu Mountain in Ming Dynasty. (by Wu Shouhua)

01 古时候，松溪河两岸苍松茂密，有"百里松荫"之称，松溪河因此而得名。松溪源头之一溪东乡溪源村 / 苏荣钦 摄

The Songxihe River got its name by the thick pine forest along its banks. The source of the Songxihe River: Xiyuan Village (by Su Rongqin)

02 历史上建溪水流湍急，礁石密布，在建瓯城关松溪建溪汇合处还留下了一处礁石激流的地方 / 涧南 摄

Rocks at the junction of the Songxi River and the Jianxi River in Jian'ou City. (by Jian Nan)

03 大布古渡是松溪古代五大古渡口之一，是舟楫往来、商贾密集的"大埠市" / 涧南 摄

Dabu ancient ferry was one of the five ancient ferries. (by Jian Nan)

04 从建瓯水南塔北望，松溪（右上）和建溪（左上）在建瓯汇合后，流向延平 / 阮任艺 摄

Viewed from the Shuinan Tower in Jian'ou, the Songxi River (upper right) joins the Jianxi River (upper left) at Jian'ou and flows to Yanping. (by Ruan Renyi)

建溪黯淡滩是历史上建溪最险之处，行船至此，稍有不慎，多颠覆，所以古代舟行者至此多登陆避之。过了黯淡滩，延平就在面前了 / 阮任艺 摄
Andan Rapids was the most dangerous place of the Jianxi River in history. Many boats capsized here. Yanping can be seen after Andan Rapids. (by Ruan Renyi)

延平湖系 1993 年水口水电站建成蓄水后在延平区建溪富屯溪汇合处形成的一个人工湖，因南平古称延平府而得名。延平湖夜景 ／ 阮任艺 陈映辉 摄

Yanping Lake is a man-made lake in Yanping district when Shuikou hydropower station was built in 1993. The night scene of Yanping Lake （by Ruan Renyi and Chen Yinghui）

延平区大洲岛是闽江上游的一个沙洲，历史上曾经是郑成功的水师营盘，二十世纪六十年代是南方最大的木材转运中心，画面右上的弧形桥梁是当年的铁路专线 ／ 阮任艺 摄

Dazhou Island is a sand island on the upper Mingjiang River. It was a navy camp of Zheng Chenggong in history. It was the largest timber transit center in 1960s. The arc-shaped bridge in the picture was a dedicated railway line. (by Ruan Renyi)

尤溪口地处闽江中游南岸的尤溪河与闽江的交汇口，历史上尤溪口是一个重要的码头，舟船上下闽江都在尤溪口停泊，因此十分繁华 / 阮任艺 陈映辉 摄
Youxikou is located at the conjunction of the Youxihe River and the River Min and it was a busy and important wharf in history. (by Ruan Renyi and Chen Yinghui)

古田溪位于闽江主流中段北侧，发源于屏南县，流经古田县，出水口镇汇入闽江。画面左侧为水口闽江大桥 / 阮任艺 摄
The Gutianxi River rises from Pingnan County and flows through Gutian County and joins the River Min at Shuikou Town. Shuikou Mingjiang Bridge (left) (by Ruan Renyi)

02

01   闽江在水口镇湾边村拐了一个大弯，水面网箱养殖密布，风光俱佳 / 阮任艺 陈映辉 摄
The River Min takes a big turn at Wanbian Village of Shuikou Town. Cage cultures cover densely on the water. (by Ruan Renyi and Chen Yinghui)

02   樟湖坂在闽江流域十分著名，除了它一年一度的蛇崇拜活动吸引观众，已经沉入水口库区的古镇历史上也是一个繁忙的码头 / 曾璜 摄
Zhanghuban is well-known in the basin of the River Min, not only because of the annual snake worship, but also its history as a busy dock. (by Zeng Huang)

古田翠屏湖古田溪一级电站 / 阮任艺 摄　Power station on the Gutianxi River (by Ruan Renyi)

雄江位于闽清县闽江边，距县城 22 公里，是水口水电站重点库区乡镇。因最接近水口电站大坝，江阔水深，水面养殖及旅游风光引人入胜 / 阮任艺 陈映辉 摄
The Xiongjiang River lies in Mingqing County, which is an important area for Shuikou hydropower station. The water is deep and wide and suitable for aquaculture. (by Ruan Renyi and Chen Yinghui)

水口水电站是华东地区最大的水电站，1993 年建成，大坝全长 870 米，高 101 米，总装机 140 万千瓦。水口水电站位于闽清县境内的闽江主流上，电站建成蓄水彻底改变了闽江闽清之上的自然状态 / 阮任艺 摄

Shuikou hydropower station is the largest hydropower station in the Eastern China. It was completed in 1993, 870 meters in length and 101 meters in height with a total capacity of 1.4 million kilowatts. The hydropower station is located on the mainstream of the River Min in Mingqing County and changed the natural condition of Mingqing reach. (by Ruan Renyi)

　　闽江进入福州闽侯上街时分为乌龙江和闽江，流经城区分割台江和烟台山的是闽江，流经上渡螺州一线的就是乌龙江，闽江两江到了马尾一带又再次合流。闽侯两江分离处　/　那兴海 摄

The River Min divides into the Wulongjiang River and The River Min at Shangjie Town of Minghou County. The River Min flows through the urban area and the Wulongjiang River flows through Shangdu Town. They converge again at Mawei area. The separation of the two rivers at Minghou County (by Na Xinghai)

历史上洪山桥是连接福州与南台岛的重要枢纽，东接西禅渡口，西止洪塘阵坂，为石梁桥，自明代始屡建屡毁，后崩毁，今桥址依稀可见 / 阮任艺 陈映辉 摄

Hongshan Bridge was an important hub linking Fuzhou and Nantai Island in history. This stone bridge has been built and destroyed and rebuilt since Ming Dynasty. The bridge site can be partly seen today. (by Ruan Renyi and Chen Yinghui)

闽江流经福州城（画面左上为乌龙江及大樟溪，右上为鼓山） / 阮任艺 陈映辉 摄
Fuzhou city at the River Min (the upper left of the picture is Wulongjiang River and Dazhangxi River; the upper right is Gushan Mountain). (by Ruan Renyi and Chen Yinghui)

闽江三江口一带（画面右侧为三江汇合处及马尾，画面左侧为乌龙江及乌龙江大桥，远处为五虎山） / 阮任艺 陈映辉 摄

The meeting of the three rivers (the right side of the picture is the meeting place of the three rivers and Mawei District; the left side is Wulongjiang River and Wulongjiang Bridge; the distance is Wuhushan Mountain). (by Ruan Renyi and Chenyinghui)

闽江口标志景点五虎礁　　Wuhu Reef, the landmark of the estuary of the River Min

闽江口四岛一礁（画面下部为粗芦岛，上中部为琅岐岛，中部小岛为壶江岛，左上为川石岛及五虎礁）
The scenery of the estuary of the River Min (the lower part of the picture is Culu Island; the top center is Langqi Island; the middle is Hujiang Island; the upper left is Chuanshi Island and Wuhu Reef)

第二章 ＋ 穿越古今的历史画卷

一条闽江串联起来的是福建的一部历史。

从三明万寿岩和明溪南山走出来的福建原始土著，一开始就选择了在水边生活，一条鱼塘溪流入沙溪河的同时，也冲刷了他们从旧石器时代走到新石器时代的脚印，甚至将他们冲到了闽江更远的下游。在昙石山闽江下游大河的水边，河水奔涌，潮汐往复，这些土著的生活书写出福建最远古的文化。

断发纹身的闽越族人从汉代伊始上演了一部悲剧，他们被迫迁徙江淮，远离故土，只剩下了几只残部隐入山林。他们被灭亡的只是部族，而文化却顽固地在武夷山的九曲洞壑和闽越古城留存下来。

闽江之水流淌到宋元，朱子理学在闽北建溪之畔的土地上渐渐养成，闽文化开始崛起。理学的智慧之光在青山绿水之间如同雨雾，四处弥漫，滋润教化着东南一隅的蛮夷之民。

及明至清，历史就如同闽江流入了下游，河水更加浩瀚壮阔，福建开始上演海丝序曲和船政故事。闽江口布满等待季风的巨帆，三宝太监郑和将闽江之水洒向了西域大洋。马尾罗星塔临江而立，纵览船政风云，闽江口万流浩淼，冲走了民族耻辱的同时也托起了民族的希望。

这就是闽江，从远古走来，奔流入大洋。

The History

The River Min is the history of Fujian Province.

The original inhabitants of Fujian chose to live by the river. The rivers witnessed their footprints from the Old Stone Age to the New Stone Age. The life of the original inhabitants records the most ancient culture of Fujian.

The history of Mingyue people was a tragedy from Han Dynasty. They had to leave their homeland and migrated to the Yangze-Huaihe region. Only few tribes stayed in deep mountains. Their tribes were perished but their cultures have been preserved in the caves of Mount Wuyi and the Mingyue ancient cities.

The Neo-Confucianism was developed in the north of Fujian in Song Dynasty and Yuan Dynasty. The culture of Fujian began to flourish and the wisdom of the Neo-Confucianism nurtured the uncivilized people in the Southeast China.

In Ming and Qing Dynasty, the history flowed down to the downstream of the River Min. The large sailboats from the Mingjiang estuary went overseas. Luoxing Tower was built at Mawei, witnessing the busy shipping transportation. The river brought the hope of the people.

This is the River Min, coming from the ancient times and running into the sea.

01 三明万寿岩古人类遗址观音洞外景 / 阮任艺 摄
The ancient hominid sites in Wanshou Cave, the outside of Guanyin Cave (by Ruan Renyi)

02 三明万寿岩古人类遗址观音洞内景 / 阮任艺 摄
The ancient hominid sites in Wanshou Cave, the inside of Guanyin Cave (by Ruan Renyi)

03 三明万寿岩古人类遗址博物馆旧石器时代遗存陈列 / 阮任艺 摄
The museum of ancient hominid sites in Wanshou Cave, the display of the Old Stone Age (by Ruan Renyi)

02

03

01

02

03

01   明溪南山古人类遗址 ／ 涧南 摄
The ancient hominid sites in Nanshan Mountain of Mingxi County (by Jian Nan)

02   明溪南山古人类遗址三号洞 ／ 涧南 摄
The ancient hominid sites in Nanshan Mountain of Mingxi County, Cave No. 3 (by Jian Nan)

03   昙石山古人类生活复原 ／ 吴寿华 摄
The recovery of ancient human life in Tanshishan Mountain (by Wu Shouhua)

武夷山具有丰富的历史文化遗存。早在四千多年前就有先民在此劳动生息，逐步形成了国内外绝无仅有的偏居中国东南一隅的古闽族文化和其后的闽越族文化，闽越文化绵延两千多年之久，留下众多的文化遗存。反映这一时期文化特征的主要有架壑船棺。坐落在武夷山九曲溪崖壁中的架壑船棺共有 18 处，经国家文物保护科技研究所 C14 测定，距今 3750-3295 年之间 / 阮任艺 陈映辉 摄

There are a lot of historical and cultural relics in Mount Wuyi. Over four thousand years ago, there were people living here. The Mingyue culture, with a history of over two thousand years, brings us rich cultural relics. The main features of this period manifested in ship coffins, which were found in 18 places in Mount Wuyi. They are supposed to be 3750-3295 years ago according to the C14 test. (by Ruan Renyi and Chen Yinghui)

01

02

01   金溪之畔将乐回头山是闽越王无诸校猎之所乐野宫的观察哨 / 涧南 摄
        Huitoushan Mountain by the Jinxi River was the hunting observation post of Minyue King Wuzhu. (by Jian Nan)

02   金溪之畔泰宁闽越王无诸校猎雕塑反映了无诸王在金铙山周边建宁泰宁明溪等地校猎的史实 / 涧南 摄
        The sculpture of the hunting of Minyue King Wuzhu (by Jian Nan)

03   武夷山城村古汉城是古越族历史辉煌的一章。从 1980 年至今，福建省博物馆组成汉城考古队进行一系列考古发掘，已
        出土四千多件可复原的重要文物。城址出土的丰富多彩的日用陶器和陶制建筑材料，烧制精良，造型别具一格。城址中还
        出土了许多文字瓦当和陶文，具有很高的书法艺术价值。宫殿中的室内浴池为我国所发现的古代最早的宫内浴池，其供、
        排水管道设施非常严整、完备，是古代宫殿建筑的典范 / 阮任艺 陈映辉 摄
        Ancient Han town in Shancheng Village is a glorious part of history. Since 1980, the archaeological team of Fujian has found
        over 4000 items of cultural relics, including domestic earthenware and building materials, calligraphy on pottery and even the
        palace bath pool. The drainage pipelines found are neat and complete, which can be the model of ancient palace. (by Ruan
        Renyi and Chen Yinghui)

04   城村古渡 / 涧南 摄
        The ancient ferry in the village. (by Jian Nan)

01

02

03

04

01 　　程门立雪的典故出自《宋史·杨时传》："至是，游酢、杨时见程颐于洛（今洛阳），时盖年四十矣。一日见颐，颐偶瞑坐，游酢（音zuò）与时侍立不去。颐既觉，则门外雪深一尺矣。" 说的是北宋大学问家杨时（将乐人），在四十多岁时与好友游酢（建阳人）一起去向程颐求教的故事，成为中国文化史上的一个传奇。将乐杨时墓 / 涧南 摄

Yang Shi (from Jiangle County), a famous scholar in Northern Song Dynasty, is a legend of Chinese culture history. The tomb of Yang Shi (by Jian Nan)

02 　　位于明溪翰仙镇龙湖村的杨时故里，目前仅余棂星门石牌坊 / 焦红辉 摄

The hometown of Yang Shi was Longhu Village of Hanxiang County. At present, only dolmen of Lingxing Gate remains. (by Jiao Honghui)

03 　　宋代著名理学家建阳县人游酢的石雕塑像如今矗立在其家乡麻沙镇的文化广场上 / 吴寿华 摄

The statue of You Zuo (from Jianyang County), a famous Neo-Confucianism scholar of Song Daynasty, in the Culture Square of Masha Town. (by Wu Shouhua)

04 　　朱熹31岁正式拜程颐的三传弟子李侗为师，专心儒学，成为程颢程颐之后儒学的重要人物。延平区夏道镇徐洋村的李侗纪念馆 / 曾璜 摄

Zhu Xi acknowledged Li Tong as his master and focused on Confucianism when he was 31 and become an important figure in Confucianism. The museum of Li Tong (by Zeng Huang)

05 　　程朱理学是福建文化的高峰、闽学之滥觞。朱熹在闽江流域的尤溪、建阳、武夷山一带讲学著述，给福建乃至中国文化留下了宝贵财富。尤溪朱熹广场朱熹塑像下妇女在练腰鼓 / 涧南 摄

Neo-Confucianism is the peak of the Fujian culture and the origin of the Fujian studies. The lectures and works of Zhu Xi are the treasure of Chinese culture. Zhu Xi Square: women are practising waist drum under the statue of Zhu Xi (by Jian Nan)

01 宋代福建雕版印刷最集中的地方，是建宁府的建安。其中又以麻沙、崇化两地更为著名，号为"图书之府"，建阳刻本称"闽本""建本"，麻沙所刻亦称"麻沙本"。书坊乡（崇化里）的沃野和覆船山上的清代白塔 / 吴寿华 摄

Masha and Chonghua were famous for woodblock printing in Song Dynasty and called "City of Books". Jianyang block printed edition is called "Ming edition" or "Jian edition"; and "Masha edition" is from Masha. The white pagoda of Qing Dynasty (by Wu Shouhua)

02 麻沙是宋代全国三大雕版印刷中心之一，素有"图书之府"、"建本之乡"之称。麻沙水南村新建的雕版印刷公园 / 吴寿华 摄

Masha is one of the three woodblock printing centers in Song Dynasty and called "City of Books". Woodblock printing park in Shuinan Village (by Wu Shouhua)

03 从宋代北苑起，中国制茶中心转移到了福建的建州（建瓯、崇安）一带，福建茶业的辉煌历史也从此时开端 / 涧南 摄

The tea manufacturing center of China moved to Jianzhou of Fujian from Song Dynasty. It is the beginning of the tea industry history of Fujian. (by Jian Nan)

04 在建瓯焙前村后的山坡上，一方记载北苑历史的摩崖石刻奠定了福建茶在中国茶历史上的地位 / 涧南 摄

The cliff inscription on the hill of Beiqian Village records the role of Fujian tea in Chinese tea history. (by Jian Nan)

03

04

02

03

01   建瓯东峰镇的一块矮脚乌龙茶园，成为百年乌龙的原产地。深刻影响了闽台两岸的茶史 / 涧南 摄
Wulong tea garden in Dongfeng Town is the origin place of Wulong tea, which has a great influence on Fujian-Taiwan tea history. (by Jian Nan)

02   建窑遗址位于建阳市水吉镇，是宋代福建烧造黑釉茶盏的著名窑场，经保护的这座古窑长达135.6米，可同时装烧10万件以上黑瓷 / 阮任艺 摄
The historical site of Jian kiln is located in Shuiji Town of Jianyang City. It was a famous kiln factory for tea-calix with black glaze in Song Dynasty. This ancient kiln is 135.6 meters long with a capacity for 100,000 items. (by Ruan Renyi)

03   建窑出土的宋盏底部，刻有"贡御"两字，说明了此盏专为皇家烧制。两宋时，因为"斗茶"的流行，建盏也风靡一时 / 阮任艺 摄
The unearthed Song calix with "Gong Yu" engraved at the bottom, which means this calix was made for imperial family. (by Ruan Renyi)

武夷山作为世界自然与文化双遗产地，有着深厚的历史积淀和丰富的文化意蕴，而这一切都能通过镌刻于碧水丹山之间的摩崖石刻得以生动、形象、直观地体现。其中朱熹的摩崖题刻，又是朱子理学遗迹的重要内容 / 李世雄 摄

Mount Wuyi, as both world natural and cultural heritage, has rich historical and cultural values. The cliff inscriptions along the river vividly embody the Chinese culture, especially Neo-Confucianism. The cliff inscription by Zhu Xi (by Li Shixiong)

建瓯文庙初建年代可追溯至北宋宝元年间，之后屡毁屡修。明洪武三十四年（1401年），文庙又毁于火，永乐三年（1405年）重建时迁至今址。现存建筑为清同治八年（1869年）重建，光绪五年（1879年）建成。建瓯文庙为闽江流域文庙之冠 / 李世雄 摄

Jian' ou Confucian Temple was built in the Northern Song Dynasty. Later it was destroyed and rebuilt. The existing one was rebuilt in Qing Dynasty and completed in 1879. Jian' ou Confucian Temple is the top of the Confucian Temples in the Mingjiang basin. (by Li Shixiong)

01

02

03

04

01　　古代于交通要塞屯兵把守，设置关隘，一方面是为了军事防御和控制交通，另一方面也是征收关税的重要设施。据《福建通志》记载：全省境内共设有 89 关 376 隘 158 寨。邵武金坑乡黄土关 / 阮任艺 摄

In ancient time, passes are set up at important fortresses for military defense and traffic control, as well as for customs collection. According to General Annals of Fujian, there are 89 gates, 376 passes and 158 forts. Huangtuguan in Jinkeng Village of Shaowu City (by Ruan Renyi)

02　　立于光泽县境四面高山险道上的"九关十三隘"是八闽一绝，遐迩闻名，其中杉关最为著名。杉关遗留的石刻 / 涧南 摄

Shanguan is the most well-known pass in Guangze County. The stone inscription of Shanguan (by Jian Nan)

03　　光泽杉关已经改建为 332 省道，这条出省大道建筑在古道的基础之上，通往江西黎川 / 阮任艺 摄

332 provincial road is built on the ancient passage to Jiangxi (by Ruan Renyi)

04　　光泽吴屯村黄岭古道黄岭亭 / 阮任艺 摄

Huangling pavilion on Huangling ancient passage in Wutun Village (by Ruan Renyi)

05　　邵武桂林乡盖竹村巫山小组村前古道 / 阮任艺 摄

The ancient passage in Gaizhu Village of Guilin County (by Ruan Renyi)

01

02

01   南平市延寿楼是延平被誉为八闽铜关的代表性建筑，该楼始建于元代，曾于 1609 年重修。延寿楼是古代重要的军事指挥机关，文天祥、韩世忠、郑成功、石达开都在此驻扎过 / 阮任艺 摄

     Yanshoulou is a representative building in Nanping City. It was first built in Yuan Dynasty and rebuilt in 1609. It was an important military demanding organ. (by Ruan Renyi)

02   延寿楼城门基部一石件刻有元至元三年字样，少数城砖印有延郡城砖楷字 / 阮任艺 摄

     The stones of the building base were engraved with some characters. (by Ruan Renyi)

03   作为古建州首府的建瓯自明代就建有威武恢弘的城墙及城楼。《八闽通志》载，明代建瓯城墙"周围两千七十九丈三尺有奇，高一丈九尺"，城墙上还设城楼 24 座。建州古城的巍峨在马可·波罗的游记中得到了赞美 / 涧南 摄

     As the capital of ancient Jianzhou, Jian' ou boasts its magnificent city wall and gate tower, which was recorded by Marco Polo during his travel. (by Jian Nan)

04   闽江流域各县自元至明开始修筑城池，浦城旧城墙砖上刻有"嘉庆拾伍年""祝徐氏捐修全城"等字迹，记录了生活在乾隆中后期至嘉庆年间，一位名为祝徐氏的妇女独立捐修浦城城墙的历史 / 涧南 摄

     On the stones of old city wall engraved the characters recording a woman named Zhuxu who donated the money to mend Pucheng city wall during Qianlong and Jiaqing periods. (by Jian Nan)

05   建于明嘉靖四十一年（1562 年）的贡川古城墙是为防倭寇而建，城墙均用青砖筑成，砖上刻有"贡川"、"贡堡"字样 / 阮任艺 摄

     Gongchuan city wall was built to defense Japanese pirates in Ming Dynasty. The city wall was built with black bricks engraved with "Gongcuan" or "Gongbao". (by Ruan Renyi)

03

04

05

01

02

01   茶市街，又名茶焙街，是富屯溪流域光泽县城区一条古街。明清年间，茶市街就是闽赣边境的一条名街。光泽茶市街目前仅存的老码头 / 涧南 摄

Tea market street, also named Chabei street, is an ancient street in Guangze County. It was a famous street during Ming Dynasty and Qing Dynasty. Only some old docks remain. (by Jian Nan)

02   梅列门是沙溪流域三明市内仅存的历史最悠久的清代古城门，城门由花岗岩铸成拱门，城门口正对古渡头，古时台阶平缓，适合抬轿直抵码头 / 涧南 摄

Meilie Gate is an old city gate of the longest history in Sanming City. The gate was made of granite, facing the old ferry. (by Jian Nan)

03   清咸丰年间（公元1851-1861年），当地的一些地位显赫官僚和一些富豪为了躲避太平军，特意雇人在武夷山悬崖岩洞建造了这种建筑物，从地理位置来看，确实做到了防守和保卫的作用，建造此建筑时，所有的木材都是以洞口可见的那些杉木为支撑架吊上去的，因而取名为天车架 / 阮任艺 陈映辉 摄

During Xianfeng period in Qing Dynasty, some local rich and powerful people built such houses in the cliff caves in order to avoid Taiping troop. All the timber used were hung to the cave supported by the furs. (by Ruan Renyi and Chen Yinghui)

01

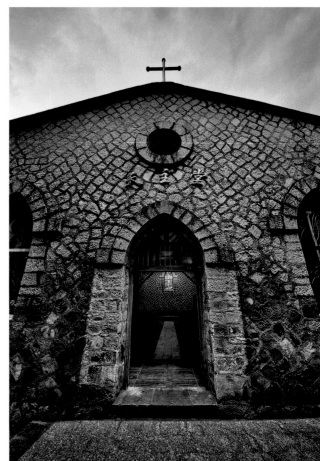

02

01 　　清末民初，随着福州开埠，外国传教士顺闽江北上，进入福建腹地，最远到达武夷山分水关。桐木天主教堂于清道光三年（1823 年），由法国生物学家、传教士罗公正筹资设立 ／ 周跃东 摄

　　During the late Qing Dynasty and early Republic of China, foreign missionaries came to Fuzhou as it opened to foreign traders. Tongmu Catholic church was built in 1823, funded by a French biologist and missionary. (by Zhou Yuedong)

02 　　桐木天主教堂构体采用哥特式建筑，至今保存完好 ／ 周跃东 摄

　　Tongmu Catholic church is of Gothic style and has been well preserved till today. (by Zhou Yuedong)

03 　　闽安古镇宋代古桥迴龙桥南北横跨邢港，全长 66 米，宽 4.8 米，4 墩 5 孔，为罕见的船形桥墩，花岗石平梁结构。迴龙桥展示着我国唐宋石刻的精湛技艺，演绎着唐宋时期繁荣的文化景象 ／ 阮任艺 摄

　　The old Huilong Bridge of Song Dynasty stretches across Xinggang Port, 66 meters in length, 4.8 meters in width. It has four piers and five openings, which is unusual. The granite flat bridge demonstrates the exquisite carving techniques of Tang and Song Dynasty. (by Ruan Renyi)

04 　　宋天圣七年（1029 年）朝廷设巡检司衙门于闽安镇，以巡察沿海县份。衙门口树立的"重修闽安协署碑记" ／ 阮任艺 摄

　　Xunjiansi office, set up by Song government, aimed to inspect the coastal counties. Tablet inscriptions at the gate of the office. (by Ruan Renyi)

03

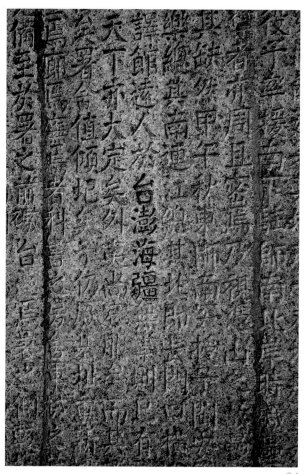

04

01

02

03

04

01   在 1884 年的中法马江海战中，长门炮台的主炮击中中法国侵华远东舰队司令孤拔的旗舰，击伤孤拔。之后，中国军民又在长门炮台顽强抗击日军侵略，屡遭日军轰炸，并最终为日军所毁 / 弗兰克 摄
The main artillery of Changmen Battery hit the flagship of French fleet during the Battle of Fuzhou. Later, the battery witnessed anti-Japanese invasion and finally was destroyed by Japanese army. (by Frank)

02   闽江北岸长门村电光山上的长门炮台，是目前中国保留下来的最古老最大的炮台，它始建于明崇祯五年，清代重建 / 涧南 摄
Changmen Battery in Changmen Village is the largest ancient battery in China. It was built in Ming Dynasty and rebuilt in Qing Dynasty. (By Jian Nan)

03   闽安炮台位于亭江镇闽安镇，清道光三十年 (1850 年) 三月，林则徐巡察闽江两岸时奏准建立，称闽安炮台。修复前的闽安炮台遗址 / 阮任艺 摄
Ming'an Battery is located in Ming'an Town. It was built in Qing Dynasty with the permission of Lin Zexu. The ruins of Ming'an Battery before restoring. (by Ruan Renyi)

04   修复后的闽安炮台与南岸炮台隔江对峙，成为船政文化旅游的重要项目 / 阮任艺 摄
The restored Ming'an Battery is opposite to Nan'an Battery, which are part of shipping culture tourism. (by Ruan Renyi)

第三章 ＋ 流水潺湲的幽静村落

村庄，在闽江源头、支流以及主流之上，如一棵大树上的果实，累累垂挂。闽江流域大地上星星点点密布着的古村落，最早的可追溯到两晋时期。这些古村落历经兴衰嬗变，绝大部分的现有格局是在明清时期完成的。这些古村落形态多样，人文荟萃，景观优美，是福建悠久历史文化传承的重要载体。

而闽江诸多源头的小村，更是山水精致、宁静宜居。可以想象在历史的长河里，闽江流域的先民们是如何顺着闽江的众多支流找到水的尽头而开垦、安居的。

源头之水，永远是那样清澈。

源水之畔的小村，还是那样安静吗？

从本世纪初开始，中国的城镇化发展造成了古村落的迅速消失。土地荒芜、人口减少形成空村化、村庄宗族与宗亲的崩塌以及当代村庄社会结构及政治生态的变化；草木的茂盛、鸟兽的繁殖、绿色生态的恢复，保存了几千年的村庄呈现出一种复杂而多元，令人眼花缭乱、目不暇接的状态。

顺着水流走到闽江的尽头，小村依然。

Quiet Villages by the River

The villages, distributed along the River Min's mainsteams and tributaries, are just as the fruits hanging on a grand tree. Those ancient villages scattered on the River Min's basin can be chased back to as early as the Jin Dynasties. These ancient village experienced rises and falls, and most of their existing structures were set in the Ming and Qing Dynasties. The ancient villages, with various structures, talents, and beautiful landscape, are important carriers of Fujian historic and cultural heritage.

In particular, the small villages at the sources of the River Min are even more delicate, tranquil and livable. You can imagine in the long history of Mingjiang River, how the ancestors chased along so many tributaries, finally find the river source and settle down.

The source water is always so clear.

Are the small villages along the river sources still quiet as before?

At the beginning of this century, China's urbanization has caused the rapid disappearing of ancient villages. Fertile land turned barren; villages became empty; clan connections broke down. Contemporary villages' social structure and ecological politics keep changing. Grass and trees grow lushly. Birds and animals breed offspring. As the recovery of the ecosystem, villages which preserved for thousands of years display a complex, diverse but dazzling state.

Walking along the riverside to the source of the River Min, you can see the villages in their stillness.

01

【光泽县司前乡岱坪村】

+

Daiping Village, Siqian Town, Guangze County

岱坪村位于光泽县东北部，距乡政府十公里，交通便利。东北部与江西省铅山县篁碧乡交界。西邻长庭村，南联西口村、干坑林场。

富屯溪北溪就发源于光泽县司前乡岱坪村北的大岐山下。大岐山气候温和宜人，总面积三万余亩，海拔八百多米，境内溪涧纵横，河床落差大，水质清冽纯美，是富屯溪最主要的源头之一。境内有著名的观光胜地金仙崖葛仙山，鸭母关自古为通往江西必经之路。

Daiping Village is located in northeast of Guangze County, ten kilometers from the township government. Transportation is convenient. It borders Huangbi Town, Qianshan County of Jiangxi Province on the northeast, Changting Village on the west, Xikou Village and Gankeng forest farm on the south.

The Beixi River of the Futunxi River originates from Daqi Mountain, north to Daiping Village. Daqi Mountain has a pleasant climate, and covers an area of over 30000 mu. It is 800 meters above the sea level. Abundant steams are running across the mountain, vertically and horizontally. The water is very clear and it is one of the main sources of the Futunxi River. There are some famous tourist resorts in the mountain, such as Jinxian cliff and Gexian hill. Yamu pass is the only way to Jiangxi.

02

01　富屯溪北溪源头之水发源于干坑 / 涧南 摄
　　The Beixi River originates from Gankeng（by Jian Nan）

02　岱坪村通往江西沿山鸭母关的古道 / 涧南 摄
　　Ancient path from Daiping village to Jiangxi through Yamu pass（by Jian Nan）

01　　小小的庙宇是茶农的皈依　/　涧南 摄
　　　A small temple is where tea farmers rest their minds (by Jian Nan)

02　　岱坪村村民将柴火垒成了墙　/　涧南 摄
　　　Daiping villagers make the firewood like a wall (by Jian Nan)

03　　干坑是武夷红茶的产地之一　/　涧南 摄
　　　Gankeng is one of the places of production of Wuyi red tea (by Jian Nan)

横坑村古道进村时的廊庭 / 涧南 摄　Ancient path stretches into Hengkeng Village (by Jian Nan)

邵武市桂林乡横坑村

+

Hengkeng Village, Guilin County, Shaowu City

富屯溪西溪源头之水在横坑村穿村而过 / 涧南 摄
The source of the Xixi River goes across the Hengkeng Village (by Jian Nan)

横坑原名嵘衢坊，为后唐工部侍郎黄峭后裔筑基建造，迄今已有一千多年的历史。横坑是一个生态优美、人文积淀深厚的乡村，也是革命老区村和省级生态村。

清澈的溪水，终日流淌在横坑的古村落中，最终汇入富屯溪源头之一的西溪，亦是闽江源头之一。

横坑村地处两省三县交界之处，由于横坑地形酷似船型马槽，四周山势俗称"五马并槽"，东西南北中，五马各聚龙势，形态各异，跑、蹲、行、奔各自显威，村庄曾兴盛一时。清朝时被人以一木横破断其盛势，故横坑一名沿用至今。

村头的黄氏宗祠（黄氏家庙）是整个邵武南部地区黄氏宗祠中保存最完整的宗祠之一。宗祠内雕梁画栋，十分精美，历经数百年的壁画色彩依旧鲜艳，栩栩如生。村中还有"流芳"学堂，以及散布在古老民居中各房大厅的"岁进仕"、"贡元"、"选魁"、"文蔚南山"、"笃厚栽培"、"惟德是馨"等大量牌匾，以其高雅的书法艺术与壮观的建筑相互辉映。

村尾顺溪流沿古道有"钟、鼓、旗、锣"四块巨石，可谓吉庆布阵，八面威风，给村子带来好风水。后来"鼓"石因为二十世纪七十年代建学校取石料被炸掉，据说破了村中风水好多年。

Hengkeng Village was named Rongqufang, which was constructed by descendants of Huangxiao, a construction minister in the later Tang Dynasty. The village has a history of more than one thousand years, with beautiful environment and profound cultural accumulation. It is also a revolutionary base areas and a provincial ecological village.

Clear stream water goes through ancient villages in Hengkeng, falling into the Xixi River, which is one of the sources of the River Min. Hengkeng Village is at the conjunction of three counties in two provinces. The shape of Hengkeng village is just as a ship-like manger. Together with mountains around, the village is commonly known as "five horses sharing one manger". The mountains surround the village just like five horses running from all directions, for which Hengkeng Village was once famous. In Qing Dynasty, the heyday of the village was broken by a person using traverse wood. Since then the name of village had been changed into Hengkeng.

The ancestral temple of Huang clan at the entrance of the village is one the best preserved temples among the Huang clans' in the whole Shaowu area. Inside the temple, carved beams and painted rafters are as vivid as they were hundreds of years ago. In the village, there is a school called Liufang Xuetang. A great many calligraphy tablets are distributed in ancient houses. The artistic calligraphy tablets and the grand architecture match well.

There are four grand rocks along the ancient path, namely Zhong (bell), Gu (drum), Qi (flag), Luo (gong). The four rocks line in a way that could bring the village fortune. However, the rock Gu was bombed apart for building schools in 1970s, thus broke the fortune of the village for many years.

建宁县均口乡张家山自然村

+

The natural village at Zhangjiashan Mountain, Junkou Town, Jianning County

张家山自然村地处严峰山西南麓，为闽江源头村。闽江源自然保护区是武夷山脉中亚热带森林生态系统保护区的重要组成部分，也是珍稀野生动植物的良好栖息地，保护区对于闽江水源涵养以及生物多样性的保护都具有重要意义，并于 2006 年 2 月晋升为国家级自然保护区。

The natural village of Zhangjiashan, located at the southwestern foot of Yanfeng Mountain, is the source of the River Min. It is the core of the nature reserve of the river source and an important part of subtropical forest ecosystem protection area of Mount Wuyi. It is a good place for rare and endangered species and of great importance for protecting biodiversity. In Feb 2006, it was upgraded as a national nature reserve.

01   站在张家山村的任何一个地方都可以看见九县石 / 那兴海 摄
The peak of Jiuxianshi can be seen everywhere in Zhangjiashan Village. (by Na Xinghai)

02   张家山村中留守的老人 / 焦红辉 摄
Elderly people left-behind (by Jiao Honghui)

山间梨花始盛开 / 那兴海 摄　Pear flowers blossom in the mountain（by Na Xinghai）

建宁县客坊乡水尾村

+

Shuiwei Village, Kefang Town, Jianning County

水尾村其实是水的源头，水尾村的溪流为都溪，是金溪源头之一。在山的另一边就是江西地界。

水尾村位于客坊乡东南部，距县城七十公里，东界中畲村；南邻江西广昌塘坊乡；西与龙溪村接壤；北靠客坊村。水尾村地势奇特，四面群山环抱，村中地势平坦，是有名的鱼米之村。水尾村又是革命老区基点村之一，至今水尾村完好地保存着闽赣红军游击队司令部、红军医院、红军银行、红军兵工厂等革命旧址。一些百姓家中还保存着当年红军和游击队留下的许多物品，极具红色旅游价值。

水尾村的白云寺自然村因白云崇圣寺而得名，白云寺始建于五代后唐同光二年（公元974年），衍北宋极盛，拥僧众三百多人。宋熙宁七年神宗命名、赐额。据说北宋名相王安石，因是水尾村谢氏门中外甥，年轻时曾投亲到此，见此风光绮丽，寺院规模之大，便在此习学一年有余，还曾作《云山十奇诗》。

Shuiwei Village has the sources of the Jinxi River. The other side of the mountain is Jiangxi Province. Shuiwei Village is located at the southeast of Kefang County, seventy kilometers away from town. The village borders Zhongshe Village on the east, Tangfang Town to the south, Longxi Village on the west, and Kefang Village to the north. With mountains surrounding, the middle of the village is flat, and the village is a land of abundance. This village sits in old revolutionary base areas. Some of the villagers' still keep those things that the Red Army and guerrilla forces left behind. Thus, the village has a great many revolution tourism resources.

The natural village is named after Baiyun Chongsheng temple. Baiyun temple was built in the later Tang Dynasty (974) and was prospered in the Northen Song Dynasty with over 300 monks at that time. The temple was named by the emperor Song Shenzong. It is said that the famous premier Wang Anshi of Northern Song Dynasty had studied in this temple for a year. Wang even wrote a series of poems known as "ten marvellous poems of Yunshan mountain".

白云寺 / 涧南 摄
Baiyun Temple (by Jian Nan)

建宁溪源乡上坪古村

+

Ancient Shangping Village, Xiyuan Town, Jianning County

上坪古村在金溪源头的大田溪末端,翻过竹叶隘就是江西的黎川了。上坪是一个山间盆地,曾经名为"六龙井"、"楚下堡",已经有一千多年的历史。明清两朝上坪是闽赣官道必经之处,为两省重要驿站,曾经商贾云集,繁华一时。

上坪古村村民均为杨姓,位于村口水尾位置的杨氏祖庙建于宋末,庙外有大树荫蔽,春季落英满地。上坪古村还有五代同堂牌坊、大夫第、古香园、司马第、得水园等多处古迹,因此成为省级历史文化名村。

上坪人说,当年朱熹曾经来此讲过学,因此上坪文风昌盛,杨姓村民以耕读传家,崇文尚学,具有儒风不衰的传统。

Ancient Shangping Village is at the end of the Datianxi River. Shangping Village is an intermountain basin with a history of over one thousand years. Shangping was an old state road connecting Fujian and Jiangxi province in Ming and Qing Dynasty. It was an important post of the two provinces and prosperous for a while with numerous merchants.

Villagers in ancient Shanpging Village are all descendants of Yang clan. The Yang clan temple, built in late Song Dynasty, is located at the entrance of the village. The temple is in the shadow of big trees outside. The village has many historic sites and became a provincial historic and cultural village.

It is said that the famous scholar Zhu Xi once gave lectures in the village. So the people in the village advocate knowledge and literature and preserve the tradition of Confucianism.

01　溪源上坪古村水塘上晒匾的木架 / 润南 摄
　　Wooden bars for drying tablets in the sun (by Jian Nan)

02　溪源上坪古村古门楼 / 润南 摄
　　Ancient gate house in ancient Shangping Village, Xiyuan town (by Jian Nan)

浦城县忠信镇坑尾村

+

Kengwei Village, Zhongxin Town, Pucheng County

南浦溪是建溪的主流，它的源流为柘溪，发源于北部武夷山脉和仙霞岭支脉处的浦城县忠信乡柘岭坑尾村。源头海拔1870米，属三江源头之一，境内溪水分别流入闽江、长江和钱塘江。

坑尾不是尾，指的是溪水的源头。坑尾村过去是闽浙两省古道上的重要隘口，有四百年历史了，由廖、刘、叶、张四大姓为主组成。村里自然资源丰富，农忙时还要到外面雇工，农户家庭的生活都还不错。高山茶叶是这里的重要资源，做茶叶生意最大的人家，年收入可达到30万元以上，2011年度评为县级文明村，同时也被评为省级生态村。

The Nanpuxi River is the main stream of the Jianxi River, whose source is the Zhexi River, originating from Kengwei Village, Zhongxin Town of Pucheng County. The source of water is one of the sources of the River Min, the Yangtze River and the Qian Tangjiang River, and is 1870 meters above sea level.

Kengwei means the source of the rivers. Kengwei Village was an important pass on the old official road connecting Fujian and Jiangxi province. The village has a history of 400 years, most of the villagers are descendants of four clans, namely Liao, Liu, Ye, and Zhang clans. Natural resource is abundant in the village. In busy seasons of farming, the village has to employ extra labour from other villages. The living condition of the villagers is pretty good. Tea industry is one of the important resources of the village. People who keep the biggest tea business have an income of 300,000 Yuan annually. In 2011, the village is honoured as the county's civilized village and the provincial ecological village.

01 坑尾村坐落在福清山下 / 那兴海 摄
Kengwei Village seats at the bottom of Fuqingshan Mountain (by Na Xinghai)

02 福清山庙民间庙会 / 涧南 摄
Fuqingshan temple fair (by Jian Nan)

03 坑尾村是新农村的样板村 / 涧南 摄
Kengwei Village is a model of China's new village (by Jian Nan)

02

03

武夷山市星村镇桐木村

十

Tongmu Village, Xingcun County, Wuyishan City

桐木村位于武夷山国家级自然保护区内，是武夷山风景名胜区九曲溪的源头。桐木村有三十三个自然村，散落分布在南北长35公里，东西宽25公里的桐木大峡谷断裂带内。

桐木村因桐木关而得名，闽赣古道贯穿其间（现为公路），系古代交通与军事要地，曾筑垣而驻戍卒，以坚防守，为武夷山八大雄关之一。立关北望，两侧高山耸峙入云，"V"形的大峡谷犹如一道天堑，直向江西沿山县伸展。

桐木关内生态良好，拥有"鸟的天堂"、"蛇的王国"、"昆虫的世界"、"开启物种生物基因库钥匙"等美誉。而最为著名的是，世界红茶的原产地在桐木，历史上出产正山小种等红茶，并流播欧洲，移植于印度及斯里兰卡等国家，是世界红茶的祖先。现代有江氏后人江元勋试制红茶新秀金骏眉，红遍大江南北。

Tongmu Village is located in Mount Wuyi national nature reserve area. It is the source of the Jiuquxi River, which goes through Mount Wuyi resort. Tongmu village has 33 natural villages, distributed along Tongmu canyon fault zone with a length of 35 kilometers from north to south and a width of 25 kilometers from east to west.

Tongmu Village is named after Tongmu Pass. An ancient road (which is now highway) connecting Fujian and Jiangxi province went through the pass. The village is an essential place for transport and military in ancient times. It is one of the impregnable eight passes of Mount Wuyi. Facing north at the pass , you can see mountains reach out high into clouds. The V-shape canyon is just like a natural chasm stretching out to Qianshan County in Jiangxi Province.

Tongmu pass boasts a sound ecological system and is honoured as "heaven for birds", "kingdom of snakes", "world of insets", etc. It is also well known as the original place of black tea. Many breeds of black tea diffused through Europe, transplanted in countries like India and Sri Lanka, etc. The black tea in Tongmu Village is the ancestor of black tea around the world. A new type of black tea called Jin Junmei, made by Jiang Yuanxuan, is now popular across the country.

02

01 桐木村制茶的箐楼 / 那兴海 摄
Tea-making house (by Na Xinghai)

02 与江西接壤的桐木关口 / 赖小兵 摄
Tongmu Pass bordering Jiangxi province (by Lai Xiaobing)

武夷山市岚谷乡樟村村

＋

Zhangcun Village, Langu Town, Wuyishan City

樟村是崇阳溪东溪的源头村，崇阳溪东溪发源于樟村和岭阳两地。樟村位于岚谷乡最北的偏远山区，北与江西上饶相连，东与浦城县接壤。樟村常年云雾环绕，气候湿润，温度适宜，雨量充沛，四季分明，弯弯曲曲的东溪，从原始森林中缓缓而下，东溪流下高山，流过平原，流到岚谷乡政府所在地，逐渐变得宽广起来。

樟村的先民从江西迁来，樟村又在明清年间从浦城划归崇安府管辖。樟村属闽赣交界革命老区基点村，全村共有186户、763人、共分樟村一、二组、碗厂、东坑、桂岭下、齐白、磨石坑、溪边八个村民小组。

樟村如同其他村庄一样，大多数轻壮年人都出去了，以致于村中小学也停办，樟村小学恩美楼是二十世纪八十年代由香港人捐建，于2004年停办。

前往樟村的路上有一个小村角岭塔自然村，村民只有五六位，清澈的溪水绕村而过，远看美丽，走近才能感受荒村的寂寞。

Zhangcun Village is the source of the Dongxi River of the Chongyang River, which originates from Zhangcun and Lingyang. Zhangcun Village lies in the extreme north of Langu Town, connecting Shangrao on the north and Pucheng on the east. Zhangcun Village is covered by clouds and fogs all year round with humid climate, mild temperature and plenty rainfall. The Dongxi River winds its way from the forest to Langu Town and becomes wider gradually.

Ancestors of Zhangcun Village came from Jiangxi Province. The village has 186 families with a population of 763 in eight village groups.

Like other villages, young people in Zhangcun leave their hometown for new lives. As a results, the primary school has to close down. Enmei building in the primary school, donated by a person from Hong Kong in 1980s, was closed down in 2004.

Lingta natural village has only five to six villagers. Clear water goes around the village. It looks beautiful at a distance, but it feels lonely when coming closer.

02

03

01　崇阳溪上游东溪源头之水发源于岚谷乡樟村村
／ 那兴海 摄
Zhangcun Village, Langu Town (by Na Xinghai)

02　留守在村里的仅剩老人妇女和孩子 ／ 涧南 摄
Elderly peole, women and children left behind (by Jian Nan)

03　展示美甲的孩子 ／ 涧南 摄
Children showing nail paintings (by Jian Nan)

建阳市黄坑镇坳头村

+

Aotou Village, Huangkeng County, Jianyang City

坳头村地处武夷山国家级自然保护区内，平均海拔 1000 米，终年云雾缭绕，气候温润，目之所及皆是绿树翠竹，是麻阳溪源头村。

北宋宣和年间江西路氏迁到此处，因村庄地处山坳顶部而得名。有五柳关、鱼洋谷、唐石涧、卧石听泉、七折三磬、竹径听蝉等八个名胜景点。

麻阳溪是建溪三大支流之一，贯穿建阳的黄坑、麻沙、莒口等地，发源于坳头村。坳头与桐木相邻，所以也是红茶正山小种的发源地，现在村里有机生态茶园 1400 亩。坳头村还拥有丰富的毛竹资源，毛竹总面积超过 8900 亩，成了名副其实的"林海竹乡"。茶叶和毛竹的收益，年年增加，村民的生活得到了改善，七成家庭有私家车，家家都过着富足的幸福日子。

Aotou Village, located in Mount Wuyi national nature reserve area, is 1000 meters above sea level at average. All the year round, the village is covered by clouds and fogs with humid climate and mild temperature. Aotou Village is the source of the Mayangxi River.

In Northern Song Dynasty, the Lu clan came here from Jiangxi. The village is named for its location, that is, on the top of a col. Around the village there are eight attractions, such as Wuliu pass, Yuyang valley, Tangshi ravine, etc.

The Mayangxi River is one of the three tributaries of the Jianxi River, going through Hengkeng, Masha, Jukou and orginating from Aotou Village. Aotou Village is close to Tongmu Village, so it is also where black tea originated. It has an organic ecological tea garden covering 1400 mu. Aotou Village has a rich bamboo resource. Its bamboo growing area surpasses 8900 mu and is renowned as the "sea of bamboos". Profits brought by tea and bamboo increased annually. Villagers' living condition has been improved greatly.

01　麻阳溪源头之水黄坝溪 / 那兴海 摄
　　The source of the Mayangxi River: the Huangbaxi stream（by Na Xinghai）

02　坳头村的竹林 / 那兴海 摄
　　Bamboo forest in Aotou Village (by Na Xinghai)

03　坳头村高山茶园 / 那兴海 摄
　　Tea garden in Aotou Village (by Na Xinghai)

01

01 清朝时村里最热闹的街道 / 那兴海摄
The most lively street in the village in Qing Dynasty (by Na Xinghai)

02 大源村南溪圣殿与文昌阁 / 涧南 摄
Nanxi Temple and Wenchang Pavilion in Dayuan Village (by Jian Nan)

Dayuan Village lies in the northeast of Xinqiao Town. The village is seated at a long basin surrounded by high mountains. On the mountains, trees and bamboos grow lushly. The Beixi River originates from Camellia Pass, flowing from north to south, slowly passing the east of village. It joins the Jinxi River after flowing through Taining gate, and become part of the River Min, heading for the sea.

Dayuan Village is situated at the boundary of Fujian and Jiangxi province, bordering Lichuan county(Jiangxi) on the north. It is the gateway of two provinces and four counties. It is also one of the essential roads from Fujian to centre China since ancient times.

Dayuan Village has a long history. According to the family tree, this village was built at the beginning of Northern Song Dynasty, dating back over one thousand years. Temples of Dai clan and Yan clan has been standing for more than 280 years. A group of stone arch bridges and official halls of Dai clan are listed in the relic protection sites. Relic sites like Wenchang pavilion, Nanxi temple, Zhou Sima Mansion, camellia pass, ancient post road, etc. are well preserved. Two historical living fossils in the village, Nuo dance (a dance to exorcise evils) and dragon dance, are listed as Fujian province's non-material cultural heritage. Thus, Dayuan Village is honoured as "China's historic and cultural village", becoming the only village possessing two non-material culture heritages in Sanming city.

大源村位于新桥乡东北部，村落位于群山合抱的狭长型盆地中，四周千米高峰竞秀，林木茂密，盛产竹笋。村东之北溪源出茶花隘，自北而南，缓缓沿村庄东侧流过，南流至泰宁城关后注入金溪，汇闽江而入海，成为闽江主要源头之一。

大源村处于闽赣交界，北接江西黎川县，是两省四县的重要门户，自古就是福建通往中原的交通要道之一。

大源村历史悠久，据族谱记载，该村始建于北宋初年，距今已有一千多年的历史。村中戴氏、严氏两座宗祠已有280余年的历史，石拱桥群、戴氏官厅等一并被纳入县级文物保护单位。文昌阁、南溪圣殿、州司马第、茶花隘、古驿道等古迹至今保存完好。如今还保存着有历史"活化石"之称的傩舞及"赤膊龙灯"，分别入选福建省第一批和第三批非物质文化遗产名录。大源村荣膺"中国历史文化名村"称号，成为三明市唯一一个拥有两项省级非物质文化遗产的中国历史文化名村。

02

第四章　＋　消逝风化的典雅宅第

当人们不再有机会站在厅堂祖先的灵位前面，亲手点燃一炷香，人生应该有的尊严和尊敬就无处汲取了。

当人们不再有机会祖孙三代围坐在厅堂里，在祖先画像的注视下进餐、议事时，人生应该有的伦常和孝道也无处学习了。

当人们不再有机会看雨水从天井淌下、听夜风从屋檐下吹过，人生那与生俱来与自然的亲近也荡然无存了。

当人们不再有机会在雕梁画栋的精致里起居长大，人生应该具有的艺术基因也从此断裂了。

这些即将遗失的，就是传统民居可以留给我们的文化财富。

闽江流域的人居建筑（包括祠堂、廊桥等）是福建人民在长期的生产和生活中逐渐形成的，既有中原建筑文化的余脉，又有本土人居文化的因素。传统民居通过千万个能工巧匠的手，被雕凿成为了一件一件的艺术品。

闽江流域的人们，长期生活在这样的屋檐下，中国人的传统居住文化、社区形态、伦理艺术、风水理念等等，都在这样的传统民居中保留着。

但是城市化的进程，毫不留情地将这一切摧毁。

于是，无所皈依的乡愁就像那一江春水。

Weathered Mansions

If people no longer worship their ancestors in front of the memorial tablet, there is no place to learn dignity and respect.

If an extended family no longer dine and discuss together in a hall decorated with their ancestors' portraits, they have little chance to learn human relations and filial piety.

If people no longer have the opportunity to watch the rain falling from patios or hear the wind blowing under the eaves, their innate intimacy with nature come to an end.

If people do not grow up in delicate surroundings, their artistic talent can be inspired from nowhere.

All those above are cultural values that traditional residents pass upon us.

Architecture along the River Min, such as temples and covered bridges, were built and developed in the long history of Fujian. These architecture preserve Central China traditions as well as local living style, designed and decorated by thousands of skillful craftsmen.

People, by the River Min, are all living in houses like that. Such traditional house maintains living styles, community patterns, human relations, and fortune worship of Chinese people.

However, all were ruined in the process of urbanization.

Therefore, the unrest homesick flows just like a never ending river.

01 富屯溪沿岸民居的门面均为砖雕。光泽县崇
仁乡古街 / 涧南 摄

Along the Futunxi River, house gates are
decorated by carved bricks. The ancient street in
Chongren Village of Guangze County (by Jian Nan)

02 闽江沿岸民居（宗祠）建筑工艺大气与细腻
并存。邵武市沿山镇古山村 / 李世雄 摄

Clan temples in Gushan Village, integrating
grandness and delicacy. (by Li Shixiong)

03 邵武市沿山镇徐溪村矗立在街坊的牌楼风光
依旧 / 曲利明 摄

A memorial arch in Xuxi Village, Yanshan
Town, Shaowu City. (by Qu Liming)

02

03

01   尤溪县桂峰村石狮厝的名称缘自他家有一座精美的青石狮子，其实他家的门楣石雕也很精美 / 涧南 摄

      Shishicuo is named after an elegant stone lion in the house. The stone carving on the lintel of the doors are extraordinary as well in Guifeng Village, Youxi County (by Jian Nan)

02   永安市青水乡沧海村客家民居的门面灵动而简朴 / 涧南 摄

      Doors of the Hakkas are simple but attractive in Canghai Village, Qingshui Town, Yong'an City (by Jian Nan)

01 　　闽江沿岸的民居经常在门前安排水塘，既有防火的作用，也有
风水聚财的效果。闽清县后垅村 / 涧南 摄

　　People live by the River Min follow a convention of digging a
pond in front of the house in case of a fire. The pond is also a symbol
of collecting fortune. (Houlong Village, Minqing County) (by Jian Nan)

02 　　闽江民居的门面白墙黑瓦在蓝天下十分协调。尤溪县双鲤村卢
兴邦宅 / 涧南 摄

　　White walls and black roofs match well under the blue sky.
(Shuangli Village, Youxi County) (by Jian Nan)

02

01   闽江民居大门的门神彩绘往往是富裕人家才有，留下了古代民间画匠的手艺 永安市安贞堡 / 焦红辉 摄

    Drawings of safe guarding gods only appear at gates of rich people's houses. The drawings preserve the ancient painting skills. (An'zhenbao, Yong'an City) (by Jiao Honghui)

02   黄土建造的房屋，门面不失风采 武夷山市五夫镇赤石村 / 曲利明 摄

    A house built by loess in Chishi Village, Wufu Town, Wuyishan City. (by Qu Liming)

03   福神登门 清流县赖坊乡 / 曲利明 摄

    Visited by fortune mascot (Laifang Village, Qingliu County). (by Qu Liming)

02

03

01 　　装饰门面的建筑理念与中国人的生活哲学密切相关　建阳市书坊乡 ／ 曲利明 摄
　　Decorating ideology is closely related to Chinese philosophy. (Shufang Village, Jianyang City) (by Qu Liming)

02 　　门神守户，进出平安　武夷山市五夫镇赤石村 ／ 曲利明 摄
　　To live peacefully in the protection of safe guarding gods. (Chishi Village, Wufu Town, Wuyishan City) (by Qu Liming)

03 　　门头虎头，辟邪纳福　清流县嵩口镇沧龙村 ／ 曲利明 摄
　　A tiger-headed tablet outside the door distracts evils and invites fortune. (Canglong Village, Songkou Town, Qingliu County) (by Qu Liming)

02

03

01　闽江流域民居的厅堂呈现出极其丰富的内容，似乎是一部从古到今的史籍　清流县赖坊乡 / 曲利明 摄

　　Houses by the River Min contain diverse contents, just like a book showing the history of the River Min from the ancient time till now. (Laifang Village, Qingliu County) (by Qu Liming)

02　厅堂一定是中国人红白喜事举办的场所 / 曲利明 摄

　　A hall is the place where Chinese people hold a wedding or a funeral. (by Qu Liming)

03　破旧的老宅，依旧保持着厅堂的威严　泰宁县新桥乡大源村 / 曲利明 摄

　　A shabby old house still shows solemnity. (Dayuan Village, Xinqiao Town, Taining County) (by Qu Liming)

04　厅堂的柱子永远要有对联　宁化县安远镇赵家源村 / 曲利明 摄

　　Inside the hall, pillars are pasted with couplets at any time. (Zhaojiayuan Village, An'yuan Town, Ninghua County) (by Qu Liming)

05　失修的庙宇将神灵寄居于民居的厅堂里 / 曲利明 摄

　　Spirit tablets in temples that are out of repair are placed temporarily in the halls of local people's houses. (by Qu Liming)

02

03

04

05

01　报纸补旧，厅堂概念基本削弱 / 曲利明 摄
　　As walls pasted by newspapers, the traditional function of halls is fading away. (by Qu Liming)

02　大厅不尽是公共场所，也是张贴各种画图的地方 / 曲利明 摄
　　A hall not only acts as a public place, but also a place to post pictures. (by Qu Liming)

03　如今村里的年轻人结婚，也还是会回到古宅里办一场婚礼　古田县杉洋镇 / 曲利明 摄
　　When young people get married nowadays, they will choose to hold the wedding in the old house of their ancestors'. (Shanyang Town, Gutian County) (by Qu Liming)

04　厅堂的墙上挂满祖先的照片　永泰县嵩口镇 / 王鹭佳 摄
　　Photos of ancestors are hung on walls in the hall. (Songkou Town, Yongtai County) (by Wang Lujia)

05　新房的厅堂，祭祀神位必不可少 / 曲利明 摄
　　Spirit tablets are essential in a new building hall. (by Qu Liming)

02

03

04

05

02

03

01   正在消失的美丽 邵武县沿山镇古山村 / 曲利明 摄
The beauty of Village is disappearing. (ancient village in Guangze County) (by Qu Liming)

02   加官进爵也是闽江民居砖雕的主要内容之一 / 曲利明 摄
The wish to be prompted to a higher rank is usually carved on bricks. (by Qu Liming)

03   墙头上的故事，文人雅士的高尚生活在闽江民居建筑石雕上也得到表现 永泰嵩口镇古民居 / 曲利明
Stories and lives of noble people are shown on the stones' carving. (old houses in Songkou Town, Yongtai County) (by Qu Liming)

01 　　壁画也是闽江民居装饰的一个主要形式　光泽县止马镇岛石村祠堂 / 涧南 摄

Fresco is another major decoration used by the people of the River Min. (ancestral hall in Daoshi Village, Zhima Town, Guangze County) (by Jian Nan)

02 　　闽江民居墙头彩绘也会将祖先故事作为主题，除了装饰，更重要是教育后人　永泰嵩口镇古民居 / 曲利明 摄

Paintings showing stories of ancestors are used to decorate the house as well, but more importantly to educate later generations. (old house in Songkou Town, Yongtai County) (by Qu Liming)

03 　　闽江民居彩绘装饰性极强　永安青水乡 / 涧南 摄

Coloured drawing is a really nice decoration. (Qingshui Tjown. Yong'an City) (by Jian Nan)

04 　　民间彩绘也会扩展到其他建筑如廊桥的装饰上　松溪县五福桥 / 涧南 摄

Local coloured drawing is also used for decoration on covered bridges. (Wufu Bridge in Songxi County) (by Jian Nan)

05 　　闽江民居墙头彩绘同时具备教化的功能　永泰嵩口镇古民居 / 曲利明 摄

Coloured drawing on walls has the function of educating people. (old house in Songkou Town, Yongtai County) (by Qu Liming)

02

03

04

05

01 精美的雕刻，记录了老宅主人曾经的辉煌 / 曲利明 摄
Delicate carvings in the old mansion record the owner's glorious life. (by Qu Liming)

02 屋梁木雕加彩绘美轮美奂 永安青水乡沧海村民居 / 涧南 摄
Wood carvings together with coloured drawing look even more marvelous. (Canghai Village, Qingshui Town, Yong'an City) (by Jian Nan)

03 屋梁彩色木雕十分精细，鹤鸟栩栩如生 永安青水乡沧海村客家民居 / 涧南 摄
Cranes on the wood carvings are so fine as if they were living (Hakka house in Canghai Village, Qingshui Town, Yong'an City) (by Jian Nan)

04 在民居木雕的窗雕中嵌入文字也是闽江民居的一种建筑装饰形式 尤溪县双鲤村卢兴邦宅花窗 / 涧南 摄
Language engraved in wood carvings of the windows. (Shuangli Village, Youxi County) (by Jian Nan)

05 屋梁支柱木刻装饰为花篮 永安青水乡沧海村客家民居 / 涧南 摄
Wood carving on the roof pillar is decorated in the shape of baskets. (Hakka house in Canghai Village, Qingshui Town, Yong'an City) (by Jian Nan)

02

03

04

05

02

03

04

02

03

01   民居建筑三大主体：厅堂、起居房和灶堂，闽江民居的灶堂大都井井有条，各种用具
整齐有序 / 曲利明 摄
Local people's house consists of three parts: a hall, a living room and a kitchen. Their
kitchens are usually very neat. (by QuLiming)

02   闽江民居灶台占用空间都很大，可以几个人同时操作 / 曲利明 摄
The hearth is large enough for a few people working on it at the same time. (by Qu Liming)

03   灶台往往与餐桌相连，宁化安远镇岩前村家际村 / 曲利明 摄
Hearths are usually connected with dinning tables. Yanqian Village, An' yuan Town,
Ninghua County. (by Qu Liming)

01

02

01　闽江民居最有生活氛围的是各种吊挂，农具和生活用具在方便使用的前提下挂在墙上 ／ 曲利明 摄
In people's life, the most interesting phenomenon is to hang farm tools and other objects on walls.（by Qu Liming）

02　农具有序排列悬挂 ／ 曲利明 摄
Farm tools hung in order（by Qu Liming）

03　千奇百态的吊挂组合 ／ 曲利明 摄
Various hanging objects（by Qu Liming）

04　蓑衣悬挂在厅堂 ／ 曲利明 摄
Straw rain cape hung in the hall.（by Qu Liming）

02

03

01　锁的故事 / 曲利明 摄
　　Stories of locks (by Qu Liming)

02　古老的锁已经十分稀少 / 曲利明 摄
　　Old locks are rarely seen.(by Qu Liming)

03　各种造型的锁显示民间锁匠的聪明才智 / 曲利明 摄
　　Different kinds of locks show the talents of lock craftsmen. (by Qu Liming)

04　关公的大刀当门闩，有辟邪防贼的功效 / 曲利明 摄
　　Using swords of Guangong as the gate lock can threat thieves and exorcise evils. (by Qu Liming)

05　铜锁是古代各种锁具中最精致的　顺昌县元坑镇槎溪村 / 曲利明 摄
　　Bronze locks is the most delicate among ancient locks. (by Qu Liming)

04

05

02

03

01   毛主席语录，一个时代的烙印 / 曲利明 摄
Quotation from Chairman Mao: mark of the time.(by Qu Liming)

02   油漆书写的标语 浦城县观前村 / 李世雄 摄
Slogan written by oil paint (Guangqian Village, Pucheng County) (by Li Shixiong)

03   选择内容合适的毛主席语录，记录了那个时代人们的精神追求 邵武市金坑乡 / 赖小兵 摄
Some of the quotations of Chairman Mao represent the spiritual pursuit of the people at that time. (by Lai Xiaobing)

04   毛主席语录和对联等形成了有趣的混搭 闽清县宏琳厝 / 曲利明 摄
Quotations from Chairman Mao and couplet match interestingly. (Honglincuo in Minqing County) (by Qu Liming)

05   "文革"时期的语录，无处不在 / 曲利明 摄
Quotations in the period of Cultural Revolution can be seen everywhere. (by Qu Liming)

04

05

第五章 ＋ 渐行渐远的农耕时代

耕种、养殖、砍伐、狩猎，延续了几千年的农耕时代，就这样渐行渐远了吗？

如果从空中俯瞰闽江流域，你会发现树根状的密集水系将武夷山脉的土地牢牢扎住。溪流江河和土地，相依相生，人类的一切，物产、生活、思想，无一不是从那里生长。

从古越族人到南迁而来的中原后裔，世世代代，这片江河土地就是他们生长繁衍的原乡。不论是善操舟楫的古越人后裔，还是那些中原子民，都选择了择水而居，闽江的万千条溪流，就像大地母亲奉献出来的乳汁，养育他们及至如今。

在田野上耕作、在江河里捕捞、在山林间砍伐、在市井中贩卖。传统农耕社会是一幅美景吗？可是现在的人们为什么要不顾一切地抛弃这些，离开土地，背井离乡，毫不犹豫地将双腿从泥巴里拔出，坐上高铁动车投入繁华？

拥抱现代化就一定要丢弃山水宁静，就一定要远离流云繁星吗？

农耕不仅仅是面朝黄土背朝天，也不仅仅是勤禾日当午、汗滴禾下土。农耕不仅仅是一种方式，还是一种心态、一种哲学、一种灵魂。

Farewell to Times of Agriculture

Farming, cultivating, timber felling, and hunting have been continued for thousands of years. Has the times of agriculture gone gradually?

Having a bird's eye view of the River Min, you will find out the drainage system stretches like roots firmly holding Mount Wuyi and the lands. Rivers and lands rely on each other, from where grew everything of the people, including their production, life and thoughts.

Both ancient Yue tribes and descendants of Central China chose to live by the River Min from generation to generation. Thousands of tributaries of the River Min, like the milk of a mother, have been cultivating the people.

People working in the field, fishing in the river, felling timber in the forest, and doing business in the market compose a picture of tradition agricultural society. Isn't that beautiful? But why do people so haste to leave everything behind? Why are they so eager to drag their feet out of mud and head for cities on high spreed trains?

Is it really necessary to embrace modernization at the cost of tranquil life and the beauty of nature?

Agriculture is not only hard labour working or a living style, but also an attitude, a philosophy, a soul.

　　用耕牛犁田在闽江农村已不多见，这个农民的牛是租来的，
耕牛也已经很稀少 / 弗兰克 摄

Farm cattle is not common in villages of the River Min. This
cattle is rent as the number of farm cattle is decreasing. (by
Frank)

02　　告别集体化生产的农村，种植已经个体化。富屯溪上游西
溪，光泽县水口乡农民在播种 / 涧南 摄

Collective farming is over. Farming is now individual
business. Farmers are sowing seeds in Shuikou Town, Guangze
County. (by Jian Nan)

02

01

01   传统的水碓舂米方式在目前闽江流域农村已经十分少见。永安市青水乡海沧畲族村农民在舂米 / 赖小兵 摄

This way of pounding rice is rare in the basin of the River Min. The farmer is pounding rice in a mortar in Canghai Shenzu Village, Qingshui Town, Yongan City. (by Lai Xiaobing)

02   收成时节，清流县长校镇留坑村农民在翻晒谷子 / 陈伟凯 摄

In harvest season, farmers are busy drying grain in Liukeng Village, Changxiao Town, Qingliu County. (by Chen Weikai)

02

01

01 　　在闽江流域农村烤烟房四处都是，烟农在烤烟
房内挂烟叶 / 涧南 摄
　　Tobacco curing house is built everywhere in the
villages of the River Min. Tobacco farmers are hanging
tobacco leafs in the curing house. (by Jian Nan)

02 　　烟叶已经成为闽江流域农民的主要收入，建溪
支流麻阳溪一家烟农全家在整理烤烟 / 涧南 摄
　　Farmers' major income comes from tobacco
industry. A family is dealing with flue-cured tobaccos.
(by Jian Nan)

01   金溪上的蛋民 / 涧南 摄
The Dan people by the Jinxi River. (by Jian Nan)

02   顺昌县溪边聚集着一个蛋民聚落 / 周跃东 摄
A community of the Dan people by the river in Changshun County. (by Zhou Yuedong)

03   蛋民在水上讨生活十分辛苦，后代均不再继承此业。邵武市富屯溪边的渔民收工回家 / 涧南 摄
The Dan people can hardly make a good living from working by the river, so their descendants all look for other jobs. Fishermen come home from work at the Futunxi River, Shaowu City. (by Jian Nan)

01　鸬鹚捕鱼是闽江流域流传了几千年的方式，建溪流域的年轻渔民在歇息 ／ 阮任艺 摄
　　Ever since thousands of years ago, fishermen caught fish with the help of cormorants. Young fishermen are resting. (by Ruan Renyi)

02　建阳弓鱼是建溪流域独特的一种生产方式 ／ 吴寿华 摄
　　Fishermen in Jianyang keep the fish live longer by curling the fish in the shape of "Gong". This is a unique method for production. (by Wu Shouhua)

03　闽江口海鲜因为处于咸水和淡水交界处而异常鲜美，闽江口的壶江岛螃蟹收获季节 ／ 涧南 摄
　　The estuary of the River Min is mixed with salt water and fresh water. thus the sea food in this area is extremely delicious. This is the crab harvest season on Hujiang Island. (by Jian Nan)

01   闽江流域毛竹种植面积极大，因此竹笋加工成为农民重要
的副业 / 王鹭佳 摄

Along the River Min, bamboo planting area is large, so
processing bamboo shoots has become an important subsidiary
production for the farmers. (by Wang Lujia)

02   传统榨油由烘干、碾碎、过筛、蒸煮、制饼、压榨等工序构成，
闽清县溪源村传统榨油作坊内农妇在过筛 / 涧南 摄

Traditional oil manufacture consists of many procedures, such
as drying, pulverizing, sieving, steaming, etc. In a traditional oil
manufacture workshop, a woman is sieving. (by Jian Nan)

01   闽江流域溪河沙质土壤形成花生种植传统，清流农民在清洗花生 / 王鹭佳 摄

In the sandy soil of the River Min, it is a tradition to plant peanuts. Farmers are cleaning peanuts. (by Wang Lujia)

02   建莲是福建建阳建宁两地的名产，中国古典小说《红楼梦》中亦有记述。武夷山五夫镇农民在剥莲子 / 涧南 摄

Lotus is a famous specialty of Jianyang and Jianning in Fujian province. This is also described in a Chinese classic novel dream of the Red Mansion. Farmers are taking the lotus seed out and striping off the covering. (by Jian Nan)

01   酿酒在民间自古存在，如今在闽江流域建溪的建瓯酿
酒已经工业化 / 李世雄 摄
        Wine making is not a new fashion. In Jian'ou, wine
making has become industrialized. (by Li Shixiong)

02   农民个人酿酒在闽江流域很普遍，古田县杉洋镇白溪
村村民在自家酒窖里忙碌 / 涧南 摄
        Farmers making their own wine is common in the basin
of the River Min. Villagers are busy in their wine cellar in
Baixi Village, Shanyang Town, Gutian County. (by Jian Nan)

02

01

01   线面是闽江下游的特色食品，永泰县梧桐镇线面制作家庭作坊 / 陈伟凯 摄

Xian noodle is a specialty in downstream area of the River Min. A family workshop for making Xian noodle in Wutong town, Yongtai County. (by Chen Weikai)

02   生猪养殖是闽江农村历史以来的主要家庭副业，邵武市金坑乡的小猪仔买卖 / 弗兰克 摄

Raising pigs is a major family subsidiary production in villages of the River Min. Porket business in Jinkeng town, Shaowu City. (by Frank)

02

01 闽江流域丰富的竹资源和稻草资源是土纸生产的基础，顺昌县大历镇岚下乡埂头村农妇在整理土纸 / 阮任艺 摄

The abundant bamboo and straw resource is the basis for paper manufacturing. A woman is taking care of the hand-made paper. (by Ruan Renyi)

02 闽江流域渔业在水库面积不断扩大时也得到很大发展，尤溪县水口镇库区的渔女在织网 / 曾璜 摄

The fishing industry of the River Min is developing with the expansion of the reservoir. A fisherwoman is weaving the fishing net. (by Zeng Huang)

第六章　+　千年留存的悠悠古意

人们说，福建的老百姓是最虔诚的一群人，只要你到闽江一带的村野宫庙去找寻，总是能遇上一群抬着神像巡游的人。

人们说，福建的老百姓是最安逸的一群人，如果你有机会在夜里飞翔着俯瞰闽江流域的山水村庄，你会发现，在那些戏台上总有笙歌回旋。

因为是善操舟楫的古越人，蛇与蛙就是他们的崇拜；因为他们也是荆楚子民，将走桥奇俗带到闽江流域的时候，也将对屈原的敬仰播撒在七闽之地；因为他们一代一代从中原迁徙而来，如风卷黄叶一般，将浙赣一带的戏剧傀儡、茶灯游艺扫进了闽江，任其顺水而下。

中原汉人敬畏五谷神，来到闽地，依然每到丰收季就到福建最高峰、闽江源头金铙山顶的五谷神庙去朝拜。从遥远的殷商跳到如今的傩舞从祠堂出发，绕村而行，以求风调雨顺，五谷丰登，人畜平安。神秘的李家五经魁、铿锵的安贞鼓；诙谐的龟蚌舞、昂扬的挑幡；热闹的游旱船、优雅的闽派古琴……纷纷繁繁，热热闹闹，千百年来如同银杏秋叶一般层层叠叠在闽江流域堆积、聚集、播散。

隆古、近古，闽江之水承载着的是那千年之前留存下来的悠悠古意。

Traditions of Thousands of Years

It is said that the people in Fujian are devout. Whenever you walk around in villages of the River Min, you will always come across a group of people carrying statues of gods parading in the village.

It is said that the people in Fujian live in a most leisure way. If you fly above their villages at night, you are sure to find out villagers singing and playing on the stage.

As descendants of ancient Yue tribe who can skillfully sail boats and ships, they worship snakes and frogs. Also they are descendants from ancient states Jing and Chu, so they brought with them a tradition to walk on bridges on the fifth day of the fifth lunar month to memorize and show respect to Qu Yuan, a great politician. While people migrated southward from Central China generation after generation, opera, puppet, tea art and entertainments originated from Zhejiang and Jiangxi spread along the River Min.

The Han people worship Crop Goddess. After migrating to Fujian, they pilgrimage to the Crop Goddess Temple on highest peak of Fujian in every harvest season. On the way to Crop Goddess Temple, they play the Nuo dance, a dance dating back to Shang Dynasty, praying for a favorable harvest safe year. Diversified folk performances, such as mysterious Wujingkui, sonorous Anzhen drum, humorous dance of turtles and clams, lively land boat dancing, and elegant ancient zither are of great culture values diffusing and settling down for centuries along the River Min.

From the time immemorial, tradition and culture keep flowing along the River Min.

01　夜空下的南平市延平区樟湖镇蛇王庙 / 那兴海 摄
　　Shewang Temple at night, Zhanghuban Town, Yanping District, Nanping City. (by Na Xinghai)

02　樟湖镇在元宵时举办游蛇灯活动 / 赖小兵 摄
　　On Lantern Festival, people in Zhanghu Town hold snake-shape lantern and parade. (by Lai Xiaobing)

02

01 　　秦汉时期，闽中各地的先人信奉蛇神为祖先之神。目前只有樟湖镇保留了完整而原始的崇蛇习俗，以蛇作为图腾，每年农历七月初七清晨，樟湖镇一年一度的游蛇活动在闽江边开始 / 阮任艺 摄

　　In Qin and Han Dynasties, ancestors of Fujian worship snakes. However, only Zhanghu Town preserves full tradition of snake worship. Snake is their totem. On every seventh day of the seventh lunar month, people in Zhanghu Town holding snake worship parades from dawn by the River Min. (by Ruan Renyi)

02 　　樟湖镇蛇王庙也称为连公庙，供奉肖、连、张三位神明 / 那兴海 摄

　　Shewang Temple enshrines three gods, namely Xiao, Lian, and Zhang, thus it is also called Liangong Temple. (by Na Xinghai)

02

01   樟湖镇溪口村崇蛙巡境要绕村行进 / 阮任艺 摄
      Frog worship parade is travelling around Xikou Village. (by Ruan Renyi)

02   溪口村崇蛙游境先要请出肖、连、张三尊神像，祭拜后出巡 / 阮任艺 摄
      In Xikou Village, people have to carefully invite the statues of the three gods before the frog worship parade. (by Ruan Renyi)

03   溪口村三圣庙前仅存的明末清初石刻蛙塑像 / 阮任艺 摄
      The remaining stone statue of frog dating back to Ming and Qing Dynasties (by Ruan Renyi)

02

03

01 光泽县鸾凤乡油溪村承安桥（夫妻桥）"走桥"活动 / 赖小兵 摄
Bridge walking activities on Chengan Bridge, which is also called Couple Bridge (by Lai Xiaobing)

02 松溪县五福桥"走桥"时，两位为自己百年后制作奈何桥的老姐妹 / 涧南 摄
During the bridge walking activities on Wufu Bridge, two old women are making their own Naihe bridge, which can be used after their deaths. (by Jian Nan)

03 政和县杨源乡花桥是闽北一座精美的廊桥，也是"走桥"活动的重要场所 / 涧南 摄
Flower Bridge in Yangyuan Village, Zhenghe County, is a delicate covered bridge and important for bridge walking activities. (by Jian Nan)

01　　　“行傩”也称之为“傩舞”，是汉民族最古老的民俗，在闽江富屯溪流域的光泽、邵武和沙溪源头的建宁以及金溪源头泰宁一带广泛留存。邵武市大埠岗镇河源村的傩舞是目前保存较好的一支 / 赖小兵 摄

　　　“Xing Nuo” is also called Nuo Dance, the oldest tradition of the Han nationality. It is widely preserved in Guangze County, Shaowu City, Jianning County and Taining County in the basin of the River Min. The Nuo Dance Troupe in Heyuan Village of Dabugang Town, Shaowu City has well kept the tradition. (by Lai Xiaobing)

02　　　河源村傩舞省级传承人龚茂发 / 赖小兵 摄

　　　The inheritor of Nuo Dance in Heyuan Village. (by Lai Xiaobing)

03　　　田野上泰宁新桥乡大源村游傩进行中 / 涧南 摄

　　　People in Dayuan Village of Taining County are playing Nuo Dance in the fields. (by Jian Nan)

02

03

02

01   五谷神崇拜在闽江流域广泛存在，泰宁县新桥乡大源村下大源自然村的五谷神祭
        在进行中 / 涧南 摄
        Crop Goddess is widely worshiped along the River Min. Worship ceremony for Crop
        Goddess in Dayuan Village, Taining County. (by Jian Nan)

02   下大源村五谷神祭时村民整理祭台 / 涧南 摄
        Villagers of lower Dayuan Village are taking care of the altar in the worship
        ceremony of Crop Goddess. (by Jian Nan)

03   下大源村五谷神祭游神队伍最前面的人头顶香火 / 涧南 摄
        In the Crop Goddess worship parade, the person at the front holds burning incense
        on head. (by Jian Nan)

03

02

03

01 顺昌县郑坊乡的大圣祭拜活动内容有打糍粑、抢供果、设道场、采圣火、祭祀、跳僮、娱神、游神、过火山、打油锅、化替身等 / 涧南 摄

In Zhengfang Town of Shunchang County, worship ceremony of the Monkey King includes making glutinous rice cake, competing for offering fruits, constructing ceremony field, making holy flame, etc. (by Jian Nan)

02 大圣崇拜及游神活动在闽江流域广泛存在。每逢农历七月十七顺昌一带就会举行大圣祭拜民俗活动，活动规模宏大、盛况空前 / 涧南 摄

Worship of the Monkey King and its parade is frequently seen along the River Min. On every seventh day of the seventh lunar month, people in Shunchang hold worship ceremony of the Monkey King. This is a grand and splendid event. (by Jian Nan)

03 郑坊乡大圣活动的最后一项"下油锅"，刺激激烈，表现大圣无所畏惧勇往直前和百折不挠的精神 / 那兴海 摄

The last activity of Monkey King worship ceremony is "to jump into the boiling oil port" as to show respect to the fearless, aggressive and indomitable spirits of the Monkey King. (by Na Xinghai)

01 　　"三月三"是尤溪县彩洋村华光帝庙会的传统节日，相传有几百年的历史。祖先的传统节日将后代子孙都召唤了回来，欢度一年之中村里最热闹的节日 ／ 那兴海 摄

Double Third Day is a traditional festival of temple fair in Caiyang Village, Youxi County. It has been existing for hundreds of years. In the village, this is the most lively festival of the year. (by Na Xinghai)

02 　　在尚未开犁的水田里戏神是庙会活动里最刺激最热闹的传统民俗，寄托了村民们丰收吉祥的愿望 ／ 曲利明 摄

Parading in unploughed paddy field is the most exciting part among temple fair activities, showing villagers' wishes for harvest and fortune. (by Qu Liming)

03 　　村民们与华光帝在水田里尽情"玩耍"之后，到清溪中洗涤干净，就要送神祇返庙归座了 ／ 曲利明 摄

After playing in paddy fields, people have to clean the god's statue and place it back in the temple. (by Qu Liming)

02

03

01

01　永安市槐南乡槐南村的张大阔公做场戏的角色之一——大魁天下是祈福百姓丰年安康 / 赖小兵 摄
　　A role of the drama, "Da Kui" acts as the prayer for harvest and safety. (by Lai Xiaobing)

02　张大阔公做场戏中唯一的女性形象 / 涧南 摄
　　The only female image in the Drama. (by Jian Nan)

01   光泽县油溪村的采茶灯是闽江流域茶灯戏的一个余脉 / 涧南 摄
        Tea picking dance is part of the tea lantern drama. (by Jian Nan)

02   村中采茶灯的女演员 / 涧南 摄
        Actress in tea picking dance. (by Jian Nan)

03   油溪村采茶灯传承人傅庆高 / 涧南 摄
        Fu Qinggao, the inheritor of tea picking dance in Youxi Village. (by Jian Nan)

01   清流县李家五经魁又称"舞大鬼"，是产生于明朝正德年间的一种融武术与医学为一体的汉族舞蹈，因流传于该县李家乡而得名。五经魁表演特征独特，寄托了百姓祛邪、避灾、祈福的美好愿望，被列入福建省第二批"省级非物质文化遗产保护名录" / 赖小兵 摄

Wujingkui of Li clan is also called holy ghost dance, which is a Han dance integrating martial art and Chinese medicine philosophy. It originates in the village of Li clan. This performance is distinct, showing people's wishes for exorcising evils and disaster, and praying for fortune. It has been included in provincial non-material cultural heritage protection list. (by Lai Xiaobing)

02   李家五经魁都是农民在表演 / 赖小兵 摄
Farmers performing Wujingkui of Li clan (by Lai Xiaobing)

02

唱不完世上喜怒哀乐

写尽人间悲欢离合

金玉满

福

01

01   浦城县传子提线木偶艺人李声森在表演 / 陈伟凯 摄
      Li Shengsen, an inheritor of marionette art is performing
in Pucheng County. (by Chen Weikai)

02   闽江流域木偶戏的存在是民间傀儡文化的余脉，宁化
县水茜乡永盛堂傀儡班 / 赖小兵 摄
      Puppet show is part of the folk puppet culture. A puppet
theatrical troupe named Yong Shengtang in Shuixi Town,
Ninghua County (by Lai Xiaobing)

03   宁化县水茜乡永盛堂傀儡班是一个父子班 / 赖小兵 摄
      This puppet theatrical troupe in Shuixi Town, Ninghua
County, is owned by a father and son. (by Lai Xiaobing)

02

03

01   闽江流域广泛保存着三角戏。三角戏的剧目内容贴近百姓，演的
是家长里短的百姓故事，表演生动、语言诙谐有趣。光泽县崇仁乡儒
堂村的三角戏班目前还在坚持演出 / 赖小兵 摄
       In the basin of the River Min, people are fond of Sanjiao Drama
(a three-role drama) as its contents are based on local people's life.
This kind of drama is still on stage in Rutang Village, Chongren Town,
Guangze County. (by Lai Xiaobing)

02   清流县的民间三角戏 / 赖小兵 摄
       Sanjiao Drama in Qingliu County. (by Lai Xiaobing)

02

02

03

01   宁化县河龙乡祁剧戏班保留的古戏本
      The old script kept by Qilian theatrical troupe

02   宁化县河龙乡祁剧戏班的老艺人伊运鼎今年 84 岁了，依然有十足的中气和嘹亮的嗓子 / 郭晓丹 摄
      This actor is already eighty-four years old, but still has a strong voice. (by Guo Xiaodan)

03   宁化县河龙乡祁剧来源于江西，是闽赣地区的民间小戏 / 涧南 摄
      Qiju Opera, originating from Jiangxi, is now a local play in Fujian and Jiangxi Province. (by Jian Nan)

01 邵武市肖家坊镇将石游旱船是闽江流域（富屯溪）的一种独特民俗 / 赖小兵 摄

Land boat dancing in the basin of the River Min (the Futunxi River) is a special folk custom. (by Lai Xiaobing)

02 建宁宜黄戏俗称大戏、土戏，由昆曲、西秦腔发展演变而成，明朝末年由江西抚州传入建宁，盛于清朝 / 涧南 摄

Yihuang Opera, originating from Kunqu Opera and QinQiang Opera, is commonly known as the big opera. It is brought from Wuzhou to Jianning in late Ming Dynasty and prospered in Qing Dynasty. (by Jian Nan)

02

01 　　永安市槐南安贞旌鼓，鼓面直径约 50cm，除了鼓心为红色外，其余均漆成黑色。在永安槐南，家家户户都有一面大鼓和小鼓，鼓被称为镇宅的"胆"，又是节庆期间营造气氛的道具 / 涧南 摄

　　Anzhen drum, fifty centimeters in diameter, is painted red in the center and black elsewhere. In Huainan, every family has a big drum and a small drum. A drum means the courage for a family. It is used as a stage property in festivals. (by Jian Nan)

02 　　花灯戏和花鼓灯均从浙江省流入松溪花桥、路桥、塘边及祖墩乡一带，至今已有数百年历史 / 赖小兵 摄

　　Huadeng Opera and Huagudeng Dance originate from Zhejiang province, which have been existing for centuries. (by Lai Xiaobing)

02

01 建宁龟蚌舞源于"龟蚌相争,渔翁得利"这一典故,是建宁县里心镇新圩等村民间流传的一种民俗活动 / 润南 摄

Turtles and clams dance is based on the story of the fight between a turtle and clam, which is frequently played by people in Xinyu Village, Lixin Town, Jianning County. (by Jian Nan)

02 延平区峡阳镇小梅村的南剑戏,原名"乱弹",清末由江西传入闽北,后来不断吸收其它戏曲的剧目和表演艺术而形成,因延平为古南剑治所,故早期将其命名为"南剑戏" / 赖小兵 摄

Nanjian Opera in Xiaomei Village, originally named "Luan Tan", came from Jiangxi province. Through learning from other operas and arts, the opera gradually formed its style. As the village is governed by ancient Nanjian County, the opera altered its name to Nanjian Opera. (by Lai Xiaobing)

02

01 建瓯挑幡是极具闽江流域民俗特色的传统文艺活动，源于三百多年前，体现了汉族劳动人民尚武精神和民族气质 / 赖小兵 摄

"Tiao Fan" in Jian'ou is a very unique traditional activity, which has a history of three hundred and forty years. This activity presents the militarism and braveness of the Han nationality. (by Lai Xiaobing)

02 "高照灯"取吉星高照之意，这种巨型纸灯，由12组灯箱和三组旋转顶灯相叠而成，形体似塔，高达四层楼房 / 赖小兵 摄

"Gaozhao" lantern is a huge paper lantern, consisting of twelve lamp houses and three rotating lights, and looks like a four-story tower. (by Lai Xiaobing)

02

第七章　+　璀璨若星辰的天工绝技

都说福建是中原文化的宝库，中原的每一次板荡，都驱使人群向南迁徙，这些仓皇鼠窜的人流中，除了皇子皇孙官宦兵勇，还有就是那些百姓，他们当中不乏手艺人。

是他们，将中原娴熟高超的手工艺带到了福建，传承了下来。或许在中原，这些技艺已经消亡，但是在福建，却如同文物一般保留了下来。每一次的流徙，就有一批手艺南来，然后沉淀，留给今天人们的，是璀璨若星辰的天工绝技。

木活字印刷、大红袍制作技艺、建盏制作技艺、木拱廊桥制作技艺、民间剪纸、脱胎漆艺、软木画等等，还有那些普通得不能再普通的竹编、腌菜、酿酒、打银、木作、雕刻等等。

中国传统文化之美，在于那些手工时代遗留下来的技艺。在闽江流域，这些农耕文明的产物，随着时代变化与现代文明产生冲突，越来越边缘化，正在逐渐消失。

闽江流域目前还留存着许多传统手工艺，我们将它们称之为文化遗产，传统手工艺的文化遗产，需要以人为载体传承，传承人的身上承载着非物质文化遗产的薪火。

纸本记录，企图"延续香火"，或许能够为即将消失的绝技做最后的挽歌。

Unparallel Techniques

It is said that Fujian province is a treasure-house of Central China culture. Every revolution in Central China drove people to the south. In the migrating group, there were royal families and soldiers as well as common people, many of whom were craftsmen.

They brought superb skills and techniques to Fujian and passed them down. Perhaps such techniques had disappeared in Central China but were preserved in Fujian as cultural relics. Each migration brought a great many techniques southwards which were maintained by their descendants.

All of these are unparallel invaluable techniques for people today, such as wooden movable-type printing, Da Hongpao tea, cup-making, wooden covered bridge, paper-cutting art, oil paint ware, soft wood painting as well as bamboo weaving, pickles making, etc.

The beauty of tradition culture maintains in those techniques. In the basin of the River Min, the production of agriculture times is disappearing and marginalized in the conflict with modern civilization. The remaining traditional craftsmanship is the culture relics only to be passed on by people. Every inheritor is another starting point of these culture heritage.

Documentary records in paper can only serve as the elegy for the weak flame of those culture traditions.

【浦城剪纸】 ＋ Paper-cutting Art in Pucheng

地处闽浙赣三省交界处，以及建溪支流南浦溪源头的浦城县，是中原文明入闽首站之一。浦城剪纸作为一种独特的地域文化，既有中原文明的印记，又见吴越源流遗风，创作手法独特，作品拙朴纯净，真实自然地反映出浦城人民内心的寄托和追求。浦城人每逢办酒设宴，当地乡亲就会互相馈赠礼品，大到浴盆，小到鸡蛋，都要贴上剪纸加以装饰，以表达主人的良好祝愿，衬托喜庆气氛。浦城剪纸 2014 年入选国家级非物质文化遗产项目。

Pucheng County, at the conjunction of Fujian, Zhejiang, and Jiangxi provinces, is the entrance of Central China culture. Paper-cutting art is a unique regional culture. It is simple but honestly reflected the wishes and pursuits of people in Pucheng. Whenever people prepare for a feast or banquet, their relatives and friends will send them presents decorated by paper-cuttings. Pucheng paper-cutting art was listed in national non-material culture heritage items.

01   浦城富岭镇双坑村剪纸艺人林莲秀 / 陈伟凯 摄
Lin Lianxiu, a paper-cutting artist in Shuangkeng Village, Fuling Town, Pucheng City. (by Chen Weikai)

02   龚淑云的剪纸作品具有浓郁的民族风 / 陈伟凯 摄
Paper-cuttings by Gong Shuyun is strongly characterized by ethnic features. (by Chen Weikai)

01

02

地处建溪支流松溪的政和县东平镇，是一个有着 1800 年历史的古镇，素有"茶乡酒镇"的美誉，凭借着特殊的地理条件、优质的水源和独到的酿制工艺，出产的东平高粱酒声名远扬。目前东平高粱酿制技艺已经入选南平市非物质文化遗产名录，并已申报福建省非物质文化遗产项目。

Located by the Songxi River, Dongping Town is an ancient town with a history of one thousand and eight hundred years. It is renowned for tea and wine, especially broomcorn wine, which is specialized by high quality water and unique brewing process. This broomcorn brewing technique has been listed in non-material culture heritage of Nanping City and also a candidate for provincial protection item

01   张步瑞在检查酒的质量 / 陈伟凯 摄
Zhang Burui is examining the quality of wine. (by Chen Weikai)

02   南平政和东平高粱酒厂的张步瑞 / 陈伟凯 摄
Zhang Burui, a worker in broomcorn wine factory of Dongping Town. (by Chen Weikai)

【政和白茶】　＋　White Tea in Zhenghe

政和白茶产自福建省政和县，政和白茶以政和大白茶品种为原料，经特有的制茶技艺加工而成，具有鲜纯、毫香的品质特征，有白牡丹、白毫银针、寿眉、白毛猴、莲心等多个优质白茶品种。政和白茶渊源极深，可追溯到唐末宋初。宋代政和已成为重要的北苑贡茶主产区，生产的银针茶备受推崇，被文人誉为"北苑灵芽天下精"。宋徽宗政和年间（1115年），当时的关隶县因进献贡茶银针，"喜动龙颜，获赐年号，遂改县名关隶为政和"。

White tea is a specialty of Zhenghe County. It is made of the white tea plant grown in Zhenghe with special manufacture procedures. It is rich in scent and pure in taste. Various types of white tea are made of this tea plant, such as Baimudan, Baihao Yinzhen, Shoumei, etc. White tea in Zhenghe can be chased back to late Tang Dynasty and early Song Dynasty. In Song Dynasty, Zhenghe became a major white tea producing area. At that time, white tea from Guandi Town was favored by the emperor, thus the town named after the emperor's reign title "Zhenghe"

01　　白茶制作技艺传承人杨丰在制茶　／　陈伟凯 摄
Yang Feng, an inheritor of white tea, is making tea. (by Chen Weikai)

02　　怀着一颗虔诚的心做茶　／　陈伟凯 摄
Making tea with a devoted heart. (by Chen Weikai)

Qingcao tea of She Clan ╋ 【畲家青草茶】

01   顺昌畲家青草茶非遗传承人兰其平 / 陈伟凯 摄
         Lan Qiping, an inheritor of Qingcao tea of She
         clan in Shuanchang. (by Chen Weikai)

02   兰其平在制作青草茶 / 陈伟凯 摄
         Lan Qiping is making Qingcao tea. (by Chen
         Weikai)

青草茶是畲族百姓经过长时间的生活实践总结出来的用青草药治病的传统医疗方式，传统青草茶制作工艺时间长、口感苦涩。其秘方以"传内不传外"的方式口口相传。畲家青草茶采摘来自深山天然林、房前屋后种植的各种珍稀药材，根据采摘、辨识、清洗、晾备、调配、搓揉、蒸制等多道传统制作工艺，按不同配比制作成畲家青草茶。

Qingcao tea is a disease healing tea produced by She clan. It tastes bitter and takes a long time to make. The secret ingredient of Qingcao tea is passed over generations through word of mouth. She families pick up various herbs from forest or their plantation, and make the tea with specific proportions through various procedures.

建阳建盏艺人蔡炳龙 / 陈伟凯 摄
Cai Binglong, a cup-making artist in Jianyang. (by Chen Weikai)

【建盏】 ✛ Jianzhan Tea Cup

　　建盏是中国宋代八大名瓷之一，是我国黑瓷的代表，曾经为宋朝皇室御用茶具。建盏产自建窑，"建窑"是我国著名的古窑之一，有大量遗址位于今建阳市各地（原隶建宁府瓯宁县，今建瓯市）。由于宋时崇尚斗茶之风，故除了必须提供优质的茶叶之外，还需要有最适于斗茶所用的茶具，建盏因此而出现。当时上至至尊、下及士大夫们都认为建盏是斗茶最佳的珍品。建盏又称为兔毫盏，其绝品有曜变、油滴、鹧鸪斑等，在国际上享有盛名。建盏技艺已失传，近年建阳有众多艺人探索恢复其工艺，该技艺获得省级非物质文化遗产项目。

　　Jianzhan tea cup is one of the eight renowned porcelains in Song Dynasty. It is the representative of black porcelain in China. Jianyao kiln, a famous ancient kiln in China, is where Jianzhan tea cup produced. Abundant historic kilns are located in Jianyang City. In Song Dynasty, people favored tea competition. Therefore, besides good quality tea, a delicate tea set was needed. That is why Jianzhan tea cup comes into being. At that time, even the emperor regarded Jianzhan tea cup as the best tea set for tea competition. However, Jianzhan tea cup technique disappeared in history. In recent years, many porcelain craftsmen try to recover the lost techniques. This craftsmanship is listed in provincial non-material culture heritage.

顺昌木拱廊桥非遗传承人徐云双 / 陈伟凯 摄　Xu Yunshuang, an inheritor of wooden covered bridge in Shunchang. (by Chen Weikai)

徐云双在自己的作品顺昌县元坑镇廊桥里 / 陈伟凯 摄
Xu Yunshuang stands in covered bridge in Yuankeng Town, which is one of her work. (by Chen Weikai)

Wooden Covered Bridge Engineering ＋ 【木拱廊桥制作技艺】

Wooden covered bridge, with timber planks bended to form an arch bridge, is supported by rocks on two riversides. Its foundation consists of ten bulky round wooden bars which vertically and horizontally jointed in a structure similar to the Chinese character "八". Without a single nail, the bridge stands firmly by its own strength, force of friction, range of diameter, building angles etc. The structure of wooden covered bridge is simple but unique.

Wooden covered bridge is a unique contribution to the world history of bridges, a living fossil of China's bridge structure containing high quality engineering and aesthetic values.

木拱廊桥，以梁木穿插别压形成拱桥，桥足支撑在两岸的岩石上，底座由数十根粗大圆木纵横拼接对拱而成"八字结构"，不用钉铆，完全靠其自身的强度、摩擦力和直径的大小、所成的角度、水平的距离等巧妙搭接，结构简单却坚固异常，是一种"河上架桥，桥上建廊，以廊护桥，桥廊一体"的古老而独特的桥梁样式。

木拱廊桥是中国在世界桥梁史上的独特贡献，是我国木结构桥梁的活化石，是中国传统木构桥梁中技术含量最高的一个品类，具有极高的传统美学价值。

01

02

【湛卢宝剑】 ✛ Zhanlu Sword

　　湛卢剑是春秋时期铸剑名匠欧冶子所铸名剑之一，五大盖世名剑之首。据《越绝书》记载，公元前496年，越王允常悬求天下第一铸剑大师欧冶子为其铸剑。欧冶子奉命之后，带着妻子朱氏和女儿莫邪，从福建闽侯出发，沿闽江溯流而上，来到了地处松溪县山高林密海拔1230米的湛卢山，在这里发现了铸剑所需的神铁（铁母）和圣水（冰冷的泉水）。欧冶子在这里住下后，辟地设炉，用了三年时间，终于炼成湛卢宝剑。

　　Zhanlu sword is a renowned sword forged by maestro swordsmith Ou Yezi. According to a book Yue Jue Shu, in 496BC, the king of Yue asked maestro swordsmith Ou Yezi to make a fine sword for him. Ou Yezi then took his family to Zhanlusan mountain---1230 meters above sea level in Songxi County, where they found iron and freezing spring water which were the essential materials for sword forging. Ou yezi then built a furnace on the mountain. After three years' hard work, Zhanlu sword was completed.

01　　湛卢剑铸造大师范志华在打造湛卢宝剑 / 陈伟凯 摄
　　　Fan Zhihua is forging Zhanlu sword. (by Chen Weikai)

02　　湛卢剑铸造大师范志华 / 陈伟凯 摄
　　　Fan Zhihua, a master swordsmith of Zhanlu sword. (by Chen Weikai)

01

01　福州竹器艺人何敏文 / 陈伟凯 摄
　　He Minwen, a craftsman of bamboo
utensil in Fuzhou. (by Chen Weikai)

02　何敏文在编制竹器
　　He Minwen is making bamboo utensils

【福州竹器】

十

Bamboo Utensil in Fuzhou

　　福州是竹子之乡。清末学者郭柏苍的《闽产录异》记载，福建的竹子品种有 51 类 95 种，所以竹器是老福州人最常见的生活用品。米筛、圆箩、酒篮、舀酒筒、竹摇篮、幼儿站车、幼儿餐椅、竹笊篱、竹筅帚等等都是福州老百姓常用的用品。而且福州人有一个习惯，每当入住新宅，都要"竹竿入屋"寓意"节节高"，还要用竹扫帚"扫屋"除邪去晦，因此编竹器、做篾匠是福州最古老的行当。

　　Fuzhou is the hometown of bamboos. A book documenting Fujian's products written by Guo Baicang, a scholar in late Qing Dynasty, has clarified 51 categories of bamboos in Fujian. Therefore, bamboo utensil is the most common articles for daily use, such as rice sieve, round basket, wine basket, cradle, baby table, baby chair, etc. There is a convention in Fuzhou that before moving to a new house, people put bamboos into the house first. This means fortune raising up like bamboos. So in Fuzhou, weaving bamboo utensil is the oldest way to make a living.

“米家船”后人林宇和老母亲合作托画 / 陈伟凯 摄
Lin Yu, the inheritor of "Mijiachuan", holding a picture
with his mother (by Chen Weikai)

【福州裱褙】 ✚ Picture Mountings in Fuzhou

历史上福州裱褙业集中于三坊七巷，因为三坊七巷集中居住了福州最多的文化人。而建于清朝同治年间（1865年）的裱褙店"米家船"是留存最久的裱褙店，至今已近138年的历史。

"米家船"裱褙店的店名是居住在大光里的福州举人、书法家何振岱起的。传说，北宋大书画家米芾喜欢沿着长江中下游漂游写生，由于江南气候潮湿，每到一个码头，米芾都把自己的书画作品挂在船头，一边晾晒，一边展示。何振岱就以"米家书画满河滩"为意起了店名。

Historically, picture mounting in Fuzhou concertrated in "San Fang Qi Xiang", where most well educated people live. The earliest picture mounting shop, "Mi jiachuan" was opened in the year of Tongzhi Emperor in Qing Dynasty, which was one hundred and thirty-eight years from now. The shop, "Mi Jiachuan", was named by a calligrapher He Zhendai, who lived in Daguangli in Fuzhou. He Zhendai was inspired by the story of a great calligrapher and painter Mi Fu in Northern Song Dynasty. It was said that Mi Fei loved to paint while travel along the humid area of Yangtze River. In every wharf, Mi Fei stopped to hang his paintings up upon the boat for drying them in the sun as well as showing them to the public. This is where the named came from.

Bodiless Lacquerware ＋ 【脱胎漆器】

01   福州脱胎漆器大师邱亨锐 / 陈伟凯 摄
       Zheng Xiangrui, a master of lacquerware in Fuzhou. (by Chen Weikai)

02   邱亨锐在工作中 / 陈伟凯 摄
       Zheng Xiangrui is in work. (by Chen Weikai)

福州脱胎漆器是继承中国古代汉族优秀漆文化发展起来的，品类之多在全国漆器行业首屈一指。大的如陈列在北京人民大会堂的漆画大屏风、彩绘大花瓶、脱胎仿古铜大狮等，小的如烟具、茶具、餐碗、盘、碟、罐等，共有十八类一千两百多个花色品种。它质地坚固轻巧、造型别致，装饰技法丰富多样，色彩明丽和谐，可谓集众美于一体，具有非凡的艺术魅力。

Fuzhou bodiless lacquerware is a development of ancient Hans' lacquer culture. It tops the nation's lacquerware industry. All together they are categorized in eighteen groups and one thousand two hundred types, including large ones like the big lacquer painting screen in Great Hall of the People, colored vast, bodiless bronze lion and small ones like smoking sets, tea sets, bowls, plates, etc. The ware is strong in texture, unique in shape, diverse in decoration, and harmonious in color. Integrating various beauties, the lacquerware has marvelous artistic charm.

郑兴利剪刀传人在打造剪刀 / 陈伟凯 摄
An inheritor of Zheng Xingli scissor is making scissors. (by Chen Weikai)

【福州剪刀】 ✛ Scissors in Fuzhou

　　在福州大部分老人的记忆里，位于福州茶亭街百年老字号郑兴利剪刀店出品的"福剪"是地道的福建名牌产品。所以有老人说："记不得是几十年前买的一把'郑兴利马头牌'剪刀，用到现在还没坏，'郑兴利'是真正的'剪刀王'"。"郑兴利"是福建唯一制作工具剪刀的老店，自光绪三十年（公元1904年）创办，至今已有上百年历史。1998年，"郑兴利"剪刀参加德国的园林器材展览会，现场制作剪刀，以第一名的成绩赢得"天下第一剪"的美誉。

　　In the memory of many local seniors, the fortune scissors made in Zheng Xingli scissor shop were the best in Fuzhou. They honor Matou brand scissors sold in Zheng Xingli scissors shop as the king of scissors. Zheng Xingli is the only old shop making scissors in Fuzhou, opened in 1904 with a history of a century. In 1998, Zheng Xingli scissor shop attended a landscape equipment expo in Germany, winning the first place in the competition of making scissors.

01　皮枕艺人金德祥在工作中 / 陈伟凯 摄
　　A leather suitcase craftsman Jin Dexiang is in work. (by Chen Weikai)

02　福州皮枕艺人金德祥 / 陈伟凯 摄
　　Jin Dexiang, a leather suitcase craftsman in Fuzhou. (by Chen Weikai)

02

Leatherware in Fuzhou ＋【福州皮具】

皮具在老福州人的生活里，扮演着重要的角色，尤其是在婚嫁之时。女方家必定在嫁妆里搭皮枕，所以有句福州俗语是"做你老婆还要贴你枕头"。十九世纪三十年代福州皮箱在上海是著名奢侈品，有钱有地位的人家都有几个福州皮箱。福州皮具在旧时算得上是中高档消费品，制作时需要上漆，所以传统的福州皮具一般都是上半年做，下半年甚至来年才拿出来贩卖，一是没有味道，二是保证皮枕皮箱质量，漆彻底阴干够老了，才不易损坏、经久耐用。

Leatherware plays an important part in life of people in Fuzhou. In particular, a bride' dowry is sure to contain leather pillows, just as the old saying goes "being your wife also giving you leather pillows". In 1930s, leather suitcase made in Fuzhou was one of the luxuries in Shanghai. Every rich family had a few leather suitcases from Fuzhou. Leatherware in Fuzhou is an upscale consumer goods. It needs to paint oil in manufacturing, so it is usually made in the first half year and sold in the second half year or even next year. On the one hand, smell of oil painting has already gone; one the other hand, the suitcase will be more durable after the oil completely dry out.

第八章 ＋ 从古至今的一缕心香

涛涛闽江，就像一条信仰之河，从涓涓细流的无数源头到广阔浩瀚的入海口，民间崇拜或顺水而下、或逆流而上，总是循着人类的足迹，到处生根发芽，流播至今。

闽越人的崇拜总是从山林水洼发生，原始而质朴；总是从恐惧开始，继而膜拜，最后完成于庙堂。一棵大树、一只蛙一条蛇，或者一块石头，都可以成为信仰的源头。

如今仅存于闽江中段樟湖镇的蛇崇拜和蛙崇拜，在远古应该遍地都是。在富屯溪的终点顺昌，有个宝山，如今被人们认为是孙悟空的家乡，在猴子比人多的时候，人们只有塑大圣像供奉献食求得安宁。闽江水边总是有溺亡，总是有病痛，人们便塑造出瘟神和千奇百怪的神灵去祈求。于是，闽江闽地原始崇拜信仰如野草般丛生。

妈祖崇拜一方面跟随福建渔船流播全球，另一方面从海洋进而到河流，随船工到达闽江的那些源头。而被民间称为"奶娘"的临水娘娘信仰伴随瘟神信仰发生，顺水传播，临水施福，也进而随出洋闽人传播世界。

汉人灭了闽越，带来了中原的信仰崇拜，佛教、道教迅速成为主流信仰，也因为有闽王这样的人推崇。

好巫的闽人坚持了自己的原始崇拜，也接受了来自中原的信仰，他们是务实的，只要能够带来福报，那一缕心香，会给每位神祇奉上的。

Folk Worship

The River Min is a stream of faith. It flows from numerous sources to the sea, carries human culture up and down, follows human footsteps, and spreads human worship non-stop. Worship of people from ancient Yue tribe originated from nature, wild and simple. It began with fear, then with respect, and ended in temple enshrinement. A tree, a snake, a frog, even a stone can be the source of worship. The worship of snake and frog only remains in Zhanghuban Town, but in the time immemorial such worship may had existed though out China. At the ending point of the Futunxi River stands Baoshan Mountain, which is regarded as the hometown of the Monkey King. In the ancient times, people prayed for safety before the Monkey King's statue. Drowning and diseases accompanied people along the River Min all the time. Therefore, people prayed to various gods they created. That is the reason why worships along the River Min grow like weeds. The worship of Goddess Matsu spread across the world through the fishing boat from Fujian; also, it flowed to every sources of the River Min. Another water goddess, "Nai Niang" emerged while the superstition of evils spirits prevailed. The worship of "Nai Niang" spread along the River and traveled to the outside world. The Hans occupied ancient Yue tribe, brought to them the worships from Central China. Buddhism and Taoism became major beliefs. The ancient people of the River Min kept their own worship as well as beliefs from Central China. They are practical, following any way to fortune with a devoted heart.

闽江流域民间信仰和闽江流域其他文化一样，呈现出丰富而复杂的状态，百姓的坚韧是信仰得以流传的基础。光泽县止马镇水口村龙安寺 / 李世雄 摄

The worships along the River Min like other culture, is rich but complex. People's persistence is the foundation for worships. Long'an Temple in Shuikou Village, Guangze County (by Li Shixiong)

入夜，每当有民间信仰活动，人们都会向庙宇聚集。顺昌县郑坊乡大圣崇拜活动 / 涧南 摄
At nights, people gather in temples when they hold worship ceremonies. The worship ceremony of Monkey King in Zhengfang Village, Shunchang County (by Jian Nan)

02

03

01   五谷神崇拜源自中原，在闽江流域广泛传播。建宁县金铙山顶（闽江正源区域）五谷神庙 / 涧南 摄
      Worship of Crop Goddess originated from Central China and spread in the basin of the River Min. Crop
      Goddess Temple on Jinraoshan Mountain, Jianning County (by Jian Nan)

02   五谷神崇拜在闽江流域民间往往和本村神祇一同供奉。富屯溪光泽县儒堂村神农庙福寿堂 / 涧南 摄
      Crop Goddess is usually worshipped in the same temple with the local god of the village. Shennong Temple
      in Rutang Village, Guangze County (by Jian Nan)

03   金溪源头泰宁上大源村五谷神祭活动中，村民们准备抬五谷神游村 / 李世雄 摄
      Villagers are preparing for parade to worship Crop Goddess. (by Li Shixiong)

01

02

03

01   妈祖信仰原为渔民崇拜，在闽江流域又演化为船民崇拜，闽江流域有水路的地方就有妈祖庙（天后宫），闽江口长门村的天后宫，应该是闽江流域第一座天后宫。有趣的是，政府有关部门界定的闽江终点，就在这座天后宫庙前的江面上 / 李世雄 摄

In the beginning, Goddess Mastu was worshiped by fishermen, gradually by water-side population. Temple of Goddess Mastu (or Tianhou Temple) was built near every waterway of the River Min. The one in Changmen Village is the earliest among those in basin of the River Min. Right in front this Tianhou Temple is the official ending point of the River Min. (by Li Shixiong)

02   马尾船政天后宫 / 阮任艺 摄
Tianhou Temple in Mawei. (by Ruan Renyi)

03   马祖妈祖庙灵穴 / 涧南 摄
Mastu Temple. (by Jian Nan)

04   据泰宁旧县志记载，泰宁妈祖崇祀，始于清朝乾隆年间。乾隆元年（公元 1736 年），福州商贾郑国良等人，于城内芦峰山丁家巷购地捐资修建庙宇，称天后宫。此外，泰宁尚有四处乡村建有天后宫。上青乡梨树坪妈祖庙为目前仅存 / 李世雄 摄

As Taining almanac recorded, worship of Goddess Mastu started from the year of Emperor QianLong in Qing Dynasty. In 1736, Zheng Guoliang and other merchants in Fujian donated money to build Tianhou temple here. Besides, four other Tianhou Temples were built in other villages in Taining. The one in Lishuping Village is the only remaining one. (by Li Shixiong)

01

01   福州三坊七巷（郎官巷）天后宫坐南朝北，清道光年间由建宁同乡会建成，也称为建宁会馆 / 李世雄 摄

The Tianhou Temple in "San Fang Qi Xiang" faces north. It was built by an association of fellow townsmen of Jianning in Qing Dynasty, so it is also known as Jianning guild-hall. (by Li Shixiong)

02   福州三坊七巷（郎官巷）天后宫同福州闽江文化有极大关联。福州内河与闽江相通，是福州早期水上交通道口。清代纸、木、茶、笋贸易红火，集贸经由内河入闽江，于是祀奉天后成为普遍现象 / 李世雄 摄

The Tianhou Temple in "San Fang Qi Xiang" is closely related with the culture of the River Min. Inland waterway of Fuzhou, as linked with the River Min, was important water transportation in Fuzhou. The trading of paper, wood, tea, bamboo shoots was popular and travelled into the River Min. Thus, the worship of Goddess Mastu is common along the river. (by Li Shixiong)

01   大圣崇拜在闽江流域主要有三个神灵，一是齐天大圣，一是通天大圣，一是弥天大圣。富屯溪支流北溪的光泽县鸾凤乡饶平村的齐天庙因为坐落在乌君山（光泽民间称为猴子山）下，更具有权威性 / 那兴海 摄

Worship of the Monkey King in the basin of River Min was popular. The Monkey King Temple in Raoping Village of Guangze County is located at the foot of Wujun Mountain (also called Monkey Mountain) and therefore has more authority. (by Na Xinghai)

02   大圣形象在历史发展中产生了很多变化。富屯溪畔的邵武市齐天宫的齐天大圣像较为古老，更接近民间风格 / 涧南 摄

The image of the Monkey King changed gradually in history. The statue of Monkey King in Shaowu City is an ancient one, but closer to the folk style. (by Jian Nan)

01 顺昌县郑坊乡武大圣庙庙会上，村民怀抱大圣神像奔跑 / 阮任艺 摄
At the Monkey King temple fair, a villager is running with the statue of Monkey King in his arms. (by Ruan Renyi)

02 闽江流域的大圣崇拜从闽江支流富屯溪建溪等地向福州流播，在福州一带广泛存在大圣庙，闽江口的闽安镇大圣庙应该是闽江流域最后一个大圣庙 / 涧南 摄
Worship of the Monkey King spread from the Futunxi River to Fuzhou. Temples of the Monkey King exist in many places of Fuzhou. The Temple of the Monkey King in Min'an town must be the last one in basin of the River Min. (by Jian Nan)

01 　　陈靖姑又称娘奶、奶娘、夫人奶、临水夫人、陈奶夫人、顺天圣母等，是闽江流域的妇孺保护神 / 李世雄 摄

Goddess Chen Jinggu is also named Nainiang, Linshui Lady, Furennai, etc., who is thought to protect women and children by the River Min. (by Li Shixiong)

02 　　陈靖姑崇拜也是闽江流域独特的民间信仰，古田县临水宫是世界陈靖姑信仰的祖地 / 李世雄 摄

Goddess Chen Jinggu is a special worship of the River Min. It originates from Linshui Temple in Gutian County. (by Li Shixiong)

02

01　　三夫人信仰也是陈靖姑信仰，辅佐陈靖姑降妖的林李两位女神为民间崇拜。尤溪福星堂供奉三夫人 / 李世雄 摄
　　Goddess Chen Jinggu was assisted by two other goddesses, and together they were known as the Three Goddesses. The Three Goddeses in Fuxing Temple, Youxi County (by Li Shixiong)

02　　光泽县司前乡清溪村夫人庙 / 李世雄 摄
　　Pilgrims are having meals happily in the Furen Temple in Qingxi Village of Guangze County. (by Li Shixiong)

01   福州鼓山涌泉寺为佛教名刹，始建于738年，历经唐宋明清，为闽刹之冠 ／ 李世雄 摄

Yongquan Temple in Gushan Mountain is a famous Buddhism temple. It was built in 738, and tops the Buddhism temples in the basin of the River Min. (by Li Shixiong)

02   观世音崇拜是福建民间最广泛的信仰，观音庙在闽江流域也随处可见，在闽江入海口的琅岐岛上一处观音庙里众多的观音神像 ／ 李世雄 摄

The Goddess of Mercy is worshiped the most in Fujian. Statues of Goddess of Mercy in a temple in Langqi Island. (by Li Shixiong)

01

01　　　　光泽县太保庙内手擎高香的老年妇女信众 / 涧南 摄
　　　　An old woman is holding a long burning incense in
Taibao Temple, Guangze County. (by Jian Nan)

02　　　　作为财神以及平安保护神的"九十九位太保"民间信仰
　　　　早已融入建瓯百姓的生活。建瓯太保殿太保神像 / 涧南 摄
　　　　People in Jian'ou worship Fortune God and Safety
Guards (ninety-nine Taibaos). Taibao statues in Taibao Temple
in Jian'ou. (by Jian Nan)

01   由于古代卫生条件落后，福建瘟疫流行史不绝书，因此瘟神崇拜普遍流行。松溪五
      显庙内打瞌睡的守庙人 / 涧南 摄

      In ancient times, plagues never stopped because of the lack of good medical care, thus
      the superstition of evils spirits was prevalent. The woman who takes care of Wuxian Temple
      in Songxi is have a nap. (by Jian Nan)

02   三圣庙遗址位于建阳市童游里，原祀奉唐朝屡立战功的李家三圣，后百姓又各自在
      家乡立三圣庙以祀。建阳黄坑三圣庙前小憩的农人 / 王鹭佳 摄

      Sansheng Temple (Three Saints Temple) site is located in Tongyouli of Jianyang City.
      Originally it was to worship the three great generals of the Li clan. Later people set up
      temples for Three Saints in their own villages. A farmer rests in hall the Three Saints Temple
      in Huangkeng, Jianyang. (by Wang Lujia)

01

闽江流域的五帝信仰从源头至福州普遍存在，《乌石山志》载："榕城内外，凡近水依寺之处，多祀疫神、称之为涧，呼之为殿，名曰五帝，与之以姓曰张、关、刘、史、赵"，松溪县东门五显庙内的五帝神像 / 涧南 摄

The Five Emperors worship is common in the basin of the River Min. Statues of Five Emperors in Wuxiang Temple of Songxi County. (by Jian Nan)

02

传说张圣君体魄健伟，精通武术，且为人急公好义、爱打抱不平，他游走于福建各地祈雨、寻找草药治病救民。闽清古堡里的张圣君神像 / 李世雄 摄

Zhang Shengjun was said to be strong and good at martial arts. He was zealous for public interests. He usually travelled around Fujian praying for rain and looking for herbs to cure sick people. Statue of Lord Zhang shengjun in an old castle, Minqing. (by Li Shixiong)

01   建阳市考亭村为历史上朱熹讲学之地，据传朱熹逝世后，人们为了纪念朱子，特在古樟树主干树缝中塑一神像，以表慎终追远之情。经年代的流逝，现今古樟树裂口已慢慢愈合，形成了如今"树洞佛"的奇观 / 吴寿华 摄

        In Jianyang City, Kaoting Village was where scholar Zhuxi gave lectures. After Zhuxi died, people carved a statue for him in a crack of a camphor tree to memorize him. The crack of that tree recovered over time, forming a special image of the statue. (by Wu Shouhua)

02   建阳考亭"树洞佛" / 吴寿华 摄
        Zhuxi's statue in the crack of the camphor tree. (by Wu Shouhua)

03   福州下池许真君祖殿位于福州市仓山区临江街道下池小区内。相传已有一千三百多年的历史，祖殿奉祀主神为许真君，系道教闾山派道祖，天府"四大天师"之一 / 李世雄 摄

        Xu zhenjun, founder of Lvshan Taoism, has been worshiped as one of the four Taoist Masters for one thousand three hundred years. The ancestor hall of Xu Zhenjun is Xiachi Xiaoqu, Cangshan District, Fuzhou City (by Li Shixiong)

03

02

01   闽王祠及闽王庙在闽江流域多有存在，尤其在福州地区有多处，邵武市卫闽镇谢坊村闽王庙烧"福"字香 / 涧南 摄

Minwang Temple is common in the basin of the River Min, especially in Fuzhou. A burning incense in the shape of the Chinese character Fu(福) at the Minwang Temple in Xiefang Village, Weimin Town, Shaowu City. (by Jian Nan)

02   董奉，侯官（今福建长乐）人。医术高明，与南阳张机、谯郡华佗齐名，并称"建安三神医" / 阮任艺 摄

Dong Feng, from Houguan (Changle, Fujian of today), was an excellent doctor and named together with Zhangji and Huatuo as "Three skilled doctors of Jian'an". (by Ruan Renyi)

03   宋代定光佛在福建就颇有影响，所谓"七闽香火，家以为祖"。在闽西地区影响更大，为客家人的守护神。清流县客家人朝圣中心灵台山定光大佛 / 陈伟凯 摄

Dingguang Buddhist is the protection god for the Hakkas in Fujian. The Dingguang Buddhist statue in pilgrim center for Hakkas in Qingliu County. (by Chen Weikai)

闽江民间信仰和闽江流域百姓生活息息相关，神像塑造充满民间色彩。政和县石屯镇石圳村临水殿百姓供奉的神像 ／ 涧南 摄
Worships is closely related to people's life in the basin of the River Min, so those statues of gods are characterized by local features. Statues of gods in Linshui Temple, Shizhen Village, Zhenghe County. (by Jian Nan)

闽江流域闽北地区百姓日常崇拜极具群休性，光泽县止马镇水口村龙安寺"念佛拜神聚庙会"上的村姑们 / 李世雄 摄
Worship ceremony is usually conducted by groups of people in the northern Fujian. Village women at the temple fair of Long'an Temple, Shuikou Village, Zhima Town, Guangze County. (by Li Shixiong)

第九章 ＋ 飘香阡陌的乡土佳肴

　　闽江流域的美食，由一个个传奇组成，食材来自乡土村野，虽然普普通通，却都有着一个个不平常的来历和传说。顺着闽江行走，吃的大多是家常便饭，而品的却是世间百态、风土人情。

　　如同福建的其他文化一样，闽江流域的饮食文化是在本土菜肴的基础之上，糅合了中原饮食的特色而形成的极其丰富多样的面貌。面食来自中原，面条、烧卖、包子、饺子在闽江一带普遍存在，但是又各具特色，一个面条在闽江上下就有多重样式，到了闽江口的福州居然出现了精细极致而凸显阴柔的线面。中原人用面粉做馒头，福建人就做光饼，一块光饼在闽江各县都有，但是大小厚薄有馅无馅或者切开夹肉夹芥菜千奇百态。

　　闽江源头区域的光泽、邵武、武夷山、浦城、建宁等地因为靠近江西而嗜辣，到了顺昌却变身为福州的甜酸口味，不能不说是闽江口味的一条分界线。

　　闽江上下民间酿酒处处飘香，从古田到福州却善用酒酿红糟做菜，乃至出现红糟酿水蜜桃的奇葩，如同酱油腌橄榄。

　　闽江入海口海鲜肥美，闽菜极品鸡汤氽海蚌俗称"西施舌"，揉入了太多宫廷趣味和文人士大夫的审美想象，"佛跳墙"其实就是乱炖，民间百姓却偏爱肉燕鱼丸。

　　一条闽江，有多少美味佳肴就有多少乡愁！

Local Food and Delicacies

　　Local food of the River Min is made of usual ingredients but is composed of unusual legends. Traveling along the River Min, you can eat daily dishes of local people and taste their life and customs.

　　Just like other culture in Fujian, food culture of the River Min preserved the characteristics of food from Central China as well as its local styles. Food from Central China like noodles and all kinds of dumplings has developed their own forms in Fujian. Take Xianmian noodles as an example, it is part of the noodle culture, but it is delicate and soft. People in Central China use flour to make steamed bread, while Fujian people make it into Guangbing pies. Guangbing pies are popular in many counties along the River Min, and they varied in sizes and stuffings.

　　Places like Guangze, Shaowu, Wuyishan, Pucheng, Jianning are closed to Jianxi Province, so people there favor peppers. However, in Shunchang, people tend to favor sweet and sour food. Here is a dividing line of people's flavors of the River Min.

　　Wine-making is common in the basin of the River Min. From Gutian to Fuzhou, people use wine and vinasse to cook dishes. They even brew peaches in vinasse, just like olives in soy sauce.

　　Sea food in estuary of the River Min is extremely delicious. A delicate dish in Fujian is "Xi Shishe", in which sea clams are cooked in chicken soups, integrating much royal interest and scholars' aesthetic imagination. Another famous dish is called "Fo Tiaoqiang", which combines various kinds of sea food in a soup.

　　The homesick is as much as the delicious food from hometown along the River Min.

01　　　闽江流域的民间美食与其他文化遗存相同，是综合了古越先人饮食以及中原风味的混合体，并且在长久的历史发展里不断变化丰富。顺昌县元坑镇村民在包烧麦 / 吴军 摄

　　　Local food of the River Min is a combination of the food made by ancient Yue tribe ancestors and that from Central China. It developed as the time moved on. Villagers are making Shaomai dumplings. (by Wu Jun)

02　　　顺昌县煮灌肠蛋菇 / 吴军 摄

　　　Sausage in mushroom-shape. (by Wu Jun)

03　　　顺昌县特色饮食灌肠蛋菇的制作，先吹气再灌蛋汁 / 吴军 摄

　　　To make mushroom-shape sausage, people first blow air into a tharm and pour in egg sauce right away. (by Wu Jun)

01

02

01   闽江流域丰富的竹林资源，为食用菌类生长提供了良好的环境。顺昌县农民采摘竹荪 / 吴军 摄

Bamboo is abundant in the basin of the River Min, providing a good environment for edible mushrooms. Farmers are picking bamboo fungus. (by Wu Jun)

02   竹荪汤 / 吴军 摄

bamboo fungus soup (by Wu Jun)

03   搓糍粑在闽江流域农村十分普遍，过年婚嫁祭神都会进行。顺昌县郑坊乡村民在祭拜大圣时搓糍粑 / 吴军 摄

Making glutinous rice cake is common in villages along the River Min. People make it for weddings and worship ceremonies. Villagers are making glutinous rice cake for the Monkey King' worship ceremony. (by Wu Jun)

01

02

03

01   追踪到蜂巢之后，火攻挖掘获得蜂巢 / 阮任艺 摄
After people find the hornets' net, they dig it out with help of fire. (by Ruan Renyi)

02   挖出的蜂巢大如脸盆，可以得到许多蜂蛹 / 阮任艺 摄
Hornets' nets are as big as washbasins and there are many hornet pupas. (by Ruan Renyi)

03   所谓油炸"毒毕"，其实就是油炸蜂蛹 / 吴军 摄
The fried food "Dubi" is in fact fried hornet pupas. (by Wu Jun)

04   乡土美食油炸"毒毕"十分美味，但是捕捉过程十分不易。要用一小块青蛙肉吸引马蜂，然后将一小片塑料袋残片挂到马蜂身上，便可以跟踪到马蜂的蜂巢 / 阮任艺 摄
The local fried food "Dubi" is very delicious, but it is difficult to make. People use a piece of frog meat to attract hornets, then put a tiny piece of plastic on a hornet in order to follow it to the hornets' net. (by Ruan Renyi)

01   邵武考粘提又称为脚跟糍，因为类似人的脚跟而得名，是用米浆烹制出的一款类似于粿类的糕点小吃 / 吴军 摄

A local food called Kaonianti looks like a human heel and is made by rice milk. (by Wu Jun)

02   邵武漾豆腐是一道名菜，以和平古镇的最为正宗 / 吴军 摄

Yangtofu is a specialty in Shaowu. The one made in Heping Ancient Town is the most delicious. (by Wu Jun)

03   光泽县司前乡清溪村夫人庙里菜姑们的快乐聚餐 / 李世雄 摄

Pilgrims are having meals happily in the Furen Temple in Qingxi Village, Guangze County. (by Li Shixiong)

01　泰宁县甘露岩寺的师父们的午餐要到山下斋堂去打，平常的斋饭是笋、长豆、豆腐、黑木耳和一碗米饭　/　吴军 摄

　　Monks at Ganluyan Temple have to fetch their lunch at the abstinence hall down at the foot of the mountain. Their average meal consists of bamboo shoots, beans, tofu, black fungus and a bowl of rice. (by Wu Jun)

02　泰宁县甘露岩寺斋堂里供奉着手握火钳的大乘紧那罗王菩萨　/　吴军 摄

　　Bodhisattva Kinnara with a fire tongs in hand in Ganluyan Temple of Taining County. (by Wu Jun)

02

02

03

01   泰宁碧玉卷又名韭菜糍，每年立夏日，泰宁城乡居民都要制作这一风味小吃，原料为纯大米和韭菜，经混合研磨后摊饼加馅制作而成 / 吴军 摄

        Biyu roll is also called glutinous leek rice cake. On every Beginning of Summer, people in Taining used pulverized rice and leek to make this local food. (by Wu Jun)

02   五谷神崇拜从中原传入闽江流域，保留了中原文化里的土地信仰，泰宁县大源村五谷神祭拜活动上，村民们吃一顿面条，祈求五谷丰登 / 涧南 摄

        Crop Goddess worship was brought from Central China, presenting culture of land worships. On worship ceremony of Crop Goddess, people eat noodles to pray for a harvest year. (by Jian Nan)

03   泰宁县大源村农民祭拜五谷神时吃面条 / 涧南 摄

        People are eating noodles on Crop Goddess worship ceremony. (by Jian Nan)

01

02

01   擂茶是流行于福建客家人生活区域的一种独特饮品，宁化县客家妇女在制作擂茶 / 吴军 摄
       Lei Tea (Pounded tea) is a popular drink of the Hakkas in Fujian. A Hakka woman is making pounded tea. (by Wu Jun)

02   擂茶虽然是客家饮品，但是在福建的不同县乡，擂茶用料又有不同，宁化县擂茶原料 / 吴军 摄
       Although Lei Tea (pounded tea) is a drink of the Hakkas, it is different in ingredients in other counties of Fujian. The
       ingredients of Lei Tea in Ninghua County (by Wu Jun)

03   泰宁县客家妇女制作擂茶 / 吴军 摄
       A Hakka woman in Taining Count is making pounded tea. (by Wu Jun)

04   闽江流域还有"摆茶"风俗，喝茶同时还有食品小吃相佐，武夷山吴屯乡红园村妇女摆茶 / 涧南 摄
       In the basin of the River Min, people eat other food and snacks while drink tea. This is the custom of "Baicai". (by Jian Nan)

04

01

02

03

01 艾草糕是客家人春季最常见的小吃，宁化县水茜乡桥墟日里农妇卖艾草糕 / 涧南 摄
Wormwood cake is a snack for the Hakkas in spring. A peasant woman sells wormwood cake on Qiaoxu fair, Shuixi town, Ninghua County. (by Jian Nan)

02 宁化勺子粉干因其取料简单、新鲜味美、又经济实惠，深受客家乡亲喜欢，几乎所有的乡镇墟场，都能见到这种小吃 / 吴军 摄
Shaozi rice noodle, simple in making, fresh in taste, and inexpensive, is loved by the Hakkas. It is sold in almost every market fair of town and village. (by Wu Jun)

03 宁化豆腐驼子要用游浆豆腐烧制，用本地特色卤汤，加一大块肥猪肉（或猪肉皮），放入香叶、八角、桂皮、辣椒干、当归、五香、生姜、酱油等佐料，将白豆腐用文火慢慢地炆成蜂窝状时味道最佳 / 吴军 摄
Tuozi tofu in Ninghua is made by tofu cooked in halogen soup, added with pork fat, myrcia, anise, cinnamon bark, dry pepper, etc. and then cook the tofu by gentle fire until it looks like a bee net for the best taste. (by Wu Jun)

01　永安市贡川有官丸、烧麦宴。如今在贡川，喜宴必上官丸、烧麦，摆盘依旧传统，按1、4、9、16成三角形状。如有男方办酒，必须请小舅子吃官丸、烧麦。如女方办酒，则必须请新郎吃　吴军 摄

In Gongchuang of Yong'an City, Guanwan meat balls and Shaomai dumplings are specialties. This two snacks are essential on wedding dinners. If the wedding is held by the bridegroom, he has to invite the bridge's brothers to eat Guanwan meat balls and Shaomai dumplings. If the wedding is held by the bride, she has to serve the bridegroom with this two snacks. (by Wu Jun)

02　永安煨豆腐，以前小吃店门口煨一大锅豆腐，冬天大家围着锅（锅底下烧着木炭）吃豆腐，两分钱一块豆腐；五分钱一块肉　吴军 摄

Stewed tofu is popular in Yongan. People used to cook a large pot of tofu in front of the snack shop decades ago. They ate tofu while stood around the pot. At that time, two cents for one tofu, and five cents for a piece of meat. (by Wu Jun)

03　沙县小吃米浆灌肠最早是沙县夏茂特有的小吃，现在成为街头巷尾小食摊上价廉物美的点心　/　吴军 摄

Sausage filled with rice milk was first appeared in Xiamao in Shaxian County. It is now a snack commonly sold by street vendors. (by Wu Jun)

04　沙县小吃滚粉豆腐丸是在传统汉族小吃豆腐丸的基础上发展而来　/　吴军 摄

Tofu balls on powder is developed from the traditional tofu balls of a Han nationality. (by Wu Jun)

03

04

01

02

01　　　　浦城木槿花，有白色的也有红色的，浦城人称之为米汤花 ／ 吴军 摄
　　　　Hibiscus flower is called Mitang flower by people in Pucheng. It has white and
red flowers. (by Wu Jun)

02　　　　木槿花煮成的米汤，香甜爽口 ／ 吴军 摄
　　　　Rice soup cooked with hibiscus flower smells sweet and tastes good. (by Wu Jun)

01

02

01   元宵佳节浦城人的餐桌上都少不了一道象征团圆的传统特色美食蛋皮燕圆。浦城蛋皮制作 / 吴军 摄
Egg sheet rolls is a traditional dish that every family eats on Lantern Festival. It is a symbol of reunion. (by Wu Jun)

02   浦城蛋皮燕细致不腻，柔而脆嫩，味鲜适口，宛如燕窝，是浦城宴客不能缺少的第一道菜 / 吴军 摄
Egg sheet rolls taste delicate and not greasy, soft and crisp, fresh and agreeable, and looks like a swallow's nest. It is an essential meal for people in Pucheng to entertain guests at a banquet. (by Wu Jun)

01

02

01   武夷山早餐常见的果仔制作 / 吴军 摄
       A chief is making Guozai, a common dish for breakfast in Wuyishan. (by Wu Jun)

02   果仔 / 吴军 摄
       A plate of Guozai (by Wu Jun)

03   武夷山市岚谷乡的熏鹅 / 吴军 摄
       Smoked goose in Langu Village of Wuyishan City (by Wu Jun)

04   笋鸭子 / 吴军 摄
       Duck filled in bamboo shoots (by Wu Jun)

03

04

03

04

01   建阳麦果是将小麦磨粉然后加红糖，搓成丸子，再用梧桐叶包裹蒸熟 / 吴军 摄

To mix wheat powder with brown sugar, then roll into balls, pack the balls with Chinese parasol tree leafs and stream them. This is how Jianyang Maiguo is made. (by Wu Jun)

02   蒸熟后的建阳麦果，是老百姓念念不忘的美食 / 吴军 摄

Steamed Maiguo of Jianyang is a dish loved by people. (by Wu Jun)

03   建瓯光饼大约流传于明嘉靖年间，戚继光由浙率部入闽抗倭之时，经过建瓯房村一带，下令赶制的干粮而流传至今 / 吴军 摄

Guangbing pie was originally made in the year of Jiajing Emperor in Ming Dynasty. It was brought to Jian'ou by a famous general Qi Jiguang in a war to resist Japan's invasion in Ming Dynasty. Guangbing pie was made for the soldiers at that time and handed down till today. (by Wu Jun)

04   光饼炒大肠 / 吴军 摄

Sausages fried with Guangbing pies. (by Wu Jun)

01

02

03

01　建瓯市民早餐少不了的是豆浆粉，用豆浆冲泡米粉，再撒点葱花、红酒、盐即可 / 吴军 摄

　　In Jian' ou City, Soybean and rice milk is a common breakfast, in which rice powder is put into soybean milk seasoned with some shallot, red wine and salt. (by Wu Jun)

02　建瓯鸡茸 / 吴军 摄

　　Mashed chicken (by Wu Jun).

03　建瓯窝底，用冬笋最嫩的部分，一碗窝底需要十斤左右的冬笋 / 吴军 摄

　　Soup base in Jian' ou uses the freshest part of bamboo shoots. Soup base for one pot needs five kilograms' winter bamboo shoots. (by Wu Jun)

04　建瓯板鸭是建瓯传统特色食品，由于其形、色、香、味俱全，制工精细、风味独特、食用方便，在清朝已久负盛名，二十世纪八十年代即被中国食品总公司收入《家禽与传统禽制品》一书，列入全国传统腌腊禽制品名品板鸭行列，（福建）建瓯板鸭与（江苏）南京板鸭、（四川）建昌板鸭、（江西）南安板鸭一起被称为中国四大板鸭 / 吴军 摄

　　Pressed salty duck is a tradition specialty in Jianou. It was very famous for its unique shape, color, smell, and taste. It was renowned from Qing Dynasty. It has been listed in Poultry and Traditional Poultry Products complied by the Food Company of China; and is also one of the most famous four pressed salty ducks in China. (by Wu Jun)

05　武夷山特色面食蜂卵汤制作手艺奇特，是将揉好的面粉放在竹笤箕背上搓制而成 / 吴军 摄

　　Fengluan soup, a pasta specialty of Wuyishan. It is made of doughs rolling on a bamboo seive. (by Wu Jun)

04　　　　　　　　　　　　　　　　　　05

01　　　尤溪拉面也称朱子面，又叫筷子面，是尤溪的传统面食之一。因为面条粗如筷子而得名，逢年过节必备，可拌可煮可炒，口感甚佳，其中手工拉面最为正宗 / 吴军 摄

　　　Youxi hand-pull noodles, also called chopsticks noodles, is one of the traditional food in Youxi. It is an essential meal at festivals because it tastes fairly good. The noodles look like chopsticks and that is where its name come from. (by Wu Jun)

02　　　古田鹤塘粿面加猪尾、罗汉肉、猪大小肠共煮，调料是醋泡辣椒 / 吴军 摄

　　　This is a dish made by cooking Kemian pasta, pig tail, streaky pork, and pig guts seasoned with pepper soaked in vinegar. (by Wu Jun)

03　　　乡村活动时，聚餐是必不可少的一个内容，尤溪县彩洋村的游神美食 / 曲利明 摄

　　　People usually dine together in village's activities. Delicious food on parade of gods in Caiyang Village, Youxi County. (by Qu Liming)

01

02

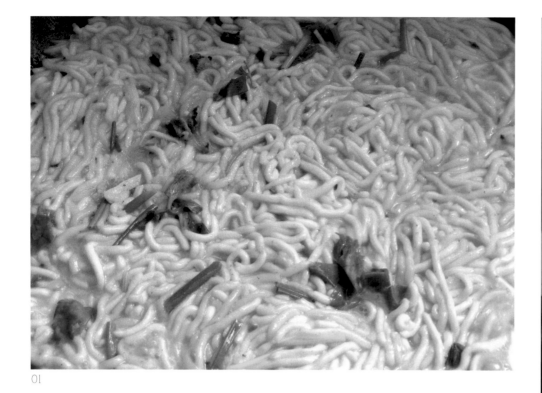

01

01 煮好的古田芋面十分诱人 / 吴军 摄
Taro noodles looks very delicious. (by Wu Jun)

02 古田芋面制作是将揉好的芋头面直接搓进锅里 / 吴军 摄
  To make taro noodles is to put taro dough directly into the boiling pot. (by Wu Jun)

03 古田豆燕坯 / 吴军 摄
Smashed soy pie in Gutian. (by Wu Jun)

04 将豆燕坯制成豆丝 / 吴军 摄
Smashed soy strip (by Wu Jun)

02

03

04

01

02

01   闽清粉干是选上好米磨成浆，压成粉团，搓成粿，用井水煮，再挤压成粉丝，晒干而成。闽清粉干久煮不烂，但入口又极为顺滑。相传郑和下西洋时曾带粉干往南洋，于是闽清"粉干"便名扬四海了 / 吴军 摄

　　　In order to make Minqing dry rice noodles, one need to choose top grade rice milk, make it into rice dough, boil it with well water, press into noodles, and dry them. It can be cooked for a long time and taste soft. When admiral Zheng He travelled southward to the Indian Ocean, Minqing dry rice noodles became world renowned. (by Wu Jun)

02   闽清粉干以茶口粉干为最佳，而炒粉干又是闽清最常见的名菜，尤其以糟菜炒粉干为绝品 / 吴军 摄

　　　The best Minqing dry rice noodles is made in Chakou Village. Fried dry rice noodles is very common in Fujian, among which dry rice noodles cooked with vinasse tops any others. (by Wu Jun)

03   白刀鱼学名长颌鲚，又称刀鲚，毛鲚，是一种洄游鱼类，与河鲀、鲥鱼并称为中国长江三鲜。而闽江白刀鱼也是最为鲜美的一种鱼类，尤其是闽清雄江白刀鱼 / 吴军 摄

　　　Coilia ectenes Jordan, also called coilia ectenes, is a migratory fish. It is one of the three most delicious fish in Yangtze River. This kind of fish in the River Min also tastes good, especial those in Xiongjiang River, Minqing. (by Wu Jun)

04   闽清清蒸白刀是宴席上不可缺少的一道名菜 / 吴军 摄

　　　Steam coilia ectenes is an essence at banquets. (by Wu Jun)

01   闽清蛋面，用蛋和地瓜粉做成 ／ 吴军 摄
Egg noodles is made from egg and sweet potato flour. (by Wu Jun)

02   闽清池园烤豆腐 ／ 吴军 摄
Baked tofu in Chiyuan Garden, Minqing. (by Wu Jun)

01

01　　　溪滑俗称花鳗鲡，生长于福建闽江流域的河溪、山涧、水库中。溪滑肉味鲜美，肉和肝的维生素 A 含量特别高，具有相当高的营养价值，历来被视为上等滋补食品，称之为"水中人参" ／ 吴军 摄

Marbled eel grows in waters of the basin of the River Min. It not only tastes good, but also contains large quantity of vitamin A. It has always been regarded as a top grade nutrient food and called "ginseng in water". (by Wu Jun)

02　　　八珍全番鸭是闽清历史悠久的菜肴，在《梅溪医话》中记载说，"闽清民间几十年以来都有吃八珍鸡、八珍鸭、八珍猪脚的习惯" ／ 吴军 摄

Braised duck with "eight-treasures" has a long history. People in Minqing have eaten this dish for decades. (by Wu Jun)

01

02

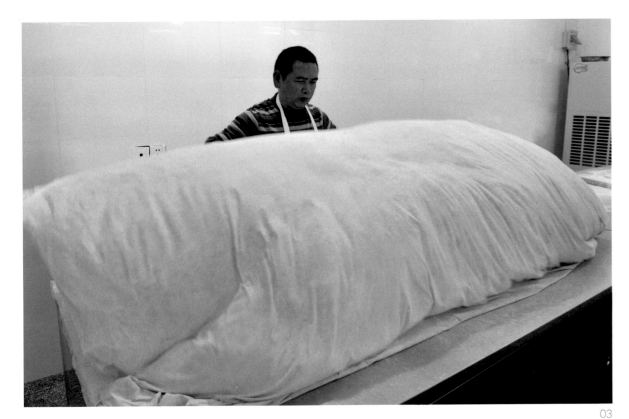

03

04

01 佛跳墙又名满坛香、福寿全，是福州的汉族名菜，属闽菜系。相传，是清道光年间由福州聚春园菜馆老板郑春发研制 / 吴军 摄

The dish "Fo Tiao Qiang" is a famous dish of Han nationality and belongs to Fuzhou cuisine. It was said to be made by a chef named Zheng Chun in the year of Daoguang Emperor in Qing Dynasty. (by Wu Jun)

02 福州佛跳墙第七代、第八代传承人罗世伟和杨伟华在福州百年老店聚春园展示佛跳墙制作技艺 / 吴军 摄

Two inheritors of "Fo Tiao Qiang" are showing their cooking skills at Juchunyuan, a restaurant of a century old. (by Wu Jun)

03 福州肉燕皮制作 / 吴军 摄

A chef is making Rouyanpi. (by Wu Jun)

04 太平燕是福州人最常食用的一道名菜，常在婚宴寿宴或年节的宴席出现。福州习俗是一放鞭炮，太平燕就要上桌了，新郎、新娘就要开始向来宾敬酒了 / 吴军 摄

"Tai Ping Yan" is a popular dish in Fuzhou. It is usually served on events like weddings or festivals. There is a custom in Fuzhou that this dish will be taken to dinner tables right away when firecracker setting off at a wedding feast. (by Wu Jun)

01

02

03

04

01 闽菜善于使用红糟调味，有红糟烹调之说 / 吴军 摄
Fujian cuisine love to used vinasse for a special flavor. (by Wu Jun)

02 红糟鱼 / 吴军 摄
Vinasse fish (by Wu Jun)

03 淡糟香螺片 / 吴军 摄
Vinasse shells (by Wu Jun)

04 醉糟鸡 / 吴军 摄
Vinasse chicken (by Wu Jun)

01

01　闽菜汤菜代表——鸡汤氽海蚌 ／ 吴军 摄
　　Sea clams in chicken soup is a representative of Fujian cuisine. (by Wu Jun)

02　福州鱼丸是富有福州地方特色的汉族小吃之一，具有天然、营养、保健的特色。口感好、
　　筋力佳、久煮不变质、色泽洁白晶亮、质嫩滑润清脆，具有特殊的海鲜风味 ／ 吴军 摄
　　Fish balls in fuzhou is a local specialty of the Han nationality. It is nature, nutrient, and
　　good for health. These fish balls, looks white and delicate, tastes smooth and crisp, has special
　　sea food flavos. (by Wu Jun)

第十章 ＋ 择水而居的美丽家园

纵观闽江流域的城市，人们惊喜地发现，居然没有一座城池不在水畔。择水而居是中国人的风水选择，也是中国人的乡土情愫。而在闽江流域，更是百姓的安居之所。

每每看着一江碧水从城际流过，都会去遥想，在很早很早以前，每座城市第一个选择在水边居住的人是谁？从一个人到一家一户，再由一家一户而一个聚落，再由一个聚落到一个村镇，进而成为一座城市。江水流动，生生不息，子民渔猎，依水而居。不能不说，是水灌溉一座城池，养育一方百姓。

借助现代技术，从空中观看闽江水流之形，江水如同血脉而流通福建大地，历史上百姓渔耕、饮用、舟楫交通，无不借江水之便利。

中国人是一个乡土观念极重的人群，"老乡"是什么？不就是同喝一江水，同居一座城而已。

水是流动的，因而顺了生命的韵律，也顺了一个城市的节奏。

闽江从群山万壑发源，流经福建大地，溪涧江河就像大树的枝桠，而城市就是这些枝桠上结的硕果。

A Beautiful Homeland by Rivers

To have a look at cities in the basin of the River Min, you will be surprised to find every city is built by the river. To live by waters is a tradition of Chinese people and the River Min is a good place for living.

Every time when watching a river winding through a city I may wonder who first came to live by the river long time ago? From a person to a family, then to a community, a town, and finally a city, this is the way a city evolves. River is a carrier of lives. People is nurtured by the rivers. To have a look from the sky, the tributaries of the River Min wind though Fujian like blood vessels firmly holding the land. Historically, people has been benefited from the river in fishing, drinking and water transportation.

Chinese people consider homeland very important. "Lao Xiang" or fellow folks is people drink from the same water or live in the same town.

Water keeps flowing carrying rhyme of life and beat of a city.

The River Min originates from various mountains and sources, flowing across lands of Fujian like a big tree. Tributaries are its branches, and the cities its fruits.

建宁县万安桥始建于南宋绍定元年（公元1228年），横跨濉溪，先后八次毁于洪水、五次毁于火，屡圮屡修，桥头朝阳门是建宁历史悠久的标志性建筑之一 / 涧南 摄

Wan' an Bridge was built in 1228 in Jianning County. Historically, it had been damaged by eight floods and five fires, and had been repaired many times. Chaoyang Gate at the bridge head is a historic monument in Jianning. (by Jian Nan)

建宁是全国重点中央苏区县之一，在红军五次反围剿过程中，毛泽东等老一辈无产阶级革命家都在此生活战斗过，目前县城还保留有红一方面军领导机关、红军三总部、红军医院、红军银行、红军兵工厂等许多革命历史遗址遗迹 / 涧南 摄

Jianning County was one of the national old revolutionary base areas. Chairman Mao and other leaders of Red Army once lived here. Places like headquarters, hospital, bank, and arsenal of Red Army still remain in the village. (by Jian Nan)

建宁县古为绥安县，唐乾元二年建镇，南唐中兴元年（958年）置县。是福建省粮食主要产区和重点林区之一，是福建省的母亲河闽江的发源地，是著名的中国建莲之乡、黄花梨之乡和亚洲最大的薄型纸生产基地。金溪上游濉溪流经建宁城关 / 阮任艺 陈映辉 摄

In ancient times, Jianning County was called Sui' an County. It was one of the major crop production and forest areas. Jianning County is where the River Min originates. Also it is the hometown of lotus and scented rosewood, and the biggest production area of thin paper in Asia. (by Ruan Renyi and Chen Yinghui)

01　　唐宋时期，南迁汉人一度汇聚石壁，蔚为壮观。石壁镇石壁村遂成客家祖地，是客家人的摇篮，有"北有大槐树，南有石壁村"之谓。石壁客家文化园 / 吴寿华 摄

In Tang and Song Dynasty, a huge wave of migrant Hans gathered in Shibi. Thus Shipi Village in Shibi County became the cradle of the Hakkas. A culture park of the Hakkas in Shibi. (by Wu Shouhua)

02　　宁化客家祖地博物馆占地500亩，建筑面积两万平方米，设有文物馆、文物库房、数字视听室、摄影展示展览馆、会议室、市民广场等设施，建设设计风格将体现客家元素和宁化特色，是一座宏扬客家精神，展示客家文化的平台 / 吴寿华 摄

The Hakkas museum in Ninghua is a comprehensive platform for demonstrating Hakkas spirits and culture. It covers an area of 500 mu with 20,000 square kilometers construction area. Inside the museum, there is relic hall, relic warehouse, digital video room, photo exhibition hall, conference room, etc. The architecture compromises elements of the Hakkas and culture of Ninghua harmoniously. (by Wu Shouhua)

03　　宁化县地处福建省西部，武夷山脉东麓，为闽赣两省交界县之一，是三江（闽江、赣江、汀江）源头之一。宁化县是第二次国内革命战争时期21个原中央苏区重点县，是中央红军长征四个起点县之一，2011年底被联合国地名专家组中国分部认定为中国地名文化遗产 / 阮任艺 陈映辉 摄

Ninghua County is located in the west part of Fujian Province at the eastern foot of Mount Wuyi, at the conjunction with Jiangxi Province. It is the source of three rivers, i.e. the River Min, the River Gan, and the River Ting. It was an old revolutionary county and one of the four starting points of Red Army's Long March. Ninghua was regarded as a culture heritage by UN experts in 2011. (by Ruan Renyi and Chen Yinghui)

01

02

03

清流县位于福建西部，武夷山脉南侧，沙溪上游。清流古属黄连峒。周、春秋末为闽越地。清流是福建最早的人类文明发祥地。自隋唐始，北方各地移民陆续迁入与土著居民融合，形成客家人聚居地。沙溪上游九龙溪流经城关，形成一个"八卦"形状 / 阮任艺 陈映辉 摄

Qingliu County lies in west of Fujian, at the south foot of Mount Wuyi, and at the upstream of the Shasxi River. It is the earliest place of origin of human civilization. From Sui and Tang Dynasty, people from north gradually migrated to Fujian and settled down. As time moved on, migrant people and the original habitants integrated as the community of the Hakkas. The Jiulongxi River winds across the city gate looking like the Eight Diagrams. (by Ruan Renyi and Chen Yinghui)

清流县立足"太极之城、大美清流"定位，建设"闽西北最佳人居地"和"休闲、度假、旅游目的地"，南滨公园等"八个公园"建设，成为城市居民休闲娱乐的中心 / 涧南 摄

The urban construction of Qingliu County is based on the concept of "the City of Taichi", and "Beautiful Qingliu". The county is to be built into the best human habitat in northwestern Fujian, and a destination for relaxation, vacation and tourism. Its eight parks such as Nanbin Park have become the entertaining center for citizens. (by Jian Nan)

定光佛又称定光古佛、定光大师，是历史上唯一被朝廷正式赐封定光佛转世的高僧。定光佛，在闽粤赣周边留下除蛟伏虎，疏通航道，活泉涌水，祈雨求阳，赐嗣送子，筑陂止水，以及屡显神异护国佑民的传奇故事，为客家保护神 / 赖小兵 摄

Dingguang Buddhist is the only monk who was announced by the government the reincarnation of Dingguang Buddhist. Dingguang Buddhist has many legendary stories, like driving evil dragon and tiger away, building channels, offering water source, praying for favorable weather, etc. Dingguang Buddhist is the protection of the Hakkas. (by Lai Xiaobing)

01 　永安贡川古镇 / 阮任艺 陈映辉 摄
Gongchuan Ancient Town in Yongan. (by Ruan Renyi and Chen Yinghui)

02 　吉山乡地处三明永安城区西南郊文川溪畔，依山傍水，地势险要，景色宜人：自古重文兴教，人文荟萃，
文物古迹众多：抗日战争时期福建省政府内迁，遂为当时福建行政、文教中心 / 吴寿华 摄
Jishan Town lies by the Wenchuan River in Yong'an. It is endowed with pleasant scenery and precipitous topography. People in the town valued education since ancient times. So here is a place gathered talents and culture relics. In the Anti-Japanese War period, Fujian provincial government move here, thus Jishan became a temporary center of politics and education. (by Wu Shouhua)

03 　永安古名浮流，分属沙县、尤溪县境。永安山清水秀，林木蓊郁。有天宝岩省级自然保护区，内有完
好的中亚热带原始森林；有列为福建省十大风景区之一的桃源洞风景区，其中"一线天"尤负盛名；有列
为省级风景区的鳞隐石林，人称之为仅次于云南路南石林的"福建石林"。此外贡川古城和槐南安贞堡为
难得的人文旅游资源。沙溪穿城而过 / 阮任艺 陈映辉 摄
The ancient name of Yong'an is Fuliu. It has picturesque scenery with lush forest. In the Tianbaoyan Nature Reserve area, there is a well preserved subtropical primeval forest. Taoyuandong resort in Yong'an is one of the ten famous resorts in Fujian, especially the site "Yi Xian Tian" enjoying great reputation. Also, Linyin stone forest is an attraction only secondary to Lunan stone forest in Yunnan Province. Besides, Gongchuan Ancient Town and Anzhen Castle are places worth seeing. (by Ruan Renyi and Chen Yinghui)

01   三明是一座新兴的工业城市，是全国创建精神文明先进城市和国家卫生城、园林城及中国优秀旅游城市 / 阮任艺 陈映辉 摄
Sanming is a growing industrialized city. It is an advanced civilized city, a state-level healthy city, nationally designated garden city and a China excellent tourism city. (by Ruan Renyi and Chen Yinghui)

02   三钢集团前身为福建省三明钢铁厂，建于 1958 年，为三明乃至福建的发展发挥了重要作用 / 阮任艺 陈映辉 摄
Sangang Group was formerly known Sanming Steel Plant, which was built in 1958. It plays an important role in Sanming and Fujian as well. (by Ruan Renyi and Chen Yinghui)

01

02

03

01　　　沙县古名沙阳，简称虬，位于福建省中部偏北，闽江支流沙溪下游，自古即为闽西北重要商品集散地，历史上中原南迁移民的著名客家历史文化之乡。沙县是国家商品粮基地县、国家南方重点林区县、福建省竹子重点产区。沙县小吃名闻遐迩 / 阮任艺 陈映辉 摄

Shaxian County was called Shayang in ancient time, located in the north to central Fujian. It is the important commodity distribution center in northwest Fujian since ancient times. Shaxian County is famous for the Hakkas history and culture. Also, it is the national commodity grain base, the national major forest zone, and the provincial bamboo production area. Snack in Shaxian county is well known. (by Ruan Renyi and Chen Yinghui)

02　　　沙县虬江大桥，横跨沙溪河 / 陈伟凯 摄

Qiujiang Bridge in Shaxi County stands right across the Shaxi River. (by Chen Weikai)

03　　　沙县小吃城展现沙县一千六百多年的闽中悠久历史和中国小吃之乡、中国小吃文化名城的饮食文化和古城风貌 / 涧南 摄

Shaxian County snack town demonstrates the 1600 years' history of China' snack town as well as its food culture in central Fujian. (by Jian Nan)

01   光泽县位于福建省西北部，闽江富屯溪上游，武夷山脉北段，与闽赣两省的武夷山、邵武、建阳、黎川、资溪、贵溪、铅山七县市交界。境内群山连绵，山高谷深，千米以上山峰有570座，有"一滩高一丈，光泽在天上"之说。画面中部高山为乌君山，富屯溪源头西溪北溪在城关合二为一始为富屯溪 ／ 阮任艺　陈映辉 摄

Guangze County locates in northwest of Fujian Province and borders seven counties or cities. It lies near upstream of the Futunxi River and northern section of Mount Wuyi. Among surrounding rolling mountains, there are 570 peaks a thousand meters above sea level. The mountain in the picture is Mount Wujun. (by Ruan Renyi and Chen Yinghui)

02   光泽边城空气清新，生态良好。光泽乌君洲公园晨练的人们 ／ 涧南 摄

Air quality and ecological environment in Guangze is favorable. People are doing morning exercise in Wujunzhou Park. (by Jian Nan)

03   光泽乌君洲公园建于1987年，位于美丽的富屯溪北溪河畔，公园成为市民锻炼娱乐的场所 ／ 涧南 摄

Wujunzhou Park was built in 1987. It is set by the Beixi River. The park has become a place for exercising and entertaining

04   光泽是福建省19个边界县（市）之一，是鹰厦铁路进入福建的第一个县 ／ 颗小兵 摄

Guangze is one of nineteen bordering counties in Fujian. It is the first county Yingtan-Xiamen Railway goes by in Fujian. (by Lai Xiaobing)

01

02

03

04

01   邵武素有"铁城"之称，地处武夷山南麓、富屯溪畔，史称南武夷。邵武历史悠久，建城已有一千七百多年的历史，曾为福建八府之一，邵武市和平古镇还是世界黄氏宗亲寻根谒祖之地 / 阮任艺 陈映辉 摄

Shaowu is known as an impregnable city in history. It is located at the south foot of Mount Wuyi, so it was once called Nan Wuyi. Shaowu has a history of more than one thousand seven hundred years. Heping Ancient Town in Shaowu is the place of origin of the Huang clan over the world. (by Ruan Renyi and Chen Yinghui)

02   邵武北门又叫樵溪门，宋代所建，保留最为完好。樵溪门位于富屯溪畔，城门为砖券拱门，门额上有贴金"樵溪门"三字，因旧时有樵溪水穿城而过，从樵溪门旁汇入富屯溪，所以此门取名为樵溪门。樵溪门外古时有码头和浮桥，门内为古代的商贸区，早在宋代即有米行街，还有县衙、学府、书院、试院等 / 涧南 摄

North Gate of Shaowu City is also called Qiaoxi Gate, built in Song Dynasty but well preserved. Qiaoxi Gate stands near the Futunxi River. Long time ago, the Qiaoxi River went through the Gate Pass into the Futunxi River. So the gate is named Qiaoxi Gate. In ancient times, outside the gate there was a wharf and a floating bridge, inside the gate was a commerce zone. As early as in Song Dynasty, there were streets that only sold rice as well as districts for government, schools and other education institutes. (by Jian Nan)

03   从福山森林公园福山阁看邵武市区 / 苏荣钦 阮任艺 摄
Looking at Shaowu City from Fushan Pavilion. Fushan forest park. (by Su Rongqin and Ruan Renyi)

04   邵武八一大桥下成为市民活动的场所 / 涧南 摄
Citizens socializes under Bayi Bridge. (by Jian Nan)

01

02

03

01   顺昌，后唐长兴四年 (933 年) 建县，据清嘉庆《延平府志》记载 "以其初顺服，故名，取顺而昌之意"。自此历代沿用。顺昌县地处武夷山脉南麓，闽江上游金溪、富屯溪交汇处，素有 "林海粮仓果乡" 之美誉，被评为 "中国竹子之乡"、 "中国杉木之乡"、 "中国竹荪之乡" 等 / 苏荣钦 摄

       Shunchang was built in 933 in Tang Dynasty. Its name means obedience and prosperity. Shunchang sits at the south foot of Mount Wuyi, at the conjunction of the Jinxi River and the Futunxi River. It is famous for abundant sources of forest, crop and fruit and is regarded as China's hometown of bamboo, cedarwood, and bamboo fungus, etc. (by Su Rongqin)

02   顺昌曾经是福州 "知青" 最密集的县区，富屯溪畔的竹乡广场上矗立的 "知青" 雕塑 / 苏荣钦 摄

       Shunchang was one a county with the biggest number of educated youth in Fuzhou. A statue of educated youths stands on Zhuxiang Square by the Futunxi River. (by Su Rongqin)

03   顺昌县元坑镇是一个历史文化名镇 / 赖小兵 摄

       Yuankeng Town of Shunchang County is a historical cultural town. (by Lai Xiaobing)

01 　　泰宁红军街原名岭上街，由于当年红军三次到泰宁，都住在这条街上，并留下了许多标语和大幅文告。街上还保存有红军留下的"红军井"等红色遗址 / 涧南 摄

　　Red Army street was named Lingshang street. The named was changed because the Red Army had been to Taining for three times and lived in this street, left behind them many banners and slogans. Relic sites like the Red Army Well is still preserved in the street. (by Jian Nan)

02 　　尚书第俗称五福堂，坐落于泰宁县城内胜利二街福堂巷，建于明天启年间（1621~1627 年）。建筑布局严谨合理，是福建现存规模最大、保存最完整的明代民居，整个府第布局严谨合理，宏伟壮观 / 阮任艺 陈映辉 摄

　　Shangshu Mansion is commonly known as "Wu Fu Tang", which is situated in Futang alley, Taining County. It was built in 1621 and completed in 1627 in Ming Dynasty. The whole buildings' architectural layout is reasonable, and it is the largest and most complete house of Ming dynasty in Fujian. The whole mansion is magnificent.

03 　　泰宁县位于福建省西北部武夷山脉中段的支脉杉岭东南，金溪上游杉溪为主要河流。泰宁素有汉唐古镇、两宋名城之美誉，明代兵部尚书李春烨府邸尚书第为国家重点文物保护单位。泰宁也是原中央 21 个苏区县之一，有红军街、东方军司令部、大洋嶂阻击战旧址等革命历史遗迹，2004 年被列入全国百个红色经典旅游景区。大金湖国家重点风景名胜区更是著名的旅游目的地 / 阮任艺 陈映辉 摄

　　Taining County is located in northwest of Fujian near central section of Mount Wuyi. Taining is an infamous ancient county. The mansion of minister of defense Li Chunye in Ming Dynasty is a protection relic at state level. Taining county belongs to old revolutionary area, preserving some monuments of the Red Army. It has been listed into the national one hundred old revolutionary resorts in 2004. Dajinhu resort is a tourist destination not to be missed. (by Ruan Renyi and Chen Yinghui)

01

02

03

01

02

03

01 将乐县，三国吴景帝永安三年（260年）置县，因"邑在将溪之阳，土沃民乐、东越王乐野宫在是"，得名将乐，是福建省最早建县的七个古县之一，也是中国26个中央苏区县之一 / 阮任艺 陈映辉 摄

Jiangle County was founded in 260 during the Three Kingdoms. It is one of the seven ancient counties in Fujian and one of twenty-six old revolutionary counties in China. It is located on the sunny side of the Jiangxi River with fertile soil. Leye Place of Dongyue King was built here, thus it was named Jiangle County. ((by Ruan Renyi and Chen Yinghui)

02 将乐简称"鏞"，新建江滨公园建起巨大的城标雕塑 / 涧南 摄

Yong is short for Jiangle. A newly built huge sculpture in Jiangbin Park. (by Jian Nan)

03 将乐玉华洞具有一千七百多年的游览史，自明代著名旅行家徐霞客探游之后，它神奇、优美的景观就随着《徐霞客游记》的流传而广为人知 / 涧南 摄

Yuhua Cave has been visited for 1700 years. A traveler, Xu Xiake, wrote about the cave's wonder and beauty in his book Travel Notes of Xu Xiake. People began to know about the cave from the book. (by Jian Nan)

04 明溪县隶属三明市，位于福建省西北部。明溪历史悠久，远在新石器时代已有人类在渔塘溪一带繁衍生息 / 阮任艺 陈映辉 摄

Mingxi County is under the jurisdiction of Sanming City. It lies in northwest of Fujian. Mingxi has a long history as even in the Neolithic Age, people began to live by Yutang River. (by Ruan Renyi and Chen Yinghui)

05 明溪"中国历史文化名村"御帘村 / 涧南 摄

Yulian Village, a historic culture village in Mingxi County. (by Jian Nan)

06 惠利夫人崇拜在明溪历史悠久，惠利夫人庙香火旺盛 / 涧南 摄

Worship of Lady Huili has a long history in Mingxi. Temple of Lady Huili is frequently visited by villagers. (by Jian Nan)

04

05

06

武夷山市是福建省唯一以名山命名的新兴旅游城市，前身为崇安县，建置于北宋淳化五年（公元 994 年）。1985 年 3 月 1 日，崇安县经国务院批准列为中国首批对外开放县市。1989 年 8 月经国务院批准撤县建市。1999 年 12 月，被联合国教科文组织批准列入《世界遗产名录》，成为中国第四处、世界 23 处世界文化与自然双遗产地之一 / 阮任艺 陈映辉 摄

Wu Yishan City is the only tourism city named after a mountain in Fujian. It was built in 994 in the Northern Song Dynasty and was once named Chong' an County. On March 1st 1985, Chongan County was authorized as one of China' s first opening counties. In August 1989, the county was upgraded to the city level by the state council. In December 1999, it was included in UNESCO World Heritage List and became the 4th site in China and the 23rd in the world of both World Cultural Heritage and World Natural Heritage. (by Ruan Renyi and Chen Yinghui)

01

02

03

01　　浦城县，中国丹桂之乡，位于福建省最北端闽浙赣三省交界处，是福建的北大门，自古为中原入闽第一关。浦城县属三江源头之一，境内溪水分别流入闽江、长江和钱塘江。北部渔梁岭和西部的铸岭头是长江水系与闽江水系的分水岭 / 阮任艺 陈映辉 摄

　　Pucheng County is the hometown of orange osmanthus in China. The county is located in the north most of Fujian Province. At the conjunction of three provinces, it is the north gate of Fujian and the first place to welcome migrant people from Central China in ancient times. Pucheng County is one of the sources of three rivers, i.e. the River Min, the Yangtze River and Qiantangjiang River. (by Ruan Renyi and Chen Yinghui)

02　　浦城古城墙及城门"登瀛门"临近南浦溪，经修复改造后成为市民晨练及休闲的场所 / 涧南 摄

　　Ancient city wall and Dengying Gate of Pucheng is near the Nanpuxi River. After reconstruction, this has been a place for morning exercises and relaxation. (by Jian Nan)

03　　浦城万安浮桥位于浦城东郊，跨越南浦溪，西接金鸡岭，东连万安乡桥头村。浮桥以舟为梁，由12只木船连接而成，独具特色 / 涧南 摄

　　Wan' an floating bridge is in the eastern suburbs of Pucheng County. The bridge crosses over the Nanpuxi River with Jinjiling hill on the west side and Qiaotou Village on the east side. The bridge consists of twelve wooden boats forming a unique style. (by Jian Nan)

01

01 松溪县是闽北山区一个颇具特色的小县，位于闽浙交界处，武夷山麓东南侧。古时沿河两岸多乔松，有"百里松荫碧长溪"之称，松溪因此而得名 / 阮任艺 陈映辉 摄
　　Songxi County is a small county in mountain areas of north Fujian. It connects Fujian and Zhejiang Province and sits at the southeastern foot of Mount Wuyi. In ancient times, Himalayan pines grew lushly on the river banks, hence its name. (by Ruan Renyi and Chen Yinghui)

02 松溪大布码头历史上曾经是商业繁华之地 / 涧南 摄
　　Dabu wharf of Songxi was once prosperous in history. (by Jian Nan)

03 松溪大布文化民俗村利用大布古埠码头改造，还原昔日商贾云集的面貌 / 涧南 摄
　　Villagers in Dabu Folk Culture Village try to reconstruct the wharf in order to achieve prosperity again. (by Jian Nan)

04 松溪西门"迎恩门"古时面临松溪河水，因城市建设发展已经失去作用，仅余砖石照壁一座 / 涧南 摄
　　Ying' en Gate is the west gate of Songxi County. It stands near the Songxi River. In modern urban development, the gate was no longer in usage, so only part of it remains. (by Jian Nan)

02

03

04

01

02

03

01   政和古名"关隶"，是一个由皇帝赐名的县城。宋代徽宗因为喝到关隶进贡的白毫银针而龙颜大悦，赐政和年号为关隶县名 / 阮任艺 陈映辉 摄
Zhenghe County was originally called Guandi. The Emperor Huizong in Song Dynasty favored its tea and altered its name by the title of his reign. (by Ruan Renyi and Chen Yinghui)

02   政和银杏装扮了深秋 / 兰斯文 摄
Gingko trees decorate the autumn of Zhenghe County. (by Lan Siwen)

03   在著名的闽浙廊桥世界里，政和廊桥占有一席之地，进入中国世界文化遗产预备名单里的政和廊桥就有岭腰后山桥、外屯洋后桥、澄源赤溪桥。岭腰后山廊桥 / 赖小兵 摄
Covered bridge in Zhenghe takes up an important part of covered bridges in Fujian and Zhejiang Province. UNESCO world heritage tentative list includes several covered bridges in Zhenghe. This is the covered bridge on the back of Lingyao Mountain. (by Lai Xiaobing)

01　建瓯"闽源文化广场"上巨大的"商代青铜大铙"地标雕塑，青铜大铙是秦汉前只有一国之君才可以享用的祭祀品。该铙于 20 世纪 80 年代在建瓯出土，把福建历史推前了一千多年 / 涧南 摄

There is a sculpture of bronze cymbal on the Minyuan culture square of Jian'ou. Before Qin and Han Dynasties, such cymbal only could only be used by the king of a country at worship ceremony. This cymbal was discovered in 1980s in Jianou, extending the history of Fujian over one thousand years. (by Jian Nan)

02　马可·波罗在其游记中这样描述建瓯，"该城范围相当大，有三座很美丽的桥，长 100 步以上，宽八步。这地方的女人美丽标致，过着安逸奢华的生活。这里盛产生丝，并且织成不同种类的绸缎"。建瓯松溪河畔通仙门前马可·波罗塑像 / 涧南 摄

Marco Polo wrote in his travel notes: Jian'ou is a fairly large county. It has three bridges and each one is a hundred steps long and eight steps wide. The women here are beautiful and graceful and they live a luxury life. The county is rich of raw silk and silk fabrics. A statue of Marco Polo stands in front of Tongxian Gate by the Songxi River. (by Jian Nan)

03　建瓯简称"芝"，历史上建宁府府衙驻地、建州州衙驻地，是一座一千八百多年建县史的省级历史文化名城，福建历史上最早设置的四个县之一 / 阮任艺 陈映辉 摄

Jian'ou is called Zhi in short. In history, Jianning government and Jianzhou government were located here. The county has a history of one thousand eight hundred years and is one of the earliest four counties in Fujian history. (by Ruan Renyi and Chen Yinghui)

建阳别称潭城，是福建省最古老的五个县邑之一。宋代曾以"图书之府"和"理学名邦"闻名于世 / 吴寿华 摄

Jianyang, also called Tancheng County, is one of the five oldest counties in Fujian. It was famous for libraries and institutes of Neo-Confucianism in Song Dynasty. (by Wu Shouhua)

01　建阳水南多宝塔建于明万历三十年（1602年），为八角七层阁式宝塔，石砖木混合结构，每层八面佛龛内均雕有佛像，是建阳县文化历史悠久的重要标志 / 赖小兵 摄

Nanduo Tower was built in 1602 in Ming Dynasty. It has seven octangle floors. The construction material is a mixture of stone, brick and wood. Each side of the floor places a figure of Buddha. It is a significant symbol of history and culture in Jianyang County. (by Lai Xiaobing)

02　建设中的建阳新区，漫步道及江边景色 / 赖小兵 摄

New district of Jianyang. Scenery by the river. (by Lai Xiaobing)

01

01　　　延平为闽北首府南平所在地，有一江三溪（闽江、建溪、沙溪、富屯溪）七十二支流纵横交织。延平历史上曾为南剑州，名重天下的延平四贤（杨时、罗从彦、李侗、朱熹）曾先后在此创建书院，讲学传道，使延平区成为名闻遐迩的东南邹鲁、理学名邦 / 阮任艺　陈映辉 摄

Yanping is located in the north of Fujian. Rivers and tributaries wind around Yangping County. Historically, four most famous scholars set up institutes here and gave lectures. Thus Yanping County became a renowned county with numerous Neo-Confucianism institutes. (by Ruan Renyi and Chen Yinghui)

02　　　闽江零公里处，双剑化龙的标志前，闽江航运线路已经停开 / 赖小兵 摄

The starting point of the River Min. Shipping routes here has been suspended in front of the sculpture of "Shuangjian Hualong". (by Lai Xiaobing)

03　　　延平新城建设日新月异 / 吴寿华 摄

New district in Yanping has changed remarkably. (by Wu Shouhua)

01

02

03

04

01   尤溪县是三明市下辖县，地处福建省中部，东邻闽清和永泰县，西连大田和沙县，南接德化县，北毗南平市延平区，有"闽中明珠"之称，是著名理学家朱熹的诞生地 / 阮任艺 陈映辉 摄

Youxi County is governed by Sanming City. It lies in the middle of Fujian Province with Minqing County and Yongtai County to the east, Datian County and Shaxian County to the south, Dehua County to the south, and Yanping District of Nanping City to the north. It is known as the pearl of the Fujian and the birth place of scholar Zhu Xi. (by Ruan Renyi and Chen Yinghui)

02   尤溪闽湖是福建地理的中心点 / 阮任艺 摄

Minhu Lake in Youxi County is the geographic center of Fujian. (by Ruan Renyi)

03   上学的少年儿童走过紫阳公园的汉白玉桥 / 涧南 摄

Children on their way to school go across a white marble bridge of Ziyang Park. (by Jian Nan)

04   尤溪紫阳公园由朱熹别号而名，紫阳公园位于尤溪县城与水东新城之间的尤溪河中，公园与两岸河滨景观公园共同组成"八园十景"。紫阳公园的朱熹讲学雕塑 / 涧南 摄

Ziyang Park is named after scholar Zhu Xi's alias. Ziyang Park is located between Youxi County and Youxi River. This is the sculpture of scholar Zhu Xi. (by Jian Nan)

01

古田县位于古田溪中下游，于唐开元二十九年（741年）建县，是千年古县，因朱熹流寓而称为"先贤过化之乡"。古田历史上以产铁、铸锅、造曲、制茶而出名，目前食用菌生产居世界第一，素有"食用菌之乡"、"华侨之乡"等称谓 / 阮任艺 陈映辉 摄

Gutian County is located downstream of the Gutianxi River. It was founded in 741 in Tang Dynasty with a history of one thousand years. Scholar Zhu Xi had ever lived here. The county was famous for iron production, pot making, tea making, etc. It now has the largest production of edible mushrooms. (by Ruan Renyi and Chen Yinghui)

02　古田临水宫 / 李世雄 摄
　　Linshui Palace in Gutian County. (by Li Shixiong)

03　古田溪水电站梯级电站 / 阮任艺 摄
　　Cascaded hydropower plant of Gutian County. (by Ruan Renyi)

02

03

01

02

03

01 　　闽清县别称"梅"，位于闽江下游，闽清县是福建省重点侨乡之一，是福建省重点林业县和南方杂果基地，橄榄、柑橘生产基地之一，是中国釉面砖重要生产基地之一和福建省最大的电瓷出口基地。梅溪由画面左面向右面穿过闽清城关流入闽江 / 阮任艺 陈映辉 摄

Minqing County is called Mei in short. It is located downstream of the River Min. It is a major county of returned overseas Chinese in Fujian Province. Minqing County is a provincial forestry county, a base of fruit production as well as olive and orange production. It is also one of China's glazed tile bases, and the biggest production base for electrotechnical porcelain exportation. In this picture, the Meixi River goes from left to right into the River Min. (by Ruan Renyi and Chen Yinghui)

02 　　水口水电站以发电为主，兼有航运、过木、防洪等综合利用效益 / 赖小兵 摄

Hydropower station of Shuikou County generates electricity and at the same time is used for shipping, controlling floods, etc. (by Lai Xiaobing)

03 　　闽清宏琳厝是闽江流域最大的传统民居之一 / 赖小兵 摄

Honglicuo Community is the largest traditional local living buildings in the basin of the River Min. (by Lai Xiaobing)

01

02

03

01　永泰县位于福建省中部。永泰水系发达，大樟溪发源于德化县，横贯全县西东，流经县内的嵩口、梧桐等乡镇，在闽侯江口注入闽江。永泰是著名的"李果之乡"、"武术之乡"、"建筑之乡"。永泰有国家级重点风景名胜区和4A级旅游区青云山，有省级风景名胜区姬岩和全国重点文物保护单位高盖山名山室 / 阮任艺　陈映辉 摄
Yongtai County sits in the middle of Fujian Province. It is a famous hometown of plums, martial art, and architecture. In the county, there are some famous resorts, like Qingyun Mountain, Jiyan Mountain, and Mingshanshi Hall on Gaogaishan Mountain. (by Ruan Renyi and Chen Yinghui)

02　永泰县嵩口古镇 / 赖小兵 摄
Songkou Ancient Town in Yongtai. (by Lai Xiaobing)

03　永泰名山室保存有宋元时期福建省仅见的浅浮雕造像，上百尊的人物、动物浮雕至今仍清晰可见 / 涧南 摄
In Mingshanshi Hall, there are relievos of people and animals dating back to Song and Yuan Dynasties. (by Jian Nan)

01

01   闽侯是中国橄榄之乡，素称八闽首邑 。1913 年由闽县和侯官县合并而成。县内著名景点有旗山国家森林公园、
          昙石山文化遗址、雪峰寺、十八重溪风景区等 / 阮任艺 陈映辉 摄
          Minhou County is the hometown of olives in China. It was combined by two counties, Minxian County and Houxian
County. In the county, there are numerous monuments and resorts. (by Ruan Renyi and Chen Yinghui)

02   福建省第一座依托于史前遗址的博物馆昙石山博物馆坐落于闽侯 / 吴寿华 摄
          Tanshishan Museum, the first museum based on the prehistorical site in Fujian, is located in Minhou. (by Wu Shouhua)

03   闽侯汤院村的老温泉澡堂历史悠久 / 阮任艺 摄
          The hotspring with long history in Tangyuan Village of Minhou. (by Ruan Renyi)

福州别称榕城、三山、左海、闽都，简称"榕"，位于福建东部、闽江下游沿岸，是福建省会、中国历史文化名城、东南沿海重要都市。福州是近代中国最早开放的五个通商口岸之一，福州马尾是中国近代海军的摇篮。福州不仅是中国东南沿海重要的贸易港口和海上丝绸之路的门户，而且是重要的文化中心 / 那兴海 摄

Fuzhou is also called Rongcheng, Sanshang, Zuohai, Mindu, and is called Rong in short. It lies in the east of Fujian. It is the capital of Fujian Province, a historic culture city, and a metropolis on southeast coast of China. Fuzhou was one of the first opening ports in Modern China. Mawei County of Fuzhou was the cradle for modern China navy. It is not only a trading port in southeast coast of China and a gateway of maritime silk road, but also an important culture center. (by Na Xinghai)

第十一章 ＋ 一个人的闽江

当年的汤姆逊，一个人行走拍摄闽江。跨越三个世纪之后，又有十几位摄影家步其后尘，再次行走拍摄闽江。

在每一位摄影家的镜头里，闽江都是极具个性的闽江：有的摄影家用最古老的拍摄方式与闽江建立起刻骨铭心的生命之约。有的摄影家以书写心经的方式，和闽江同欢喜共感叹。有的摄影家专注于艺术"造神"，和百姓同祈同祝。还有的摄影家用平民视角，以"街拍"方式记录最民间的影像。有摄影家拍福建廊桥，用精细影像述说历史。有的摄影家的镜头对准"人"，企图解说闽江的生命如何塑造一个个独特的面容。有摄影家热爱黑白记录，要为闽江留下永久的印痕。还有摄影家一路漂流，从水平面的角度解读闽江，体验大江东去的豪爽！

《闽江》的创作，直指摄影家的心灵，感动？还是震撼？深思？还是铭记？《闽江》是每一位摄影家终生难忘的生命之旅。

The River Min—a River of Many Faces

Thompson was photographing the River Min while walking along the river. Three centuries later, dozens of photographers followed his steps and photographed the river again along their journeys.

The River Min is unique in the eyes of each photographer. Some photographers build a life commitment with the river in their traditional photographing styles; some share their emotions with the river by writing Heart Sutra; some focus on the "god-making" arts and pray with the local people; some record the folk image by street snap; some retell the history by displaying the details of the covered bridge; some focus on "people" in order to illustrate how the river shapes the special countenance; some hope to keep an eternal mark for the river in their black and white image; and some like to interpret the river from the perspective of its surface while drifting on a boat.

The creation of The River Min is pointing to the soul of the photographers. It makes them moved, shocked, ponder or remember. The River Min is an unforgettable journey for each of the photographer.

Pinhole of the River Min

John Thomson, the pioneer of documentary photography in 1867, showed us the River Min and China of that time in reality with strong documentary style.

Pinhole photography is the oldest photographing technique. During the root-seeking journeys, all are presented in such original style. With innocent fearlessness, we go into the common visual spaces of the people. Dreams or desolations, all go to the films from our eyes, flowing to our homeland along the River Min.

Pinhole photographing is very unpredictable, and the dated films make the imaging process long and scary. When the film-scanned images appear before your eye, no assessment standards can be applied. You need to accept those unforgivable flaws, such as increased greyscale, less sense of depth, light leaking, etc. Of course, besides this, pinhole photography has strong perspective, which is of surreal charm.

When everything is ready, we watch the imges breathlessly, to see how this old style photography interprete the soul of the River Min and how we immerse in the lost time.

In the basin of the River Min, we came across lots of ancient symbols: ancient dwellings, bridges, ferries, pass, operas, temples, ancestral halls and old people. The water of the River Min is like an ancient hand, caressing and slapping the people by her side. We are seeking the ancient, which are dying out. The archways are teetering and folk customs are disappearing. Fortunately, some people have been making unremitting efforts to preserve the traditions. There is some way to rely on after every pure smile.

To record is to better preserve; to preserve is to better continue. Hundreds of years later, can our descendants recall the long lost memory from the images?

Guo Xiaodan

针孔·闽江 郭晓丹

慢看·闽江

此行追本溯源，从影像记录的角度，屹立着1867年的纪实摄影先驱约翰·汤姆逊。他用强烈的纪实风格，至今引领着我们更真实和理性地回顾曾经的中国，那时候的闽江流域。

针孔摄影是一种最古老的摄影术。在这场以寻根造像为目的的行走中，它用最原始的方式表达影像。带着混沌初开时候的无畏，闯进人们司空见惯的视觉空间。梦幻也好，苍凉也罢。全都从眼睛抵达胶片，顺着闽江的水流，回到故里。

针孔摄影有着很强的不可预见性，而过期胶片则更是令整个成像过程漫长和提心吊胆。当通过底扫的影像出现在你的面前，用来评价完美的标准在这里百无一用。你要尝试让自己接受那些不可原谅的缺陷：灰度增大，层次减少，药膜脱落，反差小，漏光，霉斑……当然，除此之处，还有针孔摄影本身所具备的超人般的透视，模糊与超现实的迷人风格。

当做好一切准备之后，我们再来屏息观看，看一个古老的摄影术如何诠释百年闽江的魂，看我们如何从这种反璞的摄影术中跌落回被遗忘的时光里。

在闽江流域，我们遇到许多古老的符号：古民居，古桥，古渡口，古隘口，古老的戏剧，古老的庙，祭奠先人的祠堂，守着旧民风的老人……闽江的水像更古老的手，也喂养也鞭策，也轻抚也掌掴。

我们试图追寻的过去正以疾风一样的速度在消亡，那些摇摇欲坠的牌楼，逐渐溃散的民风。幸好，还有人为了保留做出不懈的努力，在每一个纯朴的微笑后面，依然有路径可以倚顿。

记录，是为了更好地留住。留住，是为了更好地接续。一个甲子再一个甲子之后，我们的后代，是否能从影像里打捞祖先们失去的记忆？

百米落差瀑布　武夷山市岚谷乡　Fall in Langu Village, Wuyishan City

北溪水库　光泽县崇仁古镇　Beixi Reservoir, Chongren Town, Guangze County

古庙前的旌鼓队　永安市槐南镇　Drum Troupe in front of a temple, Huainan Town, Yong'an City

沿山古村　邵武市　An ancient village at the mountain, Shaowu City

高潭单孔桥　宁化县水茜乡　Gaotan single-arch bridge, Shuixi Village, Ninghua County

廊桥　Covered Bridge

伐木的江边人家 光泽县崇仁古镇 Lumberman at the river, Chongren Town, Guangze County

油茶籽的季节 建宁县 Camellia seed season, Jianning County

前洋古道 浦城县　The ancient path in Qianyang Village, Pucheng County

瑞岩禅寺烛火　武夷山市吴屯乡　The candlelight of Ruiyuan Temple, Wutun Village, Wuyishan City

大樟溪　永泰县嵩口古镇　　The Dazhangxi River, Songkou Town, Yongtai County

建于明朝的舂米房　永安市青水乡沧海村
Rice-pounding waterwheel of Ming Dynasty, Canghai Village, Qingshui Town, Yong'an City

书写·闽江 陈勇鹏

由玄奘法师翻译的《心经》，因其短小，且直指佛心，千百年来为广大出家僧人和在家文士所喜爱，成为古往今来被抄写最多的一部佛教经典，某种意义上它已经超越了宗教的范畴。

书写是人们的日常行为，但是在当下人们越来越疏于书写的情境下，书写、特别是在脱离了人们日常书写环境下的书写，就有了特别的意味。

从2006年起，我尝试在各种不同场景、不同材料上书写《心经》，希望以这种方式来探讨人与社会、与自然的一种关系。名之曰"非常心经"。2014年，应福建画报社邀请参与《闽江》大型影像文化创作工程，从闽江源头起，沿途在各种环境下书写心经，以这种特殊的艺术方式表达我对闽江这片蕴藏了秀丽自然景观和丰富人文历史的土地的敬意。

闽江流域秀丽的山水目前大多还保留着它的原生态，即使是传统民居也如自然的一部分一样和谐。我在大自然清新沁人的气息中，以山石村壁为纸，以江水调墨，用最传统的书法书写这部佛教经典，我感受到了自然造化和传统文化的双重撞击，每一次书写，身心都得到一次彻底的洗涤。

在书写闽江的过程里，我深深感悟到，人类的生存和文化创造，都要与大自然相和谐，这是最基本也是最高级的境界。

The Writings of the River Min

The most famous translation of "The Heart Sutra" by Master Xuan Zang of Tang Dynasty has been treasured by monks and scholars over the centuries as this version is concise and to the core of Buddhism. It is a Buddhist scripture which has been copied most from the ancient time. In a sense, it goes beyond the category of religion.

Writing is a kind of daily performance of human beings. Today people tend to write less. Writing is of special meaning when it is out of the everyday writing contexts.

Since 2006, I have been trying to write "The Heart Sutra" on different materials in various contexts, hoping to explore the relationship between human, society and nature. It is called "special heart sutra". In 2014, I was invited to participate the project of cultural creation of the River Min organized by Fujian Pictorial and wrote "The Heart Sutra" along the River Min in different environment. I want to honor the beautiful scenery and rich art history of the River Min in this special style of art.

Most of the mountains and rivers of the basin of the River Min maintain their original ecology. The traditional residence is also a natural part of the scenery. In such a fresh breath of the nature, I wrote the sutra on the stones and walls in the most traditional style of calligraphy. My body and mind were both refreshed in every writing, feeling the impact of nature and traditional culture.

During the process of writing along the River Min, I deeply realized that the human's subsistence and cultural creation need to be in harmony with the nature, which is the most basic and the highest realm.

Chen Yongpeng

在山洪遗留下的巨石上书写《心经》是表达对自然的敬畏
Writing the sutra on the rocks left by flood is to show respect for the nature

光泽县司前乡岱坪村河滩巨石上书写的《心经》（富屯溪北溪源头）
/ 陈伟凯 摄
The sutra written on the rock of by the river in Daiping Village,
Siqian Town, Guangze County (the source of the Beixi River of the Futunxi
River) (by Chen Weikai)

书写与村民的祭祀活动共同构成一个"艺术行为" / 陈伟凯 摄
The writing and the worship ceremony of the villagers jointly make up a
"deed". (by Chen Weikai)

光泽县止马镇水口村龙安寺烧纸炉壁上书写的《心经》（富
屯溪西溪） / 陈伟凯 摄
The sutra written on the paper burner wall in Long'an Temple,
Shuikou Village, Zhima Town, Guangze County (the Xixi River of the
Futunxi River) (by Chen Weikai)

浦城县云林禅院佛龛底座上书写的《心经》（建溪支流南浦溪） / 黄庆党 摄
The sutra written on the base of Buddha niche in Yunlin Temple of Pucheng County (the Nanpuxi River) (by Huang Qingdang)

浦城县云林禅院书写《心经》 / 黄庆党 摄
The sutra written in Yunlin Academy in Pucheng County (by Huang Qingdang)

以武夷山大王峰为背景在玻璃窗上书写《心经》（建溪支流崇阳溪） / 陈伟凯 摄
The sutra written on the glass window with the background of Peak Dawang of Mount Wuyi (the Chongyangxi River) (be Chen Weikai)

南平市延平区闽江零公里处渔船上书写《心经》（闽江）/ 陈建中 摄　Writing on a fish boat at the "0 Km" point of the River Min in Nanping City (by Chen Jianzhong)

三明钢铁厂轧钢车间钢材上书写
的《心经》（沙溪） / 陈建中 摄
The sutra written on the steal in
the rolling plant of Sanming steel plant
(the Shaxi River) (by Chen Jianzhong)

街拍·闽江 王鹭佳

所谓街拍，是纪实摄影最重要的一个组成部分。大家知道的摄影大师布列松、马克·吕布、罗伯特·弗兰克、森山大道和薇薇安，他们都是举世公认的街拍高手。他们拍的许多照片把世间美好的瞬间凝固下来，成为我们认知时代和历史的琥珀。

社会是丰富的，生活是精彩的，摄影的内容是取之不竭的。人是万物之灵，每一个人都是一个时代的符号。许多照片只有等到再回忆的时候才显得弥足珍贵，而摄影人则必须在那些珍贵的生活"瞬间"消失之前拍下必须拍到的照片。

当我沿着闽江一次一次行走拍摄的时候，闽江源头、支流、主流沿岸城乡村落的精彩瞬间扑面而来。有人觉得城市才是街拍的地方，其实，乡村也有大街小巷，乡村无疑也是街拍的好场所。摄影人只要有了人生的阅历，有了人文的情怀，就可以用平民的意识，真诚的关爱，接地气的视角，以及对生命的尊重，用手中的相机捕捉生活的真相。

一个行行摄摄的人，拍下形形色色的人。在我的眼中，每一天的人生都是不一样的，也是不平凡的。我愿意把镜头对准闽江沿岸那些有缘的陌路人，真实地反映出他们的喜怒哀乐和酸甜苦辣。

The Street Snaps of the River Min

Street photography is an important part of documentary photography. Many great photographers, such as Cartier-Bresson, Marc Riboud, Robert Frank, Daido Moriyama and Vivian are all masters of street photography. They freeze the beautiful moments in their pictures, which make us know about the time and history.

The society and the life are colorful and rich resources for photography. Human is the most intelligent creature of the universe, and every person is a symbol of each era. Many pictures become more precious in memory and photographers must press the shutter before that precious "moment" disappeared.

Every time when I walked along the River Min to take photos, the wonderful moments in the cities and villages along the mainstreams, tributaries and the source of the River caught my eyes. Many people think only city is suitable for street photography, but villages are definitely good places for street snaps. Photographers can catch the truth of life with their camera with care, love and honesty as long as they have life experience and humanistic concern.

A photographer can take pictures of different kinds of people along his journey. In my eyes, each day is different and marvelous. I would like to take pictures of the strangers along the River Min to show their pleasure, anger, sorrow and joy.

Wang Lujia

01 闽江下游闽清县水口镇江边的女孩
A girl by the river in Shuikou Town, Minqing County at the downstream of the River Min

02 建瓯市一间小店里做作业的孩子
A child who is doing homework in a shop of Jian' ou City

03 建瓯市一间老宅里的孩子
A child in an old house in Jian' ou City

04 建瓯市乡下老宅里坐在沙发背上的两个孩子
Two children sitting on the back of a sofa in an old house of a village of Jian' ou City

05 建阳市黄坑镇坳头村一个站在木桶里的孩子（建溪支流麻阳溪源头村）
A child standing in a wooden barrel in Ao' tou Village, Huangkeng Town, Jianyang City (the source of the Maxi River)

06 建阳市麻沙镇两个吃雪糕的孩子
Two children eating ice block in Masha Town, Jianyang City

07 建阳市麻沙镇一个直视镜头的孩子
A child looking in the camera in Masha Town, Jianyang City

08 建阳市麻沙镇老街孩子
Children on an old street of Masha Town, Jianyang City

09 建阳市麻沙镇骑童车的孩子
A child riding a children' s bicycle in Masha Town, Jianyang City

10 建阳市麻沙镇的一对双胞胎
A twin in Masha Town, Jianyang City

11 建阳市麻沙镇在古宅老墙下玩耍的一群孩子
A group of children playing at the wall of an old house in Masha Town, Jianyang City

12 闽江下游闽清县坂东镇宏琳厝里做作业的孩子
A girl doing homework in Honglincuo of Bandong Town, Minqing County of the downstream of the River Min

13 闽清县一个玩球的孩子
A child playing with a ball in Minqing County

14 建瓯婴儿
A baby in Jian' ou City

15 清流滑旱冰的孩子
Children going roller skating in Qinglliu County

16 三明孩子
A child in Sanming City

17 邵武和平古镇上学的孩子
Children in ancient Heping Town of Shaowu City

18 永安青水乡沧海村儿童
A child in Canghai Village, Qingshui Town, Yong' an County

19 永泰玩耍的孩子
A child in Yongtai County

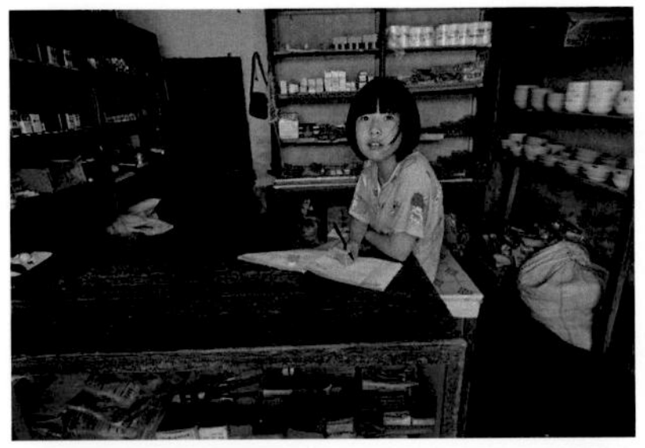
02

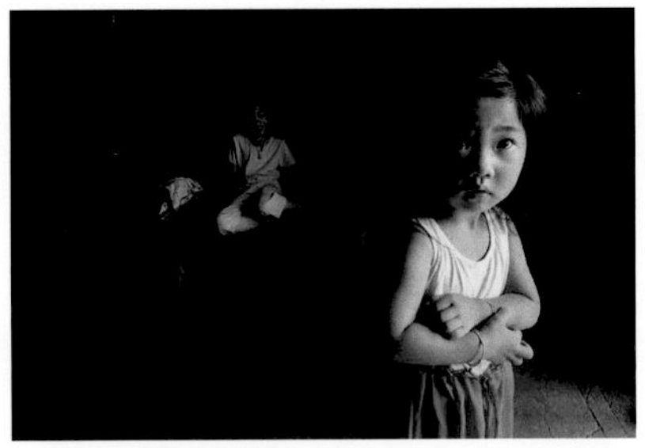
03

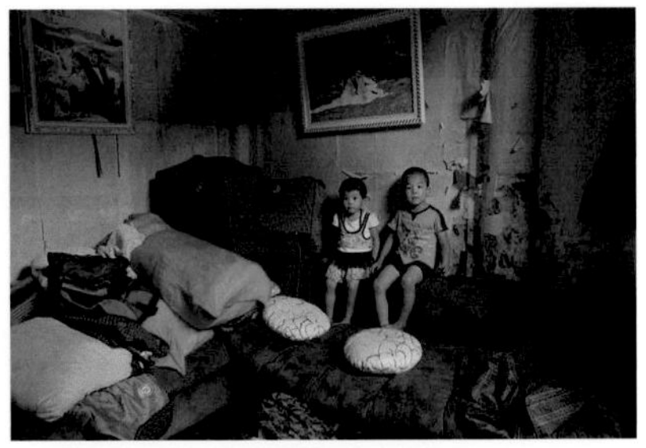
04

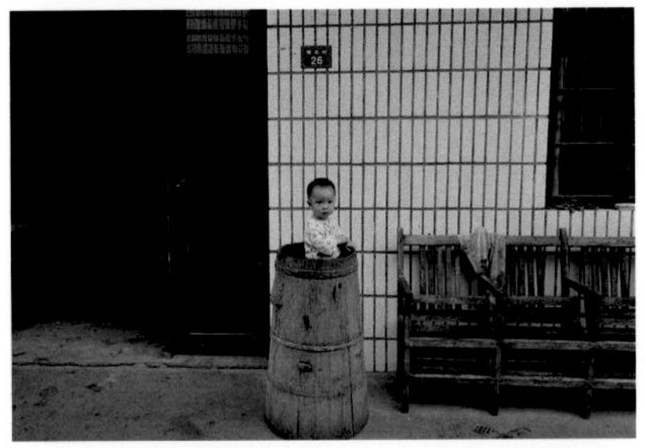
05

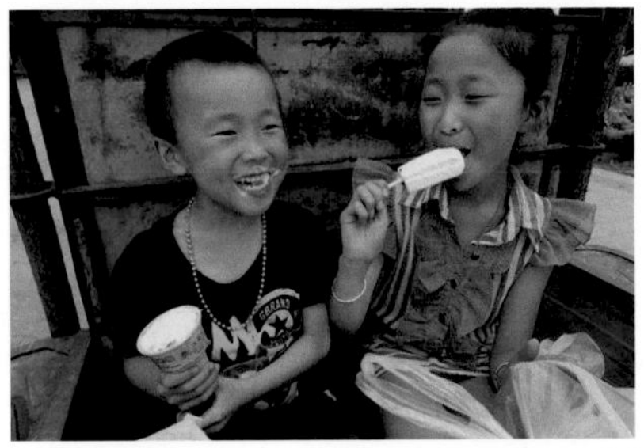
06

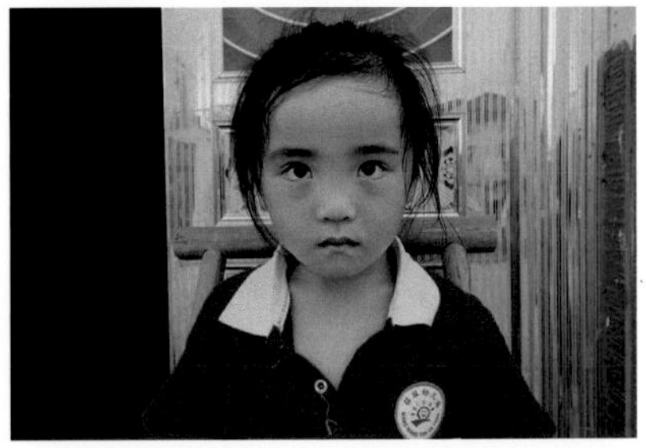
07

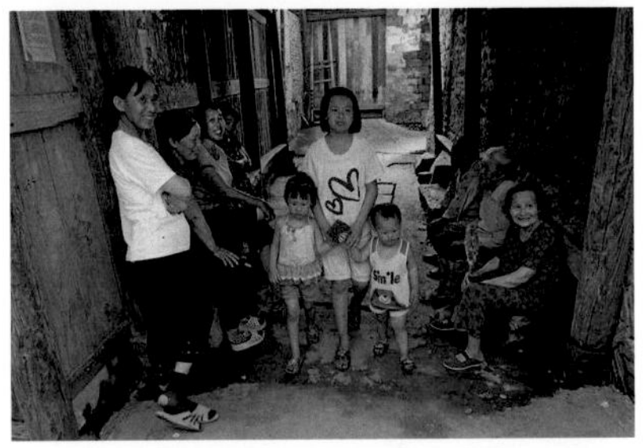
08

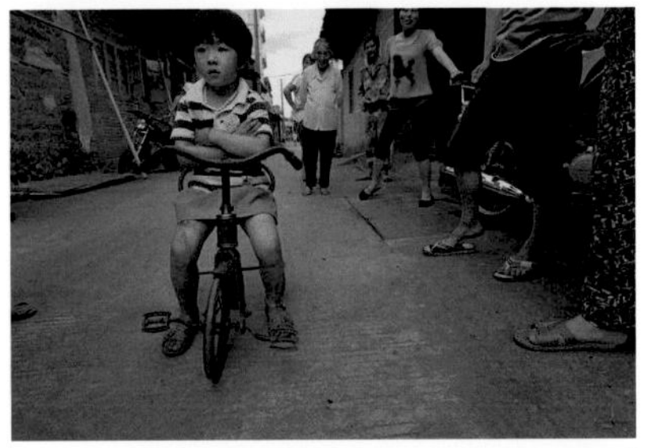
09

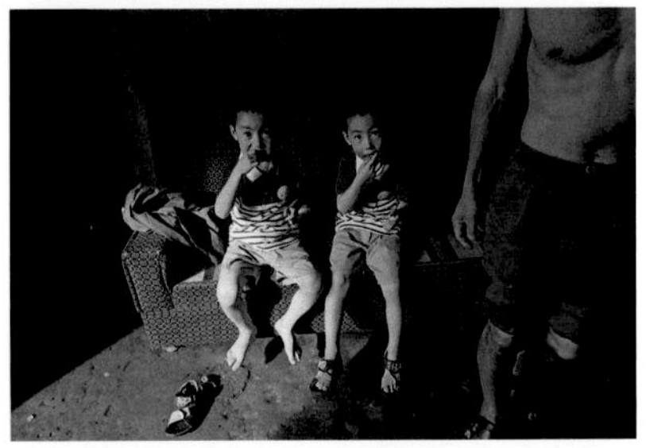
10

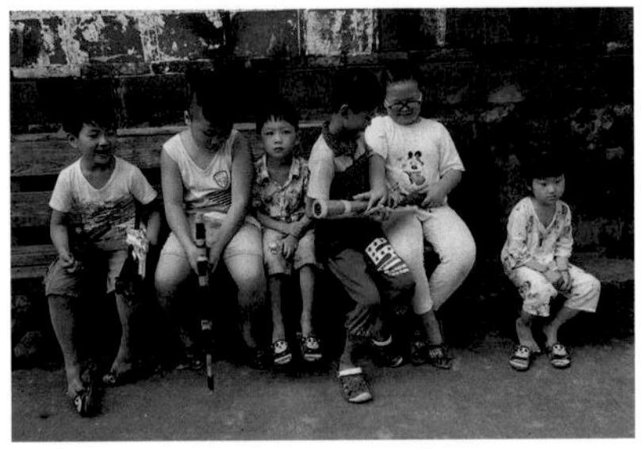
11

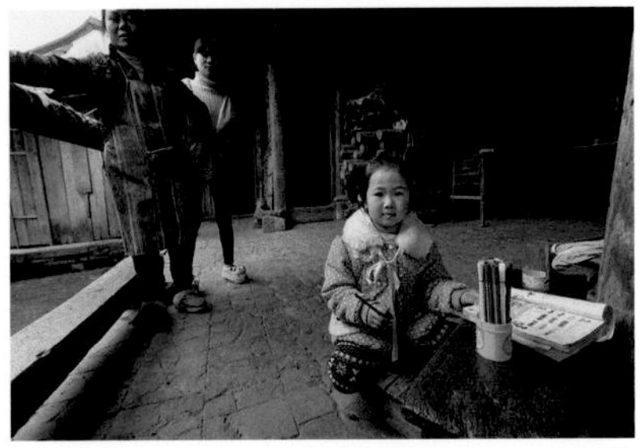
12

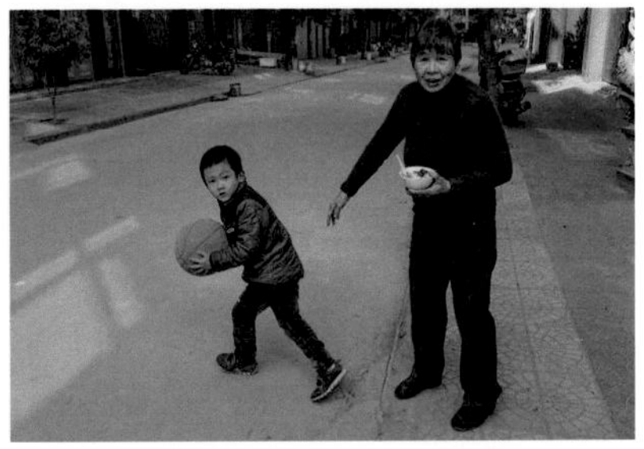
13

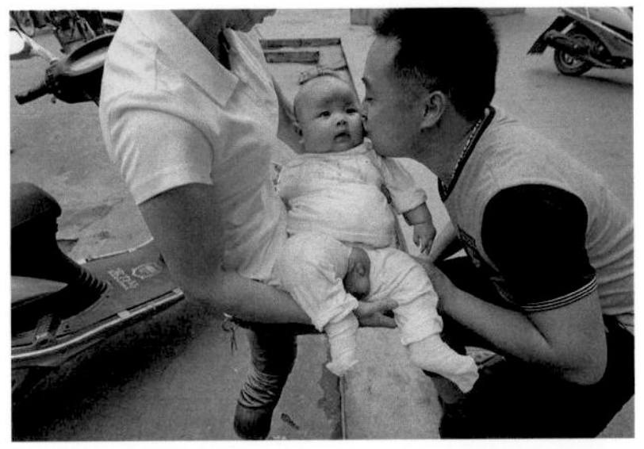
14

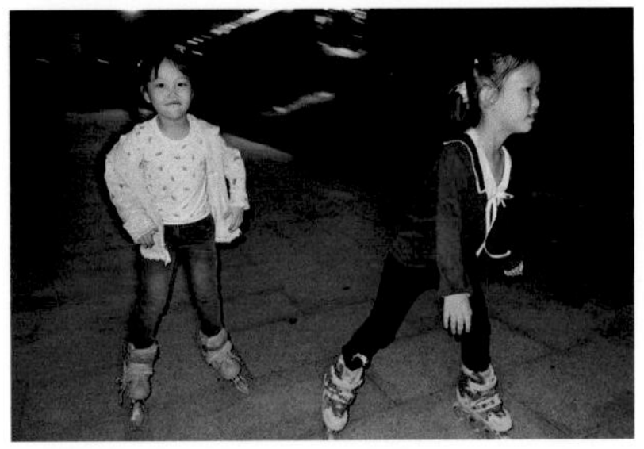
15

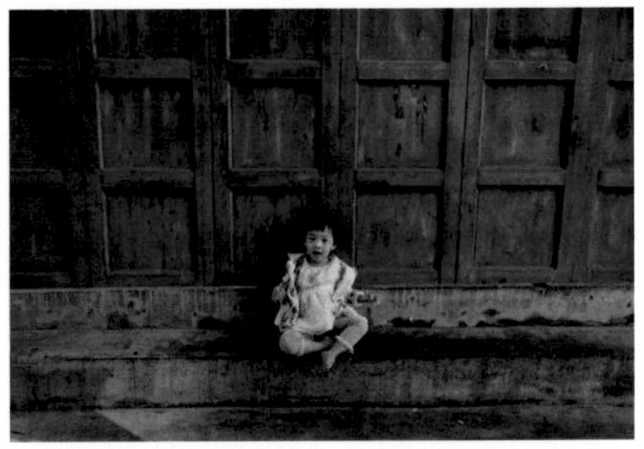
16

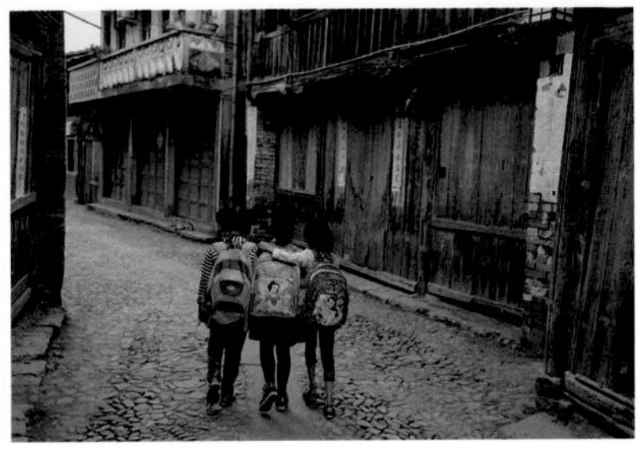
17

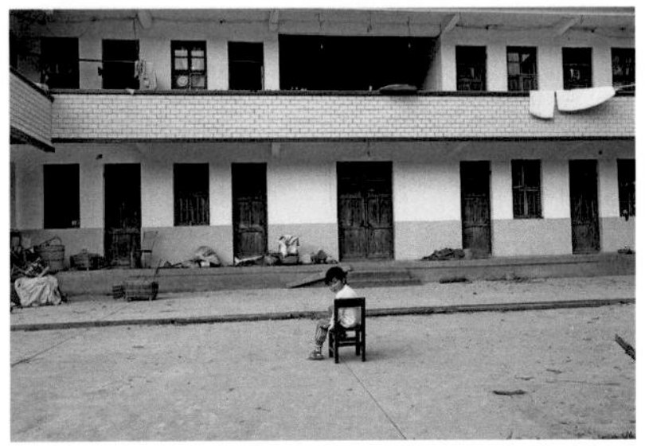
18

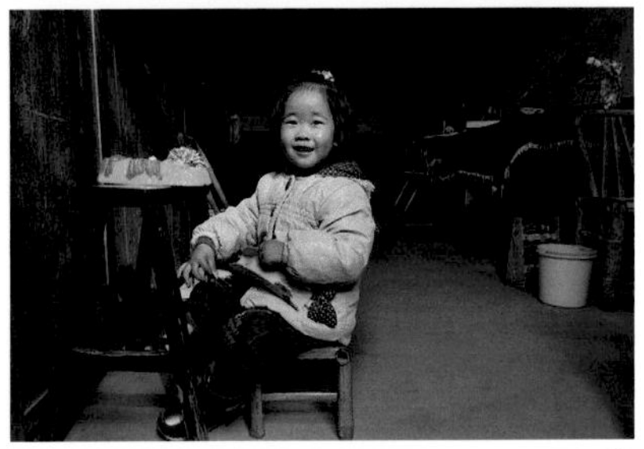
19

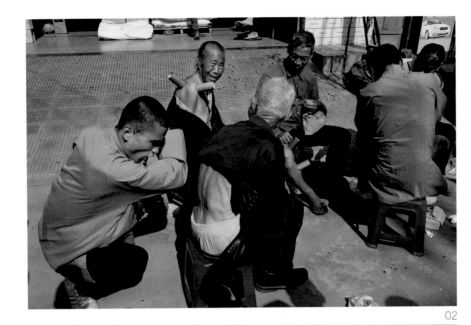

01 街头拔牙 古田县
Tooth extraction in the street, Gutian County

02 街头行医 建宁县
Practicing medicine in the street, Jianning County

03 乡村诊所 尤溪县
Village clinic, Youxi County

04 守灵 建瓯市
The wake, Jian'ou City

05 理发店 永泰县嵩口镇
Barbershop, Songkou Town, Yongtai County

01

02

03

01   竹躺椅　尤溪县
　　　Bamboo deck chair, Youxi County

02   外婆
　　　Grandma

03   打毛衣　永泰县
　　　Knitting, Yongtai County

04   轮椅　永泰县
　　　Wheel chair, Yongtai County

04

01   打电话的女人　建瓯市
A woman on a phone, Jian' ou City

02   泡温泉的男女　闽清县黄楮林
Young people in a hot spring,
Huangchulin, Minqing County

03   补鞋的女孩　建瓯市
A girl having her shoe fixed, Jian' ou City

04   纹身的女子　建瓯市
A woman with tattoo, Jian' ou City

05   土墙前的美女　浦城
A beauty at the wall, Pucheng County

Canoeing along the River Min

Few people can observe the River Min on the its surface. What effect can it be when watching the river from its source to estuary on its surface?

Our journey began from Fuzhou. We came to the source of the River Min in Zhangjiashan, Junkou Town of Jianning County by a van with two canoes tied up on the top.

The stream from the mountain slope is the baby of the River Min. Like the eyes of all the babies, the stream is clear and pure. Standing at the source of the river, we were imaging the steam, after running all its way for over 500 kilometers and covering an area of half Fujian Province, becomes a mighty river running into the sea. This is the rhythm of the life of the River Min.

Canoeing is the best way to explore the River Min. Going slowly with the touch of the water, you can explore every corner of the river with the feeling of its pulse. You can see its beauties as sun rises and sets, clouds gather and spread; you also can feel its pains with dams, rubbish and sewage.

The canoeing is part of the cultural creation project of the River Min. We were drifting the mainstreams of the river till its estuary as well as its three main tributaries: the Futunxi River, the Shaxi River and the Jianxi River, with a total run of over 1000 km, crossing 98 dams. We took over ten thousand pictures with cameras fixed on the head of the canoes

The canoeing on the River Min is an unforgettable and fantastic journey for us. Nobody in the future may know that there once a canoe drifting along the river. But what we took on the surface of the water records the truth of the river in this time, which is hardly seen by most people.

Hundreds of years later, we believe that the River Min will be clearer. People may get shocked and moved when they see the pictures we took today as we see the pictures took by John Thompson over a hundred years ago.

Wish the River Min running forever.

Ruan Renyi

漂流·闽江 阮任艺

很少有人能在贴近水面的高度来观察闽江，若是能从这个角度来看闽江，而且是从源头一直看到入海口，那会是什么感受？

我们的行程从福州开始。汽车上绑着两条皮划艇，沿着江边的公路，从国道到省道再到县道和乡道，最后是一条羊肠小山路带着我们到了闽江源头，建宁县均口镇张家山自然村。

从山坡上滴灌出的这一泓泉水是闽江的婴儿时代，就像所有婴儿的眼睛一样，泉水清澈宁静纯洁。站在源头，我们想象它在经过五百多公里之后，包容了半个福建面积的水流，变成了一条滔滔大河奔腾入海，这就是闽江的生命律动。

划艇，是探索江河最好的形式。静下心来慢慢前进，与江水肌肤相亲，你能深入这条河的每一个角落，随着它的脉搏起伏。你看到它的美：日出日落、云卷云舒。你也看到它在承受的痛苦：大坝、垃圾和腥臭的污水，尽管你感受到的痛苦远不及它受到的伤害的千万分之一。

作为"闽江"大型影像文化创作工程中的一个子项目，我们漂过了闽江主流延平至入海口以及三大干流富屯溪、沙溪和建溪，总行程一千余公里，共计翻越了 98 座大坝，用固定在船头的摄影机拍摄了数万张延时摄影图片，留下了珍贵的图片资料。

闽江漂流之于我们，将会是一个永难忘怀的奇幻旅程。水过无痕，未来不会再有人知道、记得曾经有这样一条小艇在江上划过。可我们从水面的高度记录了这个时代闽江的全景，记录了人们难以深入看到的真实。

几百年乃至很长很长时间以后，我们相信闽江将会重新奔腾、更加清澈，那时的人们看到这些图片，会和我现在看到约翰·汤姆逊先生一百年前拍摄的闽江图片一样震撼和感动。

愿闽江澎湃如昨。

闽江源头建宁县均口镇张家山自然村　　The natural village of Zhangjiashan, Junkou Town, Jianning County, the source of the River Min

From the Caojiawu section of the Shuixixi River, the flow is big enough to carry the canoe. We entered the river at Gujin Bridge and began our canoeing. Several hundred meters away, the first dam appeared in front of us unexpectedly. The dam, less than two meters high, might be built for agricultural irrigation. Our little canoes could not go through it, so we had to carry our canoes and went across the dam.

It took us more than one hour to go across the little dam. We entered the water again and found another dam less than one kilometer away. We proceeded only three kilometers this afternoon and there was a dam appearing per kilometer. We spent over one hour in mud for crossing each dam. When we arrived at Ninghua County, it was late of the day.

在闽江正源水茜溪曹家屋河段，水流终于大到可以载舟了。我们在"古今桥"下水，正式开始闽江漂流。划出几百米之后，第一道水坝就出乎意料地横亘在我们眼前。这道高度不到两米的水坝，也许是为了农业灌溉而设。我们的小艇无法逾越这种障碍，只好靠岸扛船翻坝。

用了一个多小时才翻过了这道小水坝。再次下水，只划出了不到一公里，前方河面传来哗哗的落水声，又是一道大坝。在这个下午，我们只前进了三公里，平均每公里一个水坝，而每个水坝都要耗费一个多小时的时间在烂泥中摸爬滚打来翻越。等我们接近宁化县城时，天色已晚。

在宁化县的水茜溪下水开始漂流　The starting point of the canoeing: the Shuixixi River in Ninghua County

进入宁化县城突遇雷暴雨　The thunderstorm in Ninghua County

安砂水库风光迷人　The scenery of Ansha Reservoir

1970年，安砂水电站动工修建，1975年开始蓄水发电。随着水位渐渐升高，九龙溪昔日兴风作浪的九条龙从此深埋水底。一路划去，碧绿的江水和两岸青山让人心旷神怡。过了中游后，网箱养鱼密集了起来，我们仿佛闯进了一个大迷宫，在密集的尼龙网线中划行，格外吃力。

安砂水库右岸正在开挖新307省道，原本是原始森林的山地被拦腰开挖，粗暴地毁灭了山腰以下的植被，数吨重的土石不停地从山上翻滚砸进水里，雷鸣般的落水声在山谷中回响。我们胆战心惊地贴着左岸划行，以防被哪个跳石砸中。一直划到最后五公里，两岸森林密布，终于没有了人类活动的痕迹。水面弥漫着森林的草木芬芳，深山中不时传来几声猿啼鸟叫。我想，这可能是闽江流域最后的原始地带了。

Ansha Hydropower station was built in 1970 and began to operate in 1975. With the rising water level, the Jiulongxi River gets quiet. The green water and mountains along the bank are pleasant and relaxing. After the middle reach of the river, cage fish culture gets dense. We seemed be in a labyrinth and paddled hard in the net.

On the right side of Ansha Reservoir, 307 provincial road is under construction. The mountain with primeval forest was dug open from the middle. The vegetation on the lower part of the mountain was destroyed. Tons of stones and earth were rolling into the river with thunderous sound. We rowed along the left side carefully, fearing some stones might fall on us. Until the last five kilometers, no traces of human activities were found on either side of the bank. Fresh smell of the grass and the singing of the birds came from the deep mountains. I think this is probably the last primeval area of the reach of the River Min.

划过永安市贡川镇会清古桥　Huiqing Bridge in Gongchuan Town, Yong'an City

沙溪三明段，与溪岸边的鹰厦铁路并肩而行　The Sanming section of the Shaxi River, paralleling with Yingtan-Xiamen Railway

Rowing along the Shaxi River, we can see lots of rubbish and dams. The residents living along the river use to dumping rubbish at the bank. The River Min is a cleaner of zero cost to them. During the rainstorm season, the rising water level will wash away their rubbish into the river and bring it to the next dam.

After the Shaxian County, we followed the yellow flow till the Shaxikou Hydropower station. After rowing 250 km and crossing 25 dams, we came to the end of the Shaxi River. Nanping City was insight.

在沙溪上一路划来，垃圾和水坝，是两个最常见的现象。沿江居民们习惯将生活垃圾倾倒在岸边，闽江对他们来说这是一个零成本的"清道夫"。每到暴雨时节，江水上涨就会把垃圾冲走，一直运到下一个大坝前。

经过了沙县，我们跟随着这股黄色的水流直到沙溪口水电站。划过了250公里水路、翻过了25座大坝。越过沙溪和富屯溪交汇的河口，沙溪水路终于走到尽头，南平市区遥遥在望了。

武夷山建溪源头的漂流拍摄，是整个闽江水系漂流中最让我期待的一部分。行前做漂流计划，用谷歌地球鸟瞰这片郁郁葱葱之地，绝大多数地方是完全看不到人类活动痕迹的。卫星图上桐木的这一片核心保护地带，大地就像一块揉皱了的巨大绿色地毯，你可以看到无数涓涓细流、林间飞瀑慢慢汇聚成小溪、河流，一条江，就是这样诞生的。

武夷山自然保护区1979年创建，是福建省最大的自然保护区。这片五万六千多公顷的保护区中，保留了最原始的植被和丰富多样的生物种类。

在桐木的山谷小片空地中，村民们见缝插针地种植了小块茶园。没有化肥与农药的茶树，也保持了野生的自然生长状态，和我们印象中整齐排列的茶园很不一样。

当村民们领悟到生态环境对他们的生活有多么重要时，和大自然的良好互动就开始了。在桐木的村落中，你见不到一片纸屑，河道中也见不到任何垃圾。曾经的盗伐林木也早已绝迹，因为一株茶树带来的经济效益远远超过了砍伐一棵大树。

当这一切变成良性循环时，我看到了美丽、和谐。

漂流在清澈见底的桐木溪中，有一种久违了的愉悦和感动：这才是山水的纯真之态，这里才是人类发祥的源头，深藏在细胞中的原始记忆被唤醒，我原来只是回到了家乡。

The source of the Jianxi River in Mount Wuyi is the most anticipated part of the whole canoeing trip. Looking down from above by Google Earth when planning the trip, we could not see any human traces in most part of this area. The core protection area in Tongmu looks like a giant green carpet. Many tricklets and falls in the forest gather together and form a creek, a steam and then a river.

Wuyishan Nature Reserve was built in 1979 and it is the largest nature reserve in Fujiang Province, covering an area of 56,000 hectares with most original vegetation and diversified species.

In some small spaces of the valley in Tongmu, villagers plant their patches of tea gardens without chemical fertilizer. The tea gardens are naturally grown, which are different from our impression of the large and neatly arranged tea garden.

When the villagers realize that ecological environment is so important to their life, favorable interactions with the nature begin. In the villages of Tongmu, you will not find any litter. Illegal lumbering disappeared because the economic benefit of a tea tree is bigger than felling a tree.

The virtuous circle makes me see the beauty and harmony.

The long lost feeling of pleasure and touch came to me when we were drifting on the clear water of the Tongmuxi River. This is the purity of the mountains and rivers, the origin of human being, my hometown.

划过桐木村清澈的溪水　The clear water of Tongmu Village

漂流进入武夷山核心景区，与九曲溪上的竹排一同前行　　The core scenic spots of Mount Wuyi: drifting with the bamboo rafts on the Jiuquxi River

在1994年出版的《南平市志·总述》中，开篇首句说道："南平，地处八闽喉襟。"这句豪迈的宣告并不算夸张。不论从哪个角度看，福建省南平市市区都是整个闽江水系的交通中心和枢纽。沙溪、富屯溪与建溪在南平市区一带汇合，形成闽江。从古至今，南平也是福建省陆上交通的交汇之处，南平古"剑浦驿"是省城福州北上出省必经之处。这里也是鹰厦铁路（江西鹰潭－福建厦门）和横福铁路（江西横峰－福建福州）两大福建出省铁路的交汇处，是205国道和316国道的交汇点，京台高速公路也在市郊穿过。

在南平延福门外江面上，有"双剑化龙"雕塑，代表"干将"、"莫邪"两剑的两块方尖碑交错直指天穹。精确地说，在南平市区延福门码头三江汇流"双剑化龙"雕塑处，才是这条叫"闽江"的河流零公里起点处。

三水合一，江面豁然开朗，浩浩荡荡奔涌流向远方的东海，我们的"闽江漂流"终于可以实至名归。

Nanping City is the throat of Fujian Province. It is the transport center and hub of the water system of the River Min. The Shaxi River, the Futunxi River and the Jianxi River converge in Nanping City and form the River Min. Since the ancient time, Nanping has also been land transport hub in Fujian. The ancient Jianpu Post was the only passage to the north from Fuzhou. It is also the junction of two major provincial railways: Yingtan-Xiamen Railway and Hengfeng-Fuzhou Railway. As for highways, it is the junction of National Highway 205 and 316 as well as Beijing-Taipei highway.

There is a sculpture named "Shuangjian Hualong" on the river by Yanfumen dock of Nanping City. The two swords of the sculpture represent "Gan Jiang" and "Mo Xie", connected at the top and pointing to the sky. To be exact, the sculpture is the starting point of the River Min.

The three rivers converge in one surging to the East China Sea in the distance. Our canoeing on the River Min finally deserves the name.

01 南平闽江零公里标志处
    The starting point of the River Min

02 闽江零公里处"双剑化龙"雕塑
    Statue of "Shuangjian Hualong" at 0 km point of the River Min

03 延平湖，一座纪念碑式的桥梁底座
    Yanping Lake, a monumental bridge base

04 水口水库，正在修建的库区大桥
    Shuikou Reservoir bridge is under construction

05 水口水库，樟湖坂至溪口的客船
    Shuikou Reservoir, a passenger ship from Zhanghuban to Xikou

01

01　　闽江入海口遥遥在望
　　　The estuary of the River Min in sight

02　　福州，中洲岛
　　　Fuzhou, Zhongzhou Island

03　　福州，福厦高铁闽江大桥
　　　Fuzhou, Fuzhou-Xiamen Railway Minjiang Bridge

04　　2014 年 8 月 30 日，闽江漂流队完成正源沙溪和闽
　　　江主流的漂流拍摄，顺利在福州琅岐岛南面海滩登陆
　　　On August 30 2014, Minjiang canoeing team
　　　completed the photographing work along the Shaxi
　　　River and the mainstreams of the River Min and landed
　　　successfully on the Langqi Island of Fuzhou.

02

03

摆脱了水口大坝，闽江终于回归正常，江水一泻而下奔腾流淌过闽清、闽侯，直到福州。我们终于感受到了些许痛快淋漓的漂流快感。

头顶上方是无数高大的桥梁。"海西三纵八横高速公路"、"八横九纵省级干线公路"、"温福高速铁路"、"福厦高速铁路"、"向莆铁路"……密集高效的交通网络覆盖了闽江下游的丘陵地带。皮划艇小心翼翼地穿过了繁忙的马尾港，趁着退潮的水流，冲过了"双龟锁江"，在琅岐岛面向东海的滩涂登陆。

至此，我们的闽江漂流终于正式结束。

After Shuikou Dam, the River Min returns to normal. The river is running through Minqing, Minghou and reached Fuzhou. We finally experienced the exciting canoeing.

The downstream of the River Min is overlapped with intensive bridges, railways and highways. We carefully rowed through the busy Mawei Harbor. With the help of the falling tide, we landed on Langqi Island.

This is the official end of our canoeing on the River Min.

04

神灵 · 闽江 李世雄

　　都说闽江神奇，我说最神奇的莫过于闽江流域民间信仰中的众神交错与灵迹异动的民俗景象。学术上将宗教信仰分为正统宗教和民间崇拜，但在这里的老百姓眼里，"拜拜"都是一回事，念经或可借用佛语，而拜神则是一视同仁。自原始崇拜至宋元理学，这种兼容并蓄的文化性格致闽江民间信仰呈现众神交错与纠缠迁移的混象，而之后全闽范围声势浩大的造神运动更为史上罕见。或者说，因宋元以来朱熹理学长期强有力的抑制和影响，又在各朝政府支持下的乡族经济的阶段性不断冲击下，加之闽江地理交通的障碍，导致正统宗教主导化进程缓慢，在区域文化中地位尴尬，而地方神明在地域分布上又显得零散，缺乏影响面特广的大神，故而官宦名儒信仰节外有枝，故而各路神仙偶像同室合供……但若说闽江流域在闽地灵迹异动特色中的特色，当属女性神明的迎引与塑造，例如妈祖天后缘江逆进山乡，例如临水夫人全能保育护幼……这是一个很有意思又独一无二的现象。

　　民间造神是社会生存中公众利益与价值观的表达．其创造与膜拜的心理依据是平等合作或休戚与共的归属感。而我用影像的方式介入其中，并不想止于满足文献性的视象记录，而是期望借助影像数码科技的当下话语特性，参与敬神造像和灵迹"改造"。从民间造神到摄影照神再到数码媒介的再造神，这一脉相承的本质意义不仅是同步与协调的，而且是能相应与互动的。

The Gods of the River Min

The most amazing thing of the River Min is the folk beliefs in the river basin, where people worship different gods and have spiritual experiences. Academically religious beliefs include orthodox religions and folk worship. For the people here, all the worships are the same. From the original worship to the Neo-Confucianism of Song and Yuan Dynasties, its inclusive cultural feature led to the overlapping and mixing of gods among folk beliefs. And later an influential province-wide god-creating movement was carried out, which is rarely seen in history. The orthodox religions were making slow progress in the region due to the restrain and influence of the Neo-Confucianism, the impact of township economy and the geographic situation. At the same time, the local gods are scattered around without too much influence. The most unique phenomenon is the introduction and creation of goddess, such as the Goddess Mazu and Lady Linshui.

Folk creation of god is an expression of the public interest and value of social existence. The mental basis for creation and worship of god is fair cooperation or the sense of belongings. I would like to participate into the process of god creating and spiritual "reform" with digital images rather than the traditional documentary records. The essence of the folk creation of god and the recreation of god by digital media is coordinating and interactive.

Li Shixiong

建瓯光孝寺　Guangxiao Temple of Jian'ou County

古田水口天柱山将军庙　　Jiangjun Temple of Tianzhushan Mountain, Shuikou Town, Gutian County

古田临水宫祖庙　　Linshuigong Temple of Gutian County

福州陈靖姑出生地　The birthplace of Chen Jinggu of Fuzhou

邵武和平古镇延喜宝庵　Yanxibao Temple of ancient Heping Town, Shaowu City

闽清兴隆大王殿   Dawang Temple of Minqing County

邵武和平坎头村惠安祠　Hui'an Temple in Kantou Village, Heping Town, Shaowu City

永泰嵩口寿春堂　　Shouchun Temple in Songkou Town, Yongtai County

武夷山瑞岩禅林　Ruiyan Buddhist Temple of Mount Wuyi

建瓯光孝寺　Guangxiao Temple of Jian'ou County

廊桥·闽江 周跃东

我自幼生活在闽北山区，有关廊桥的记忆是儿时家门口的那座每日上学的必经之桥。这桥不仅能遮风挡雨，桥内还能嬉戏打闹，逢年过节大人们在此烧香拜佛……长大后，才知道这种桥叫廊桥。

福建位于东南沿海，境内山高林密、地势险峻、河道密布，自古即有"闽道更比蜀道难"之说，修路筑桥成了历代闽官开发福建的重要举措。自隋唐以来福建建桥无数，有着"闽中桥梁甲天下"和"闽中桥梁最为巨丽"的说法。福建廊桥就像构建了一座时空隧道，有过惊人的技术成就，创造出灿烂的桥梁建筑艺术。在深山峻岭之中，频频出现"山穷水尽疑无路"之际，仿若彩虹飞架南北，引来"柳暗花明又一村"的惊叹。站在桥屋之中，遥望远山如黛，近听流水潺潺，鸟鸣山幽，给人如诗如画之感，令人心旷神怡，劳累顿消。总之，它们横亘如虹，上履廊屋，饰以重檐，挺然秀出，饶有画意。事实上，廊桥不仅是交通设施，还兼有驿站、祭祀、社交、贸易等大量民俗、文化、经济、社交、风水景观等功能，还代表着一种文化和乡土情感。可以说，古廊桥就是一个载体，见证着当地亘古文明的发展历程，无声地叙说着过往的人、事、物。

现如今拿起手中的相机拍摄闽西北的古廊桥，不只是想将那些依旧不朽的廊桥逐一记录，更是追忆着被其默默承载的印记和感情。

The Covered Bridge of the River Min

I was brought up in the mountainous area of the northern Fujian Province. The covered bridge in my memory was a bridge in front of my home that I had to go through to school every day. It was a place where Kids could play and adults could worship. I didn't know it is called covered bridge until I grew up.

Fujian Province is located in the southeast coast of China. The high mountains, thick forests and numerous rivers inside the province make it hard to get access to other places. Building bridges and roads was an important move to develop Fujian in the past dynasties. Since Sui and Tang dynasties, numerous bridges were built and great achievements have been made in the covered bridges, which are like time tunnels, demonstrating the splendid bridge architectural art. The bridges in the thick forests look like rainbows, bringing pleasant surprise to the travelers who thought there was no way out. Standing in the bridge, you can relax and enjoy the picturesque scenery around. In fact, the covered bridges are not only traffic facilities, but also used for pass, sacrifice ceremony and trade with integrated functions. It is a cultural carrier, witnessing the past people, events and objects.

When taking the pictures of the ancient covered bridges in the northwestern Fujian, I not only record the amazing bridges, but also recall the memory and feelings that they bring to me.

Zhou Yuedong

光泽汕溪廊桥　　The covered bridge in Youxi Village, Guangze County

油溪廊桥　Youxi Covered Bridge

油溪廊桥内景　The interior of Youxi Covered Bridge

宁化滑石廊桥外景　The exterior of the covered bridge in Huashi Village, Ninghua County

浦城临江桥桥头　The bridgehead of Linjiang Bridge in Pucheng County　　　　　　　浦城临江摄桥外景　The exterior of Linjiang Bridge in Pucheng County

永安贡川会清桥　　Huiqing Bridge in Gongchuan Town, Yong'an City

永安贡川会清桥内景　The interior of Huiqing Bridge in Gongchuan Town, Yong'an City

延平区宝珠村瑞龙桥　Ruilong Bridge in Baozhu Village, Yanping district

古田杉洋洪湾亭下桥　　The covered bridge in Hongwan Village, Shanyang Town, Gutian County

闽清合龙桥内景　The interior of Helong Bridge in Minqing County　　　　　　　　闽清合龙桥外景　The exterior of Helong Bridge in Minqing County

面容·闽江 涧南

　　凡是看过汤姆逊作品的人，都会感慨什么是"沧海桑田"，汤姆逊镜头里出现最多的就是"人"，闽江沿岸各种各样的人，他们的表情、他们的衣着、他们生活的环境、他们使用的生活器皿，都成为了我们今天阅读的视点。

　　今天闽江流域各种各样的人的影像，也会成为一百年后我们的后代阅读的视点吗？！

　　行走闽江，我拍摄了近一百个人，男人和女人，老人和孩子，各种各样职业的人。村长、街道主任、教师、乡村医生、导游、厂长、商人、学生、司机、厨师、民工、小贩、民间艺人、方丈、养殖专业户、疍民、退休工人等等。

　　一百年后，或许不再有这样的职业、不再有这样的表情、不再有这样的穿着、也不再有这样的生活环境。

　　一切都在不知不觉中悄悄变化，而镜头凝固的是那永远的一刹那，永远的记忆。

The People of the River Min

When you see the pictures taken by Thomson, you will feel how the time change the world. "People" are most common topic in his pictures. All kinds of people along the River Min; their expression, clothes, living environment, daily utensils are the focus for us today.

Will the images of different people today become the focus of our descendants a hundred year later?

Along the River Min, I took pictures of nearly a hundred persons, men and women, the old and the young, people from all walks of life, such as village head, teacher, rural doctor, tourist guide, factory director, businessman, student, driver, cooks, migrant worker, craftsman, monk, farmers, retired worker, etc.

There would no longer be such occupations, expressions, clothes or living environment one hundred years later.

Everything is changing unconsciously. The moment in the camera will be an eternal memory.

Jian Nan

雷绍泉和老伴　Lei Shaoquan and his wife

雷绍泉，畲族，司前乡梅坪自然村人，76 岁。

光泽在没有通公路之前，交通主要靠水路，光泽素有"一滩高一丈，光泽在天上"的说法，司前乡在历史上就是联系江西福建两省的一个重要码头。

梅坪妈祖庙建在北溪河边，庙前是公路，庙后是当年的老街。村民说，过去梅坪码头非常热闹繁华，有酒楼驿站，甚至还有妓院。但是现在的梅坪老街除了一些老房子和那条由卵石铺的老街之外，已经看不到昔日富贵的景象了。

妈祖庙是一个木结构的建筑，单层翘檐，庙前供奉弥勒佛，后面安放着妈祖的塑像，如同所有庙宇一样，神像对面是一个戏台。

雷绍泉不仅是梅坪自然村的村民小组长，同时也是妈祖庙的管理者。雷绍泉 1958 年 22 岁的时候就是梅坪的生产队长，1970 年改为了村民小组长，农村基层干部他一做就是 54 年。

目前雷绍泉老俩口靠每月一千多的企业退休金生活，可以过得去。因为雷绍泉以前在乡里经委做过，搞企业办厂，所以享受退休金。

Lei Shaoquan, She nationality, from the natural village of Meiping Village in Siqian Town, 76 years old.

Water way was the major transportation in Guangze County before roads were built. Siqiang Town was an important dock connecting Jiangxi and Fujian Provinces in history.

Mazu Temple in Meiping Village was built by the Beixi River. There is a road in front of the temple and an old street at its back. The local villager said that Meiping dock used to be very busy and there were hotels and even brothels around. Today there are only some old houses and an old cobbled street without any hint of the past luxury.

Mazu Temple is a timber structure building. Maitreya Buddha is worshipped in front of the temple and Mazu statue is at the back. Like all other temples, there is a stage opposite to the Buddha statue.

Lei Shaoquan is a team leader in Meiping Village and the administrator of Mazu Temple. He was a production team leader in Meiping Village when he was 22 in 1958 and later changed to be a villager team leader in 1970. He has been grass-roots leader for 54 years.

At present, this old couple live on the pension of over 1000 yuan, which is not bad. He can enjoy the pension because he once worked in the village economic committee.

光泽县司前乡梅坪村村民小组长、妈祖庙管理员雷绍泉
Lei Shaoquan, the villager team leader in Meiping Village and the administrator of Mazu Templer

林明琴带游客上金铙山　Lin Mingqin is guiding the tourists to Jinraoshan Mountain

林明琴，1987年生人，属兔。长得黑乎乎的一个开朗的女孩子。可能是因为做导游吧，所以晒得这样黑。

林明琴做导游时间不长，2014年6月6日开始。她是建宁县伊家乡澜溪村人，毕业于厦门集美轻工业学校会计电算化专业。林明琴学校毕业后去过很多地方，也做过很多事情。她一毕业去湖南工作了一阵，后来到上海，在上海工作了三四年，可是被父母亲叫回来。林明琴说：建宁的机会不多，只好当一名导游。做导游还好，如果游客友好，就蛮好玩，工作才有兴趣。

林明琴的家境还好，有个弟弟。父亲种烟，还种水稻。烟叶每年种一万多株，有一个烤房，收入有七八万元，属于中等收入。家里2013年盖了新房，花了三四十万，其中买地120平方米。

Lin Mingqin, born in 1987, is an optimistic girl. She got tanned maybe due to her job as a guide.

Lin Mingqin has been working as a guide since June 6 of 2014. She is from Lanxi Village, Yinjia Town, Jianning County. After graduation from Xiamen Jimei Light Industry School, she had been to work in many places, such as Hunan and Shanghai, where she worked for three to four years. Her parents asked her to come back. She said she can only work as a guide as there is not many opportunities here in Jianning. If tourists are fun, she also enjoys her work.

The family financial situation of Lin Mingqin is quite good. She has a younger brother. Her father is planting tobacco and rice, with an annual income of 70 to 80 thousand yuan, which is the middle income of this area. In 2013, they bought a piece of land of 120 square meters to build a new house at a cost of 300 to 400 thousand yuan.

林明琴，导游，金铙山风景区
Lin Mingqin, a tour guide at Jinraoshan Scenic Spot

释惟荣（叶长荣）师傅带客人参观开平寺　Master Shi Weirong (Ye Changrong) showed visitors around Kaiping Temple

释惟荣出家前俗名叫叶长荣，1945 年生人，今年 70 岁了。释惟荣 1983 年出家，算一算他 38 岁才出家，他的人生一定有故事。

释惟荣师傅是建瓯人，最早在顺昌狮峰寺出家，1984 年到福州鼓山涌泉寺，1988 年从涌泉寺来到开平寺当家，1989 年担任南平佛教协会会长，2006 年退出当家人位置，将方丈禅让给当今的方丈释传雄。

开平寺是延平区著名的寺庙，最早建于五代梁开平年间，至今已有一千多年的历史。而在惟荣师傅 1988 年到的时候，因为文化大革命寺庙已经破败不堪，他几乎重建了开平寺。开平寺的布局结构很像鼓山涌泉寺，因为释惟荣是从涌泉寺来的，所以扩建开平寺时，惟荣师首先想到的模版就是涌泉寺。

释惟荣原来是当兵（解放军）的，1964 年入伍，在山西太原陆军部队司令部警卫营，给司令员当警卫员。他当兵前叫叶增寿，是司令员让他改名，改为了叶长荣。惟荣师傅不仅被司令员改了名，还被看上招了婿。

Shi Weirong was named Ye Changrong before becoming a monk. He was born in 1945 and has become a monk since 1983 when he was 38. He must be a man of stories.

Master Shi Weirong is from Jian' ou and became a monk at Shifeng Temple in Shunchang County. He moved to Yongquan Temple on Gushan Mountain in Fuzhou in 1984 and then to Kaiping Temple in 1988. He was the head of Nanping Buddhism Association. In 2006, he handed over the title abbot to Shi Chuanxiong. Kaiping Temple, a well-known temple in Yanping district, has a history of over one thousand years. The temple was seriously damaged during the Cultural Revolution and he rebuilt the temple when he arrived in 1988. The layout of Kaiping Temple is similar with Yongquan Temple, where he came from. Therefore, he thought of Yongquan Temple as a model when he rebuilt Kaiping Temple.

Shi Weirong was a soldier (PLA) and joined the army in 1964. He was a safeguard of the commander of the army in Taiyuan, Shanxi. The commander changed his name from Ye Zengshou to Ye Changrong and asked him to marry his daughter.

释惟荣，南平市延平区来舟镇开平寺原方丈
Shi Weirong, former abbot of Kaiping Temple in Lazhou Town, Yanping District, Nanping City

卢有永在祖父的照片前留影　Lu Youyong, in front of the picture of his grandfather

卢有永，72岁，民国时期尤溪著名人士卢兴邦的直系孙子。

卢有永的祖父卢兴邦按照民间的说法是一个大土匪。作为一个大土匪的孙子，卢有永没有享受到祖父带来的任何荣耀和好处，相反是吃尽了苦头。卢有永的父亲叫卢胜威，是一个教书匠，1951年被人民政府镇压，奶奶被游街，全家被赶出卢氏公馆，那个时候卢有永九岁。

因为是孙子辈，动荡过去，卢有永还有正常的生活。他在双鲤读完了小学，就到城关读中学，初中毕业读不下去了，就回到双鲤务农。

卢有永是1971年才结的婚，那个时候他已经快三十岁了。幸运的是，他找到了一个好老婆。卢有永说，那个时候去修水库，在工地上有许多周围村子的人，他们就是那样认识了。后来他也问了老婆为什么会喜欢上他，老婆说，在工地上看他勤劳，就认为他是一个可以依靠的人，岳父岳母也这样认为，乡下人就看吃苦耐劳。

做了一个平常百姓，卢有永家庭和睦，他有两个男孩一个女孩，都已经成家立业。

卢有永现在有时常回到公馆里来，给人们讲解这座公馆的历史。

Lu Youyong, 72 years old, grandson of Lu Xingbang, a well-known person in Youxi County during the period of Republic of China

It is said that Lu Xingbang, Lu Youyong's grandfather, was a bandit. Therefore, Lu Youyong suffered a lot as the grandson of a bandit. His father, Lu Shengwei, was a teacher and suppressed by the People's Government in 1951 and his whole family was evicted from Lu's Mansion when he was only 9 years old.

After the movement, he led a normal life. He finished primary school and middle school. Then he became a farmer in Shuangli Village.

He got married in 1971 when he was nearly 30. He is lucky to have a good wife. He said they met each other when building the reservoir. The girl and her family believed he is a reliable person since he was working hard at the reservoir.

Lu Youyong enjoys a happy family, with two boys and one girl. All of his children get married and have their own career.

Now Lu Youyong often comes to Lu's Mansion to tell the history of the house to the visitors.

卢有永，尤溪县新阳镇双鲤村人
Lu Youyong, from Shuangli Village, Xinyang Town, Youxi County

李仲达在择日的小摊前等生意   Li Zhongda, waiting for business at his stand

李仲达，64岁。他家祖上五代人都是做"择日"生意，有堂号叫"富春堂择日馆"。他说他的父亲最厉害，曾经多次被人请去泉州等地择日，而且和当地的择日同行"竞争"，以争辩的方式赢得了生意。而李仲达自己是从三十几岁才开始学做择日。

关于择日，很多人已经不知道是个什么行当，因为在1949年以后，这些东西都当做封建迷信被清除了，但是在民间，还悄悄地存在。改革开放以后，社会越来越开放宽容，这些曾经的迷信又"死灰复燃"了。比如李仲达也敢公开摆摊了。

李仲达祖上是泉州洪氏，后来分支到尤溪县钟仙镇，算是钟仙人了。他原来都在乡下做，自从2000年儿子在县城水南的丽景公寓买了房子，就一直叫他上城里来住，他到今年才来，住了几日就想摆摊了，到今天他出来四天，接了六个生意，感觉还不错。

问他一个生意多少钱，他说算一次五十元。

Li Zhongda is 64 years old. His family has been doing "date selection" business for five generations. He said his father is the best and was invited to Quanzhou and other places to select dates. His father won business through debates with competitors. Li Zhongda began to learn how to select date in his 30s.

Many people do not know what "date selection" is because this fortune-telling business was eliminated as superstition after 1949. But it do exist privately among local people. Since the reform and opening up, such superstitions are revived as the society become more inclusive. Li Zhongda began to set up his business in public.

Li Zhongda is from Zhongxian County. He used to do his business in the village. Since 2000, his son bought an apartment in town and asked him to live with them. He didn't go until this year. And he has been doing his business for four days and got six businesses done.

He earned 50 yuan for each business.

李仲达，尤溪县钟仙镇人，择日算命师
Li Zhongda, date-selection fortune teller from Zhongxian Town, Youxi County

村忆·闽江 焦红辉

今天的很多村落，早已不是儿时记忆中的印象。空寂、凋敝、荒凉……成为我所见到的古老村落的共同现象。年轻劳力在都市物质文明强大磁场的吸引下倾家远行，渴望改变人生命运。老人、弱妇及小孩成为乡村的守护者。

许多有着百年历史、建筑特色明显、有着深厚传统文化底蕴的老宅院，现已空空荡荡，毫无生气。不少房屋因历经风化，年久失修，亦已摇摇欲坠。就连农家养的狗，可能也嫌人气太缺而显得少有的温顺、亲和。

当我透过相机镜头，俯拍到一位老年农妇沿着一道残缺的古垣向上爬行，撑满画面的村落与其几乎忽略不计的孑影形成强烈对比时，一种悲悯感油然而起。当我面对几千年农耕文明传承下来的各种传统农具被当作废物堆弃在一边时，两眼木讷、难以抑制内心的忧伤和惘然。

当我走进位于闽江正源的张家山小村时，这个与外界疏离的原始村落，仿佛把我带回到另一个时空里。村里仅有的几位老人在默默的守护着自己的家园，坚持陪伴着祖屋走完最后一程。

随着时间的流逝，随着村里的老人们一个个终将离去，很多古老的村落也将很快消失，多数长年在外打工的年轻人将彻底告别曾经养育他们的土地。闽江流域历史悠久的农耕文明也将渐渐远去。

The Villages of the River Min

Many villages today are no longer the same as those in our memory. Deserted, lonely, desolated…are common phenomenon of the ancient villages I have seen. Young labors, attracted by the urban material life, leave home for city, hoping to change their life. The old, women and children become the guardians of the village.

Many old houses with long history and profound traditional culture look lifeless today. Some of them are in danger without repair for years. Dogs seem gentle and obedient with fewer people around.

When I took a picture from above of an old woman climbing up along an old and broken wall, her lonely shadow shaping sharp contrast with the village taking up most of the picture, a strong feeling of sorrow and pity came over me. When I am seeing the traditional farm tools be put away like rubbish, it is difficult to control of the feelings of sadness and frustration as the agricultural civilization of thousands of years' history is gone.

When I came to the small primitive village in Zhangjiashan, which is isolated from the outside world, I seemed to go into another space. The only left old farmers in the village guard their homeland and old houses till the end.

As the time goes by, the old people in the village will finally pass away. Many ancient villages will soon disappear and the young people working outside will say farewell to their homeland forever. The agricultural civilization of long history in the basin of the River Min will disappear gradually.

Jiao Honghui

01   尤溪县洋中镇桂峰村
Guifeng Village of Youxi County

02   建宁县均口镇张家山自然村
The natural village of Zhangjiashan
in Junkou Town, Jianning County

03   将乐县万全乡良地村
Liangdi Village, Wanquan Town,
Jiangle County

建宁县均口镇张家山自然村　The natural village of Zhangjiashan in Junkou Town, Jianning County

01   尤溪县洋中镇桂峰村
       Guifeng Village, Youxi County

02   宁化县曹坊镇下曹村
       Xiacao Village, Caofang Town,
Ninghua County

03   清流县沙芜乡龙地自然村
       The natural village in Shawu
Town, Qingliu County

清流县沙芜乡龙地自然村　The natural village in Shawu Town, Qingliu County

宁化县曹坊镇下曹村　Xiacao Village, Caofang Town, Ninghua County

The Endless River The Immortal Journey

    In Nov 2015, a dozen photographers took the last group photo at the old town of Taining County, declaring the successful end of the two-year journey for the large-scale image culture creation project "the River Min".

    The sun is shining and the earth is warm. Satisfactory and delighted smiles are shining on the face of every photographer.

    The first journey of photographing started from the Futunxi River on May 4 2014. We took seven journeys in the past two years: the Jianxi River in June 2014, the mainstream of the River Min in Dec 2014, the Futunxi River (2nd) in May 2015, the Songxi and Jianxi River in June 2015, the Jinxi River in Nov 2015. During the seven journeys of photographing, we have been to Guangze, Shaowu and Shunchang along the Futunxi River; Mount Wuyi, Pucheng, Jianyang, Jian'ou, Zhenghe and Songxi along the Jianxi River; Jianning, Ninghua, Qingliu, Yong'an, Sanming, Shaxian along the Shaxi River; Nanping, Youxi, Gutian, Minqing, Yongtai and Fuzhou along the mainstream of the River Min. The canoeing team and the aerial photography team went through the whole basin of the River Min.

    We took pictures of numerous sources of the River Min and its vegetation, the quiet villages, colorful folk beliefs, customs, traditional residence, all kinds of people, traditional handicrafts and local food in the basin of the River Min.

    The River Min is the source of Min Culture. The unique and valuable culture along the river as well as the natural heritage need to be kept in photos as a record, a file and a reality in history.

    Like Thomson, the River Min is unique in each photographer's work. They record, appreciate and love the River Min with their own understanding.

    The River Min has flown into the bottom of our heart and becomes the covenant of our life.

不竭的闽江水 不朽的闽江行

2015 年 11 月，"闽江"大型影像文化创作工程团队的十几位摄影家聚集在金溪流域的泰宁县的古城前，拍下了最后一张合影，宣告长达近两年的行走采访拍摄圆满结束。

阳光很耀眼，大地温暖。

满足和欣慰的笑意在每一位摄影家的脸上灿烂着。

从 2014 年 5 月 4 日开始第一次的富屯溪行走拍摄，近两年来，我们一共出发了七次：2014 年 6 月行走拍摄建溪；2014 年 10 月行走拍摄沙溪；2014 年 12 月行走拍摄闽江主流；2015 年 5 月补拍富屯溪；2015 年 6 月拍摄松溪建溪；2015 年 11 月行走拍摄金溪。七次行走拍摄，我们走过了富屯溪的光泽、邵武、顺昌；建溪的武夷山、浦城、建阳、建瓯、政和、松溪；沙溪的建宁、宁化、清流、永安、三明、沙县；闽江主流的南平（延平区）、尤溪、古田、闽清、永泰和福州。我们的漂流团队漂完了闽江的全流域，我们的航拍团队从空中飞遍了闽江的全流域。

八千里路云和月，我们拍摄了闽江众多的源头和生态植被，拍摄了闽江源头和沿岸那些美丽安静的村庄，拍摄了闽江沿岸丰富多彩的民间信仰、民情风俗、传统民居，拍摄了闽江流域各种各样的人，拍摄了闽江流域还留存的传统手工艺和目前还生存于民间的丰富物产饮食。

闽江流域溪涧密布，森林茂盛，闽江是闽文化的发源地，闽江流域沉淀留存了大量独特而珍贵的文化。闽江的这些自然遗产和文化遗产需要用影像将它保留下来，为历史留下一份记录、一份档案、一份真实。

像汤姆逊一样，呈现在每个摄影家的作品里的闽江，都是"一个人的闽江"，他们用自己的理解，阅读着、记录着、欣赏着、沉醉着闽江的每一朵浪花。

闽江，已经流进我们的心底。

闽江，成了我们的生命之约。

01　2015 年 1 月 4 号，"闽江"采访团到达闽江终点长门村，团旗铺在了长门炮台上
　　On Jan 4 2015, the team arrived at Changmen Village, the end of the River Min, with the team flag on the battery.

02　2014 年 5 月 3 日，"闽江"采访团开始首次闽江大型采访，出发前在出版大楼前合影
　　On May 3 2014, group photo in front of the publishing house before startting off.

03　2014 年 5 月 5 日，"闽江"采访团在富屯溪源头光泽县司前乡岱坪村采访，与村民合影
　　On May 5 2014, group photo with villagers of Daiping Village, Siqiang Town, Guangze County

04　2015 年 5 月 7 日，"闽江"采访团在邵武市桂林乡盖竹村前往茶花隘途中
　　On May 7 2015, on the way to Chahua Pass in Gaizu Village, Guilin Town, Shaowu City

05　2014 年 7 月 2 日，新华社著名编辑曾璜在教基层干部如何用手机摄影
　　July 2 2014, Zeng Huang, famous editor at the Xinhua News Agency, taught the grass-roots leader how to take pictures with mobile phone.

06　2014 年 10 月 29 日，"闽江"采访团在清流采访三角戏，摄影家焦红辉在拍摄
　　Oct 29 2014, photographer Jiao Honghui is taking pictures when interviewing Sanjiao Drama.

07　2014 年 10 月 28 日，"闽江"采访团在建宁县均口乡采访，福建画报社副社长曲利明在街头拍摄
　　Oct 28 2014, deputy head of Fujian Pictorial is taking pictures when interviewing in Junkou Village, Jianning County

08　2014 年 10 月 27 日，"闽江"采访团部分成员到达闽江正源
　　Oct 27 2014, some interviewing members arrived at the source of the River Min

09　2015 年 1 月 3 日，"闽江"采访团在永泰梧桐镇采访，厦门摄影家李世雄借三轮车高点拍摄
　　Jan 3 2015, photographer Li Shixiong is taking pictures on a tricycle when interviewing in Wutong Town, Yongtai County

02

03

04

05

06

07

08

09

01

02

01 　　2014 年 10 月 26 日，"闽江"采访团到达建宁县金铙山顶，厦门摄影家陈伟凯在拍摄晚霞
　　On Oct 26 2014, photographer Chen Weikai is taking picture of sunset glow at the top of Jinraoshan Mountain in Jianning County

02 　　2014 年 10 月 27 日，"闽江"采访团登上建宁县金铙山顶
　　Oct 27 2014, interviewing team arrived at the top of Jinraoshan Mountain in Jianning County

03 　　2014 年 6 月 30 日，"闽江"采访团部分成员在浦城县忠信镇坑尾村采访，福建画报社社长崔建楠与坑尾村班子成员合影
　　June 30 2014, Cui Jiannan, head of Fujiang Pictorial, took a group photo with the village leader of Kengwei Village, Zhongxin Town, Pucheng County

04 　　2014 年 10 月 27 日，"闽江"采访团登上建宁县金铙山，美国摄影家弗兰克对中国传统建筑十分好奇
　　Oct 27 2014, on Jinraoshan Mountain, Jianning County. Frank, an American photographer, is very interested in the traditional Chinese architecture.

05 　　2014 年 6 月 27 日，"闽江"采访团部分成员在武夷山自然保护区桐木村采访，福州摄影家郭晓丹在桐木溪边留影
　　On June 27 2014, Fuzhou photographer Guo Xiaodan at the Tongmuxi River

06 　　2014 年 6 月 30 日，"闽江"采访团在浦城拍摄传子木偶
　　On June 30 2014, marionette at Pucheng County

07 　　2014 年 7 月 2 日，"闽江"采访团在建阳采访，福州摄影家周跃东在拍摄烤烟一家
　　On July 2 2014, Fuzhou photographer Zhou Yuedong is taking pictures of a family making flue-cured tobacco.

08 　　2014 年 6 月 28 日，"闽江"采访团在浦城县忠信镇坑尾村采访，福建画报社编辑欧阳丽敏和村中儿童合影
　　On June 28 2014, Ouyang Limin, editor of Fujian Pictorial, took group photos with the children in Kengwei Village, Zhongxin Town, Pucheng County

09 　　2014 年 6 月 29 日，"闽江"采访团在浦城县忠信镇坑尾村采访，福州摄影家那兴海在村中庙堂里午休
　　On June 29 2014, Fuzhou photographer Na Xinghai is taking a nap in the temple of Kengwei Village, Zhongxin Town, Pucheng County

10 　　2015 年，福州摄影家那兴海在建宁县均口乡台田村拍摄闽江第一桥
　　In 2015, Fuzhou photographer Na Xinghai is taking pictures of the first bridge on the River Min in Taitian Village, Junkou Town, Jianning County.

11 　　2014 年 5 月 8 日，"闽江"采访团在邵武和平古镇采访，团长崔建楠在访问建设黄氏祠堂的民工
　　On May 8 2014, Cui Jiannan, head of the team, is interviewing the rural workers who are building Huang's ancestral hall

03

04

05

06

07

08

09

10

11

01　2015 年 1 月 1 日，"闽江"采访团在闽清黄楮林过了一个有意义的新年
Jan 1 2015, a meaningful new year in Huangchulin of Minqing County

02　2014 年 7 月 21 日，"闽江"采访团漂流小组合影
On July 21 2014, group photo of canoeing team

03　福建画报社社长助理吴寿华在邵武航拍
Wu Shouhua, head assistant of Fujian Pictorial, is taking aerial photo in Shaowu City

04　"闽江"航拍团队在桐木关与武夷山自然保护区哨卡工作人员合影
The aerial photo team is taking group photo with the staff working in Wuyishan Nature Reserve

05　"闽江"漂流团队户外运动摄影师李朝阳正在拍摄桐木溪漂流
Photographer Li Chaoyang is taking picture of canoeing on the Mutongxi River

06　"闽江"漂流团队苏荣钦、杨波、阮任艺在闽江主流闽侯白沙合影
The canoeing team at Baisha Town, Minhou County

07　"闽江"航拍团队在建阳交警保护下在高速公路上拍摄
The aerial photo team is taking pictures on highways with the protection of traffic police in Jianyang

08　"闽江"漂流团队在连日大雨之后车陷泥泞
The van of the canoeing team got stuck in the mud after days' storm.

09　"闽江"漂流团队在桐木溪用航拍器自拍，右起户外摄影师李朝阳、纪录片制作人苏荣钦、福建画报社记者阮任艺
The canoeing team is taking a selfie with aerial apparatus

01

02

01　　　2014 年 10 月 28 日，"闽江"采访团在建宁县均口乡鸳鸯湖采访
　　　On Oct 28 2014, interviewing at Yuanyang Lake, Junkou Village, Jianning County

02　　　2014 年，"闽江"采访团再次到达顺昌县，采访团成员与当地宣传部领导在富屯溪金
　　　溪汇合处合影
　　　In 2014, group photo with local leaders of Shunchang County at the conjunction of the
　　　Futunxi River and the Jinxi River

03　　　2014 年 5 月 8 日，"闽江"采访团由邵武桂林乡前往和平古镇的路上，厦门摄影家陈
　　　勇鹏教美国摄影家弗兰克打太极
　　　On May 8 2014 Chen Yongpeng is teaching Frank to do Tai Chi on the way to Heping
　　　County

04　　　2014 年 10 月 28 日，"闽江"采访团在建宁县均口乡采访宜黄戏，采访团成员自得其乐
　　　On Oct 28 2014, interviewing Yihuang Drama in Junkou Village, Jianning County

05　　　2015 年 11 月 26 日，"闽江"采访团在泰宁采访擂茶时品尝擂茶
　　　On Nov 26 2015, tasting Lei Tea in Taining County

06　　　2015 年 1 月 4 日，"闽江"采访团到达闽江出海口壶江岛，部分成员在码头合影
　　　On Jan 4 2015, group photo at Hujiang Island, the estuary of the River Min

07　　　2014 年 5 月 8 日，"闽江"采访团纪录片摄影师林雷炜在和平古镇拍摄视频
　　　On May 8 2014, Lin Leiwei, the cameraman, is shooting in ancient Heping Town

08　　　2014 年 10 月 31 日，"闽江"采访团在清流县与三角戏剧团演员合影
　　　On Oct 31 2014, group photo with Sanjiao Drama players in Qingliu County

09　　　2014 年 6 月 27 日，"闽江"采访团在武夷山下梅村合影
　　　On June 27 2014, group photo at Xiamei Village, Wuyishan

10　　　2015 年 1 月 4 日，"闽江"采访团走完闽江全程，在闽江终点长门炮台合影留念
　　　Jan 4 2015, group photo at Changmen battery, end of the journey

11　　　2015 年 11 月 26 日，"闽江"采访团结束闽江全流域采访，在泰宁古城合影
　　　Nov 26 2015, group photo in ancient Taining Town, end of the journey

03

04

05

06

07

08

09

10

11

"闽江" 大型影像文化创作工程摄影家
The Photographers of the Large-scale Image Cultural Creation Project "the River Min"

曾璜，美国 Syracuse 大学传播摄影硕士；Corbis 图片社签约摄影师，新华社高级编辑。在几十家国外主流媒介发表照片，其中包括美国《新闻周刊》，香港《南华早报》等；出版中国第一本个人战地新闻摄影作品集《波黑：战火浮生》，主编中国唯一的《图片编辑手册》和北京电影学院《报道摄影》教科书。在包括清华大学、北京大学、中国人民大学、北京电影学院、北京外国语学院，新闻出版总署培训中心、新华社、中国摄影家协会、总政治部、国家外文局培训中心、时尚集团、财经集团、三联生活等十多所大学和几十家传媒集团开设报道摄影讲座。在法国阿尔勒国际摄影节，金边国际摄影节，EPSON 影艺坊等展出作品，并入选 2015 版 The Culture History of Photography（摄影文化史）。

Frank Folwell（弗兰克），美国《USA TODAY》前图片副总编辑，富布莱特基金会签约专家、美国密苏里大学新闻学院国际项目讲座教授，曾负责报道索马里和巴尔干地区冲突、苏联解体和美国总统大选等重大新闻事件，并在多个国家担任顾问和媒体培训师。

焦红辉，福建省摄影家协会副主席。1999 年出版个人纪实摄影集《客家祖地》，曾任海风出版社社长、总编辑，现为《两岸视点》杂志编委。

李世雄，任教于厦门大学传播学院，长期从事摄影专业教学、摄影理论研究、摄影艺术创作、摄影组织工作及摄影商务运作，曾获中国摄影家协会授予"德艺双馨"和"中国摄影事业突出贡献工作者"称号，获厦门市委市政府授予"厦门文艺突出贡献奖"，获福建省摄影家协会授予"福建摄影 50 年贡献奖"。现为世界华人摄影学会执行委员、中国摄协摄影教育委员会委员、世界闽籍摄影家研究会副会长、福建省摄影行业协会副会长、福建省艺术摄影学会副主席、福建省高教摄影学会副会长、厦门市摄影家协会常务副主席（社团法人）。

　　曲利明，福建画报社副社长，副总编辑、编审。1982年从事专职摄影工作，1990年开始出版工作。多年来，出版过个人专辑，策划、拍摄、编辑出版过图书、系列丛书、大型画册，分别获得过省、华东地区及全国图书奖。

　　周跃东，自由摄影人，1961年11月出生于福建福州，1983年毕业于厦门大学经济系，后任教于福建广播电视大学，是二十世纪八十年代厦门大学"五个一"摄影团体的重要成员。1988年留学日本学摄影，学成归来"悄无声息"地游摄于闽水山川、古村老宅、街头巷尾，始终执着于用影像堆砌生活。

　　那兴海，1957年3月出生，知青、军人、中国摄影家协会会员。

　　郭晓丹，中国摄影家协会会员、福建省摄影家协会会员、福建青年摄影家协会常务理事、华夏针孔艺术影像委员会（CPPC）委员、中国全球图片总汇签约摄影师、新华社签约摄影师、福建画报特约摄影师。

　　参加的影展有：《惟孔·天下》针孔影像三人展（2011）、《跨越三个世纪的影像》大理国际影展（2011）、《梦回晚清》三坊七巷主题摄影展（2012）、《百年家园》凤凰国际双年展（2012）、《中国·留住》艺术影像邀请展（2013）、策展《静·悟·灵·光》郑忠油画作品展（2013）等。

"闽江"大型影像文化创作工程摄影家
The photographers of the large-scale image cultural creation project "the River Min"

陈伟凯，中国摄影家协会会员、美国摄影学会会员、福建省旅游摄影协会副主席、厦门市摄影家协会副秘书长。

1999年、2007年、2011年分别举办个人摄影艺术作品展，被福建省摄影家协会授予"福建摄影十佳"称号和福建青年摄影协会授予"福建青年摄影十佳"称号。获福建省摄影家协会授予的"福建摄影五十年优秀工作者"称号。

徐希景，福建师大美术学院教授、硕士生导师，先后任中国摄影家协会理论委员会、摄影史研究委员会委员，《中国大百科全书》第三版摄影卷民国摄影主编。主要著作和教材有《中国摄影艺术史》、《中国影像史》（第四卷）、《大学摄影》等八部，《大学摄影》被评为"十二五"国家规划教材。主持过多项省社科规划课题和教育厅重点课题，在《中国摄影》、《中国摄影家》、《中国艺术时空》等刊物发表近三十篇摄影史论和影像文化研究论文，获福建省第八届、第九届社科优秀成果三等奖。参加中国摄影家协会主办的第六届至第十届全国摄影理论研讨会并获优秀论文奖、摄影作品入选全国影展，获中国·杨柳青第一届国际民俗摄影大展展览大奖、福建省第七届百花文艺奖等。

王鹭佳，祖籍山东、出生于厦门鼓浪屿。当过知青、工人、法官、企业人。现为中国摄影家协会会员，厦门市摄影家协会副主席，曾任厦门市青年摄影家协会主席，福建省青年摄影协会副会长，厦门鹭风报社常务副社长。曾在厦门、上海、北京、福州、澳门、平遥等地举办过六次摄影个展，三十余次摄影联展，曾荣获"福建摄影十杰"、"福建十大时尚人物"、首届"厦门十大杰出青年"称号。

陈勇鹏，供职于建设银行厦门市分行。

二十世纪八十年代初开始参与组织民间摄影群体，1987年4月，参与策划在香港举办的《5个1》影展。

1988年，《人的历程》组照在中国美术馆展出引起关注。有专家评论其人体摄影："以思辨的手法处理人体题材无疑是中国人体摄影表现的一大历史性突破。"（顾铮《人体摄影150年》）

2006年和2007年，《纪念碑》等作品在曾在北京华辰拍卖公司组织的摄影专场影像拍卖中上拍并成交。

2006年开始探索以《心经》为主题，融合摄影、书法和行为的艺术活动。2013年连续两次举办《非常心经》艺术展。

2015年10月，部分1980年代人体摄影原作入选北京三影堂举办的"中国摄影：20世纪以来"展览。

　　崔建楠，福建画报社社长、总编辑。福建新闻摄影学会副会长，福建艺术摄影学会副会长。1978年考入福建师范大学中文系，1986年进入《福建画报》任记者编辑，从事专业摄影及出版事业三十多年。主编的《福建戏剧丛书》荣获首届国家出版大奖"中国出版政府奖"提名奖。坚持多年拍摄福建传统地方戏剧系列影像作品《千秋梨园》，该作品曾经参加鼓浪屿摄影画廊2010年春季展、第二届大理国际影会、2010年平遥国际摄影节，都得到了较高评价和较大的影响。

　　赖小兵，福建泉州人，1989年毕业于厦门大学中文系外宣班，现任福建画报社副社长、副总编辑。福建华侨摄影学会副会长、福州市摄影研究会副会长。长期拍摄福建人文专题，拍摄、编辑的《福建戏剧丛书》获得首届"中国出版政府奖"提名奖，《菲华精英》系列丛书获得福建省优秀图书编辑奖。专题作品多次获得福建省对外新闻奖、全国画报评比优秀奖。

　　吴寿华，1956年7月出生，祖籍福清，武汉大学新闻系艺术摄影专业毕业。1991年至今历任福建画报社编辑部记者、编辑部副主任、主任、副总审、社长助理。2001年荣获"首届福建杰出青年摄影家"光荣称号，2002年荣获"福建省新闻双十佳记者"光荣称号。1996年参加组建福建省青年摄影协会，历任副秘书长、秘书长、会长、荣誉会长，现为中国摄影家协会会员、福建省摄影家协会常务理事，数十年来，计有上百组摄影专题在全国画报行业评选中入选、获奖，有百余幅摄影作品在省级、全国及国际摄影艺术展览中入选、获奖。

　　吴军，福建画报社记者，长期从事民俗摄影。先后在《福建画报》开设"小村""民间艺人""福建海岛""寻味"等栏目。2005年出版图书《绝活》。

　　阮任艺，2004年毕业于厦门大学艺术教育学院美术学专业。热爱摄影、人文、地理、旅行。曾任福建画报社美术编辑、《户外探险》杂志编辑、特约撰稿，现任福建画报社编辑部副主任。曾著图书《闽古道》，图文并茂地记录了福建独具特色的古驿道系统，另有文章、图片散见于国内各大人文、旅游杂志。在《闽江》影像工程中，主要承担"闽江漂流"以及"闽江航拍"的拍摄，水空并进为闽江流域的地理、风光作了全方位的记录。

行走拍摄记录 / 第一次闽江行走拍摄线路
The Photographing Itinerary - The First Journey:

2014 年 5 月 4 日：
上午大部队福州出发，经福银高速转武邵高速到达邵武，经 316 国道中午到达光泽。
午餐后，在光泽城区及周边拍摄。
返回光泽城区晚餐。

2014 年 5 月 5 日：北溪
一早（7：00）出发，前往司前镇方向。
到崇仁，留下一组小分队拍摄三角戏和采茶灯（请崇仁乡镇派一辆车，并组织三角戏和采茶灯表演人员）；
到寨里，早餐。早餐后留下一组小分队（1-2 人），前往拍摄肖家坑水库、木活字传承人（落实能否在寨里拍还是要请到光泽博物馆拍）（请寨里乡镇派一辆车）。
早餐后大部队前往司前乡。
一组小分队前往云际村，拍摄马岭关，云际关（请司前乡镇派一辆车）。
其余人员前往岱坪、干坑、高家水库（请司前乡镇派两辆车）。
中午各小分队及大部队在寨里镇汇合，吃午餐。
午餐后大部队至历史文化名村崇仁乡，拍摄明清古街、葛仙庙、夫人庙等。
傍晚返回光泽城区晚餐。

2014 年 5 月 6 日：西溪
一早（7：00）出发，前往止马镇方向，在止马早餐。
早餐后一个小分队前往杉关拍摄（请止马镇派一辆车）。
大部队在止马镇拍摄半天（止马街、药材种植、岛石二组种田能手何典勇、白门楼村、永济桥）。
中午前大部队前往李坊午餐，午餐后经上观、贯庄、管密（管密瀑布、曾氏古建筑、波罗禅师塔）、水口（码头驿站、水口古街"豆角街"、排下屋桥等）沿路拍摄。
下午 5 点 30 分左右到达邵武晚餐，住邵武。

2014 年 5 月 7 日：金坑（西溪）
一早（7：00）早餐后从邵武出发，前往金坑方向。
路经沿山镇（拍摄"舞龙灯"、"三角戏"等民间传统优秀小戏，古建筑等以及徐溪村的梅坊大桥，下排元大桥，延寿大桥，索家桥两座大桥）。
到金坑，留下一组小分队去隘上村（请金坑乡镇派一辆车）。
金坑午餐。下午金坑拍摄（古民居、非遗擂茶：苏区文化；文昌阁、儒林郎、九阶厅、基督教堂、大夫第、李太簪、风雨桥、危氏宗祠第等一批重点明清建筑文物和典型建筑），晚上食宿桂林乡。

2014 年 5 月 8 日：和平古镇（上清溪）
一早（7：00）早餐后，留两个小分队分别前往西溪源头盖竹村和横坑村拍摄（请桂林乡镇派两辆车）。
大部队离开桂林，前往和平，以中国历史文化名镇和平为中心拍摄（和平以北上清溪源头坎下、朱源；和平特色：城堡式大村镇、古街巷南北 600 米、古建筑民居群、和平书院、李氏黄氏廖氏"大夫第"、碎铜茶；愁思岭隧道）。
到达肖家坊后留一个小分队前往天成岩漂流、将石保护区拍摄（请肖家坊乡镇派一辆车）。
到达和平后留一个小分队前往大埠岗拍摄（请大埠岗乡镇派一辆车）。
同时再分出一个小分队前往清溪源头坎下、朱源拍摄（请和平乡镇派一辆车）。
和平午餐，拍摄至傍晚由高速返回邵武。
邵武晚餐。

2014 年 5 月 9 日：邵武
一早（7：00）邵武拍摄（富屯溪沿岸），早餐后大部队沿富屯溪一路拍摄至顺昌。
留一个小分队前往大竹（烟叶种植，烟叶烤制）拍摄（请邵武宣传部派一辆车）；

大部队从晒口（煤炭工业基地）、拿口（宝林寺）、卫闽、洪墩一路拍摄，中午抵达顺昌大干镇，邵武方面拍摄结束。
中午进入顺昌地面，大干午餐。
午饭后大干留下一个小分队前往来布村、富文村拍摄（请大干乡镇派一辆车）。
大部队沿仁寿溪前往洋墩、仁寿拍摄至傍晚。
仁寿乡派一个小分队前往桂溪村拍摄仁寿溪源头及村落（请仁寿乡镇派一辆车）。
傍晚拍摄队伍汇合，返回顺昌晚餐，住宿顺昌。

2014 年 5 月 10 日：
一早（7：00）在顺昌分出一个小分队前往元坑镇拍摄槎溪及万佛宿（请顺昌宣传部派一辆车）。
大部队出发沿鸳鸯溪流域前往洋口、建西、大历、岚下拍摄。抵达洋口镇早餐。（在洋口镇拍摄古码头、谢家渡渡口、旧大桥、"福州会馆"旧址、陈宝琛题匾的"天后宫"以及闽剧团。到建西镇拍摄建于上个世纪六七十年代的森林小铁路）。到大历分出一个小分队前往岚下夏墩村拍摄鸳鸯溪源头（请大历乡镇派一辆车）。
中午统一返回顺昌午餐。
下午在顺昌周边拍摄。顺昌火车站、双溪区、文化墙、全景、工业（炼石水泥厂、富文化工厂、白林村富宝化工厂、欧普灯液晶面板公司等）、"大爱村"——2010 年后灾后由台湾慈济会援建的重建村以及华阳山风景区等（请顺昌宣传部派一辆车）。
（注：顺昌有登云桥、新龙桥、廊下厝桥等廊桥遗迹，并有徐云双"闽北木拱廊桥传承人"——能否组织拍摄制作？）
晚上顺昌食宿。

May 4, 2014:
    Set off from Fuzhou: arrive in Shaowu through highways:
arrive in Guangze at noon through the National Highway 316:
photograph in Guangze and nearby places after lunch:
return to Guangze for dinner

May 5, 2014: the Beixi River
    Set off at 7am to Siqian County:
Arrive in Chongren: a team left to photograph Sanjiao Drama
and Tea Picking Dance
Arrive at Zaili Town for breakfast: a team left to photograph
Xiaojiakeng Reservoir and the inheritor of wooden types:
The main body head for Siqiang Village after breakfast:
A team head for Yunji Village to photograph Maling Pass and
Yunji Pass:
The rest head for Daiping, Gankeng and Gaojia Reservoir:
All the members meet at Zaili Town for lunch.
After lunch, the main body go to Chongren Village to
photograph the old street of Ming and Qing Dynasties,
Gexian Temple, Furen Temple:
Return to Guangze County for dinner

May 6, 2014: the Xixi River
    Set off at 7am for Zhima Town and have breakfast in Zhima
Town:
After breakfast, a team head for Shanguan:
The main body photograph in Zhima Town for half day:
Head for Lifang for lunch: after lunch, photograph along the

road through Shangguan, Guanzhuang, Guanmi, Shuikou:
Arrive in Shaowu at 5:30 and dine and stay in Shaowu for
the night

May 7, 2014: Jinkeng (the Xixi River)
    Set off at 7am after breakfast from Shaowu to Jinkeng:
Go through Yanshan Town and photograph traditional
dramas and bridges along the road:
Arrive at Jinkeng: a team head for Aishang Village:
Lunch at Jinkeng: photograph at Jinkeng in the afternoon
(ancient houses and buildings)
Dine and stay at Guilin Village

May 8, 2014: Heping Ancient Town (the Shangqingxi River)
    Set off at 7am after breakfast: two teams head for Gaizu
Village and Hengkeng Village, the source of the Xixi River:
The main body head for Heping Town and photograph the
historical and cultural town:
Arrive at Xiaojiafang: a team left to photograph at Tianshiyan
and Jiangshi Reserve:
Arrive at Heping, a team left to photograph at Dabugang:
Another team go to Kanxia and Zhuyuan:
Lunch at Heping and photograph till evening:
Return to Shaowu through highway and dine at Shaowu

May 9, 2014: Shaowu, Shunchang
    Photograph in Shaowu from 7am: after breakfast, the main
body photograph along the Futunxi River till Shunchang:

A team go to Dazu to photograph tobacco planting:
The main body photograph along the way through Shenkou,
Nakou, Weimin, Hongdun and arrive in Shunchang at noon:
the end of photographing in Shaowu
Arrive in Shunchang at noon and lunch in Dagan Town:
A team left to photograph Laibu Village and Fuwen Village:
The main body go to Yangdun and Renshou Village:
In Renshou Village, a team go to Guixi Village to photograph
the source of the Renshouxi River:
All the members meet in Shunchang for dinner

May 10, 2014:
    Set off at 7am: a team go to Yuankeng Town to photograph
the Chaxi River and Wan Fo Cave:
The main body head for Yangkou, Jianxi, Dali and Gangxia
along the Lucixi River: arrive Yangkou County for breakfast
(photograph ancient dock, ferry, bridge, Min opera troupe,
etc.)
When arrive at Dali, a team go to Xiadun Village to
photograph the source of Lucixi River:
All go back to Shunchang for lunch:
Photograph around Shunchang in the afternoon, including
Shunchang Railway Station, Shuangxi Town, Culture Wall,
industries, etc:
Dine and stay in Shunchang for the night

行走拍摄记录 / 第二次闽江行走拍摄线路
The photographing itinerary - The second journey

2014年6月24日：福州
　　福州集中，下午至晚上观赏第一次行走拍摄成果及座谈第二次行走路线。宿福州。

2014年6月25日：武夷山
　　福州出发，经南平，直达武夷山。晚上召开座谈会，安排武夷山行走拍摄计划。宿武夷山。

2014年6月26日：武夷山
　　全体出发前往崇阳溪，分两队以岚谷乡为基点西北面走到最远的村子（丘岭、岭阳、山坳），东北面最远的村子（东坑、樟村、客溪）。午餐岚谷乡。下午吴屯乡，晚餐吴屯乡。宿武夷山。

2014年6月27日：武夷山
　　分三支队伍一队前往黄岗山（武夷山自然保护区），拍摄黄岗山、桐木村、星村。一队前往长滩伐木场方向。
　　一队前往梅溪（上下梅）。宿武夷山。

2014年6月28日：武夷山
　　上午崇安城与度假区，全体下午拍摄古粤城村、闽越王城、五夫镇。由五夫上G3京台高速前往浦城。宿浦城。

2014年6月29日：浦城
　　分三队，一队去渔梁岭（渔梁），一队前往忠信镇，查找源头，最远到海溪村（关口）。一队去富岭溪（富岭）方向。宿浦城。

2014年6月30日：浦城
　　一队去临江溪至永平镇（最远龙岭下水库之远尚有几个自然村），再返回至观前，一队留关拍摄。下午由观前汇合由302省道前往水北街道，浮桥村过河沿南浦溪至曹村、至朱墩、至丘源、至旧馆、至石壁。上G3京台高速前往建阳，宿建阳。

2014年7月1日：建阳
　　全体一路经莒口（分一队至书坊）、麻沙、直达黄坑镇，北上至源头高堂，西北上至竹窠、大竹岚。宿建阳。

2014年7月2日：建阳、建瓯
　　上午建阳城关拍摄，下午前往建瓯，北上由G3高速转G1514至水吉。拍摄水吉、小湖，下至南浦溪与崇阳溪汇合处。前往建瓯，宿建瓯。

2014年7月3日：建瓯
　　分两队拍摄，一队前往东峰东游，一队留建瓯城关拍摄。宿建瓯。

2014年7月4日：建瓯、延平区
　　建溪拍摄开始。前往南平一路拍摄，东面支流小桥溪太平至小桥，西面支流高阳溪房村至高阳乡西尾村。宿南平。
　　到达延平区，16:00拍摄延平城区。分两组拍摄，一组拍摄九峰山、双剑化龙、延平全景、剑州大桥、三江合流；
　　二组拍摄九峰索桥、江滨公园、延寿楼郑成功军事指挥中心、南平剑津中学郑成功军营和宋碑亭。

2014年7月5日：延平区
　　8:00，统一乘车到峡阳，峡阳镇安排两名工作人员。分两组拍摄，一组在集镇拍摄峡阳土库、风火墙、下马坪、屏山书院、百忍堂、峡阳小吃制作、溪中公园等。二组前往小梅村采访南剑戏、杜溪村千年古樟等。
　　12:00，在峡阳江汇村用午餐。
　　13:00，午餐后，采访浪石新村、江汇新村、峡阳水电站；
　　14:00，全体成员前往王台镇上溪口村，拍摄苏维埃革命旧址。
　　15:00，赶往王台镇，分两组拍摄。一组拍摄越王台、八角楼（王台谈判旧址）、太平鼓、黄龙队；二组前往溪后村拍摄丰产林、杉木王、珠宝庵。

2014年7月6日：延平区
　　8:00，统一乘车到赶往茫荡镇，茫荡镇安排两名工作人员。先前往三千八百坎坎头村拍摄后回茂地村拍摄瑞龙桥。
　　11:00，前往宝珠村拍摄晴雨树、雪杉、廊桥、越王亭、别驾第。
　　12:00，在茫荡镇宝珠村用午餐。
　　13:00，从宝珠村经来舟镇赶往西芹镇沙溪口水电站，西芹镇安排两名工作人员。分两组拍摄，一组采访沙溪口水电站、高坪森林人家、竹林畲歌、白粿制作过程、鸳鸯石、红旗顶；二组采访玉封庙、开平寺、新亭新村。

2014年7月7日：
　　8:00早餐后结束采风活动返福州。

June 24, 2014: Fuzhou
    gather in Fuzhou and discuss the route of the second journey; stay in Fuzhou for the night

June 25, 2014: Wuyishan
    set off from Fuzhou; arrive at Wuyishan via Nanping; preparation meeting at night; stay at Wuyishan for the night

June 26, 2014: Wuyishan
    set off to the Chongyangxi River; divide into two teams; one team go to the northwest villages (Qiuling, Lingyang, Shan'ao); the other team go to the northeast villages (Dongkeng, Zhangcun, Kexi); lunch at Langu Village; go to Wutun Village in the afternoon and dine there; stay in Wuyishan for the night

June 27, 2014: Wuyishan
    divide into three teams; one team go to Huangganshan Mountain to photograph Huangganshan Mountain, Tongmu Village, Xing Village; one team go to the logging camp in Changtan; one team go to the Meixi River; stay in Wuyishan for the night

June 28, 2014: Wuyishan
    go to Chong'an Town and resort in the morning; all photograph ancient Yue village, King Minyue, Wufu Temple in the afternoon; go to Pucheng through highway; stay in Pucheng for the night

June 29, 2014: Pucheng
    divide into three teams; one team go to Yuliang; one team go to Zhongxin Town and Meixi Village; one team go to Fuling; stay in Pucheng for the night

June 30, 2014: Pucheng
    one team go to the Linjiangxi River till Yongping Town and return to Guanqian; the other team stay in town; two teams meet in Guangqian in the afternoon and head for Shuibei Jiedao through provincial road 302, then to Cao Village, Zhudun, Qiuyuan, Jiuguan, Shibi; go to Jianyang through highway; stay in Jianyang for the night

July 1, 2014: Jianyang
    go to Jukou (one team to Shufang), Masha, Huangkeng Town, northward to Gaotang, northwestword to Zuke, Dazulan; stay in Jianyang for the night

July 2, 2014: Jianyang, Jian'ou
    photograph in Jianyang in the morning; go to Jian'ou in the afternoon, then to Shuiji; photograph Shuiji and Xiaohu; go to the convergence of the Nanpuxi River and the Chongyangxi River; go to Jian'ou and stay for the night

July 3, 2014: Jian'ou
    divide into two teams; one team go to Dongyou; the other team stay in Jian;ou; stay in Jian'ou for the night

July 4, 2014: Jian'ou, Yanping district
    photograph the Jianxi River; go to Nanping, then to Xiaoqiao in the east and Gaoyang in the west; stay in Nanping for the night; arrive in Yanping district and photograph Yanping at 4pm; divide into two teams; one team photograph Jiufengshan Mountain, Shuangjian Hualong, panorama of Yanping, Jianzhou Bridge, convergence of three rivers; the other team photograph Jiufengsuo Bridge, Jiangbin Park, commanding center in Yanshou Building, Jianjin Middle School

July 5, 2014: Yanping district
    8:00 All go to Xiayang by bus; divide into two teams; one team photograph in town; the other team go to Xiaomei Village and Duxi Village;
    12:00 lunch in Jiangsi Village, Xiayang Town;
    13:00 after lunch, interview in Langshi New Village, Jiangsi New Village, Xiayang Hydropower station;
    14:00 all go to Shangxikou Village of Wangtai Town to photograph former site of Soviet revolution;
    15:00 go to Wangtai Town and divide into two teams; one team photograph Yuewangtai, Bajiao Building, Taiping Drum, Huanglong team; the other team go to Xihou Village.

July 6, 2014: Yanping District
    8:00 set off to Mangdang Town; go to Maodi Village to photograph Ruilong Bridge;
    11:00 go to Zhubo Village;
    12:00 lunch at Zhubao Village;
    13:00 go to Shaxikou hydropower via Laizhou Town; divided into two teams; one team interview at Shaxikou hydropower, She song, Yuanyang stone, etc; the other team interview at Yufeng Temple, Kaiping Temple, etc.

July 7, 2014: 8:00 return to Fuzhou after breakfast

闽江
大型影像文化创作工程

行走拍摄记录 / 闽江正源采访拍摄路线
The photographing itinerary - Journey to the source of the River Min

2014 年 10 月 26 日：建宁
　　福州出发至泰宁（动车站接厦门摄影家），至建宁，绕道溪源乡（金溪支流大田溪）拍摄竹叶隘及上坪村，拍摄大岭村傩舞。
　　晚上宿建宁。
　　建宁拍摄题材：建莲、报国寺、红色旅游、鸳鸯湖、万安桥、宜黄戏。

2014 年 10 月 27 日：建宁
　　分五路前往1、黄坊乡（黄坊溪）邱家隘。2、杉溪村百丈隘。3、里心镇（桂阳溪）甘家隘、船顶隘，拍摄打银舞，新坪村花钵灯舞、龟蚌舞。4、客坊乡苏茜隘、大子峒，拍摄伞舞。
　　晚上宿建宁。

2014 年 10 月 28 日：建宁、宁化
　　上午前往均口台田村闽江源，经过龙头村拍宜黄戏，台田村拍摄马灯舞。
　　午餐后前往宁化县。
　　下午在宁化安远镇（宁溪）拍摄稻草龙、岩前赤壁等。
　　晚上宿宁化。

2014 年 10 月 29 日：宁化县、清流县
　　分两队拍摄，一队赴闽江主流水茜镇（水茜溪），拍摄踩地故事、水茜藩维桥已有 500 余年历史、沿口木偶戏班、铸造）以及河龙（石门山祁剧、贡米、辣椒干、鲤鱼干）、中沙（叶坊傀儡戏）。
　　一队赴客家祖地石壁拍摄。（治平乡下坪村茜坑组胡兰山玉扣纸）、

活字印刷，夏坊村古游傩等内容。
　　前往清流，晚上宿清流。

2014 年 10 月 30 日：清流县
　　一队以沙芜乡为中心，拍摄九龙湖风景区（清流人）。九龙溪支流长潭河，过赖坊，最远达李家，拍摄李家五经魁。
　　一队赴长校，拍摄长校打银打锡，灵台山定光大佛、十番锣鼓、冷泉。
　　一队北上至嵩溪、林畲。拍摄嵩溪豆腐皮制作、返回龙津镇拍摄三角戏。
　　晚上宿清流。

2014 年 10 月 31 日：永安
　　由清流前往永安，经安砂镇（安砂双塔步云塔和仰世塔），至九龙溪与文川溪交界处，至文川溪小陶镇，拍摄甘乳岩、抗战第一村石峰村、拍摄正远楼、允升楼、永峙楼、固吾圉堡、永盛楼等五座土堡）、洪田镇（林改第一村、大科畲族村祖传图、黄坑土堡、东山土堡、易安楼洋尾土堡等土堡）。
　　晚上宿永安。

2014 年 11 月 1 日：永安市
　　一队拍摄贡川镇，拍摄廊桥、临水宫、陈氏大宗祠、草席、燕西街道办事处吉山村的上吉山土堡、文龙村的复兴堡，以及桃源洞风光。

一队拍摄槐南镇（尤溪上游安贞堡、安贞旌鼓、张大阔公做场戏）、青水畲族乡（青水大腔戏、傩狮、畲族竹竿舞、过坑村福临堡、光坑村岗陵堡、曲尺丘村敦仁堡、三房村福安堡、炉丘村成志堡治元堡等古建筑）。
　　晚上宿永安。

2014 年 11 月 2 日：三明市
　　由永安前往三明，一队前往三元区岩前镇、莘口镇（忠山村历史文化名村：百年栳格式栳、千年寨忠山村十八寨、万年居万寿岩、旧石器时代遗址、浮桥式石桥）。
　　一队拍摄三明钢铁厂。
　　一队拍摄沙溪水上公园以及自行江边寻找拍摄内容。
　　晚上宿三明。

2014 年 11 月 3 日：沙县
　　拍摄淘金山长达 38 米的华夏第一岩雕卧、罗岩山风景区佛、东南沿海现存最大的城隍庙，以及"十里平流"、"七峰叠翠"、"洞天瀑布"、"二十八曲"等自然景观，拍摄琅口古码头。
　　拍摄沙县肩膀戏。拍摄沙县小吃城、小吃制作。
　　宿沙县。

2014 年 11 月 4 日：沙县
　　上午拍摄青州镇及青州造纸厂。
　　下午返回，结束闽江正源采访拍摄。

Oct 26, 2014: Jianning
    set off from Fuzhou to Taining; arrive in Jianning; go to Xiyuan Village to photograph Zuye Pass and Shangping Village; then Nuo Dance in Daling Village;
    Stay in Jianning for the night

Oct 27, 2014: Jianning
    Divide into five teams to 1) Qiujia Pass in Huangfang Village; 2) Baizhang Pass in Shanxi Village; 3) Ganjia Pass, Chuanding Pass in Lixin Town, folk dances in Xinyu Village; 4) Zhuyu Pass in Kefang Village;
    Stay in Jianning for the night

Oct 28, 2014: Jianning, Ninghua
    Go to the source of the River Min in Taitian Village, Junkou Town; photograph Yihuang Drama in Longtou Village and Madeng Dance in Taitian Village;
    Go to Ninghua County after lunch;
    Photograph in Anyuan Town, Ninghua County in the afternoon;
    Stay in Ninghua for the night

Oct 29, 2014: Ninghua, Qingliu
    Divide into two teams; one team go to Shuiqian Town to photograph Fanwei Bridge of over 500 years' history, as well as Helong Village and Zhongsha Village; the other team go to Shibi Village, the origin of the Hakkas;
    Go to Qingliu and stay there for the night

Oct 30, 2014: Qingliu
    One team photograph Jiulong Lake Resort in Shawu Village;
    One team go to Changxiao and Lingtaishan Mountain;
    One team go to the Songxi River and Linshe Village and Longjin Town;
    Stay in Qingliu for the night

Oct 31, 2014: Yong' an City
    Go to Yong' an from Qingliu via Ansha Town; go to the convergence of the Jiulongxi River and the Wenchuanxi River; go to Xiaotao Town to photgraph Ganru Cave, Shifeng Village, etc., and Hongtian Town;
    Stay in Yong' an for the night

Nov 1, 2014: Yong' an City
    One team go to Gongchun Town to photograph covered bridge, ancestral hall, Fuxingbao, etc.;
    One team go to Huainan Town, Shezu Village;
    Stay in Yong' an for the night

Nov 2, 2014: Sanming City
    Go to Sanming from Yong' an; one team go to Yanqian Town and Shenkou Town;
    One team photograph Sanming Steel Plant;
    One team photograph Shaxi Water Park;
    Stay in Sanming for the night

Nov 3, 2014: Shaxian County
    Photograph Taojinshan Mountain, Luoyanshan Mountain, City God Temple and other natural scenery, Langkou dock;
    Photograph the opera and snacks in Shaxian;
    Stay in Shaxian for the night

Nov 4, 2014: Shaxian County
    Photograph Qingzhou Papermaking Plant in the morning;
    Return in the afternoon

闽江

大型影像文化创作工程

行走拍摄记录 / 第四次闽江行走拍摄线路

The photographing itinerary - The fourth journey:

2014 年 12 月 26 日：福州，延平

　　上午福州、厦门人员在福州集中出发前往南平。南平午餐（延平区）；下午采访拍摄南平市区（以"闽江零公里"为拍摄主题），宿南平（延平区）。

2014 年 12 月 27 日：延平

　　前往夏道镇（大洲贮木场、安济村、铁路新旧线），太平镇沿线拍摄风光，太平镇拍摄地理和民俗。太平午餐。宿南平。

2014 年 12 月 28 日：延平

　　上午前往樟湖坂，分两组，一组前往小支流武步溪经巨口到达洋后。一组在樟湖镇拍摄。下午一组前往尤溪口镇拍摄，一组前往西滨镇拍摄，傍晚前往尤溪县。宿尤溪。

2014 年 12 月 29 日：尤溪

　　尤溪拍摄。宿尤溪

2014 年 12 月 30 日：古田

　　前往古田，上午在黄田镇拍摄，下午前往平湖镇拍摄，一小组前往屏南长桥镇。宿古田。

2014 年 12 月 31 日：古田，闽清

　　前往水口镇拍摄。傍晚前往闽清，路经雄江。宿闽清黄褚林。

2015 年 1 月 1 日：闽清

　　休整，上午讨论 2015 年《闽江》工程后续事宜。下午出发前往水口电站拍摄。宿闽清。

2015 年 1 月 2 日：闽清，永泰

　　上午前往闽清（坂东宏琳厝等）拍摄。宿永泰。

2015 年 1 月 3 日：永泰，福州

　　上午前往嵩口镇拍摄，途经梧桐镇。宿福州。

2015 年 1 月 4 日：福州

　　前往琅岐岛，完成全部闽江拍摄。宿壶江岛（全程采访结束总结会）。

2015 年 1 月 5 日：全体人员返回福州，厦门人员返程。

Dec 26, 2014: Fuzhou, Yanping

Set off from Fuzhou to Nanping in the morning; lunch in Nanping; Photograph Nanping in the afternoon; stay in Nanping for the night

Dec 27, 2014: Yanping

Go to Xiadao Town and Taiping Town; lunch at Taiping; Stay in Nanping for the night

Dec 28, 2014: Yanping

go to Zhanhuban; divide into two teams; one team go to the Wubuxi River and arrive at Yanghou via Jukou; one team photograph in Zhanghu Town;

In the afternoon, one team go to Youxikou Town and one team go to Xibing Town;

Stay in Youxi County for the night

Dec 29, 2014: Youxi. photograph Youxi County and stay there for the night

Dec 30, 2014: Gutian

go to Tutian; photograph in Huangtian Town in the morning and Pinghu Town in the afternoon; one team go to Changqiao Town, Pingnan County; stay in Gutian for the night

Dec 31, 2014: Gutian, Minqing

go to Shuikou Town; go to Minqing via Xiongjiang Town in the evening; stay in Huangchulin of Minqing

Jan 1, 2015: Minqing

rest and discussion in the morning; Go to Shuikou Hydropower Station in the afternoon;

Stay in Minqing for the night

Jan 2, 2015: Minqing, Yongtai.

go to Minqing in the morning; stay in Yongtai for the night

Jan 3, 2015: Yongtai, Fuzhou.

go to Songkou Town via Wutong Town; stay in Fuzhou for the night

Jan 4, 2015: Fuzhou

go to Langqi Island and finish the photographing of the River Min; Stay in Hujiang Island for the night

Jan 5, 2015: all members return to Fuzhou

行走拍摄记录 / 第五次闽江行走拍摄线路

The photographing itinerary - The fifth journey:

分组：

漂流航拍小组：阮任艺　小陈　林雷伟　阿苏

城市小组：崔建楠　赖小兵　吴寿华　郑巍　小辛

补拍小组：那兴海

2015 年 5 月 16 日、17 日：富屯溪光泽

　　光泽（16 号下午及傍晚城区航拍看点、17 号清晨城区航拍，清晨至
　　下午从源头司前岱坪漂流至城关，18 号清晨补拍城关后离开光泽，
　　沿溪漂流航拍，晚餐前到达邵武。航拍人员跟拍一段漂流，中午前
　　到达邵武）

　　1、河流与城市：梅树湾道路改造，北溪铁路桥、县政府、南部新区（16
　　号下午拍摄，傍晚拍摄）、两溪交会处高楼带全景（17 日清晨拍摄），
　　傍晚夜景。

　　2、企业：圣农集团航拍

　　3、水电站：漂流中选择合适电站拍摄，人物、设备。（雷伟、小陈）

　　4、乡镇：岱坪源头山景、司前乡全景、寨里高家水库、崇仁乡。

5、街巷、城关西南茶市街（酒厂、码头、古桥）

6、八月补拍油溪量桥（七月初六至初七）。

补拍内容：1、源头小村岱坪。2、光泽民俗馆馆长。3、城关水边。

2015 年 5 月 18 日、19 日：富屯溪邵武

　　漂流组 18 号出发一天到邵武过夜，19 号由邵武至卫闽，20 号由卫闽
　　到顺昌。航拍组 18 号一早出发往邵武，沿途拍漂流，午餐后前往和
　　平古镇航拍河流与乡镇、傍晚返回城关航拍、19 号清晨航拍城区，
　　然后追漂流至卫闽。专号组 18 号全天洽谈（赖总主谈）及城区补拍，
　　19 号专号补拍。

　　1、城市基础设施建设：全景（早晚）、夜景。人民广场、"太极景
　　　　观文化墙"工程、火车站、市政府。

　　2、企业：国家"小三线"工业建设基地。

　　3、乡镇：和平古镇（航拍）、拿口镇、卫闽镇。

　　4、补拍信仰内容：博物馆（宝岩寺）、齐天宫、惠安庙（福建最早
　　　　的土地庙）。邵武民间无诸庙。坎下五通庙（五通神）。晒口街
　　　　道水塔山妈祖庙。东关张王庙（张巡）。

2015 年 5 月 20 日：富屯溪顺昌

　　漂流组 20 号傍晚到达顺昌、21 号驱车前往建宁，中午到达建宁。航
　　拍组 20 号下午到达顺昌，傍晚城关两溪汇合处航拍、21 号清晨航拍
　　城关全景然后前往建宁中午到达。专号组 20 号一早出发至顺昌，20
　　号顺昌全天洽谈专号及补拍，21 号专号补拍。22 号前往泰宁。

　　1、城市基础设施建设：全景，两溪相交处（早晚）、城关夜景。市政府。

　　2、乡镇：洋口古镇（航拍）、浦上镇、大干镇。燕子坪畲族自然村

　　3、补拍信仰内容：宝山大圣崇拜。

　　4、补拍城关水边、合掌岩石雕师傅个人及合影、

　　注：受强降雨影响，闽江水超过警界水位，闽江采访团取消了建宁之
　　后的计划。

Teams:

Canoeing team: Ruan Renyi, Xiaochen, Lin Leiwei, Asu

Urban team: Cui Jiannan, Lai Xiaobing, Wu Shouhua, Zheng Wei, Xiaoxin

Make-up team: Na Haixing

May 16 and 17, 2015: Guangze, the Futunxi River

Guangze: on 17th: aerial photograph of the city; canoeing from Daiping to city gate;

On 18th: make-up photograph in city and canoeing till Shaowu in the evening

1. river and city: road reconstruction in Meishuwan, railway bridge in Beixi, county government, panorama of the convergence of the two rivers, night scenes

2. enterprise: Shengnong Group

3. hydropower station: during canoeing

4. town and village: mountain view of Daiping Village, Siqian Village, Gaojia Reservoir, Chongren Village

5. streets, docks, ancient bridges

6. make-up photograph in Youxi

Make-up photographing contents: 1. Daiping Village; 2. Yang Mengling, head of folk museum; 3. City gate

May 18 and19, 2015: Shaowu, the Futunxi River

The canoeing team set off on 18th to Shaowu, from Shaowu to Weimin (19th), from Weimin to Shunchang (20th);

The aerial photo team set off on 18th to Shaowu; to Heping Town after lunch; photograph urban area and follow the canoeing team till Weimin on 19th; make-up photograph urban area on 18th and 19th.

1. urban infrastructure facilities: panorama and night scenes: People's Square, cultural wall, railway station, municipal government

2. enterprise: industrial construction base

3. town and village: ancient Heping Town, Nakou Town and Weimin Town

4. belief make-up photographing contents: Baoyan Temple, Qitiangong, Hui' an Temple, Wuzhu Temple, Wutong Temple, Matsu Temple, Zhangwang Temple

May 20, 2015: Shunchang, the Futunxi River

The canoeing team arrive in Shunchang in the evening of 20th; arrive in Jianning by van on 21st;

The aerial team arrive in Shunchang in the afternoon of 20th and photograph at the convergence of the two river; panorama of the city gate on 21st; arrive in Jianning at noon; the special issue team set off on 20th to Shunchang; make-up photograph on 21st and leave for Taining on 22nd.

1. Urban infrastructure facilities: panorama, convergence, night scenes of city gate, municipal government

2. Village and town: Yangkou Town, Pushang Town, Dagan Town, Shezu natural village

3. belief make-up photographing contents: worship of Monkey King in Baoshan

4. city gate, rock carving worker

Due to the heavy rainfall, the water level of the River Min exceeded its warning line. The interview plan after Jianning was cancelled.

行走拍摄记录 / 第六次闽江行走拍摄线路
The photographing itinerary - The sixth journey:

分组：
漂流组：小阮、阿苏等
闽江组：政委、焦社、伟凯、李世雄（21号加入）、郑巍
专号组：赖社、吴寿华等

2015年6月10日：漂流组出发到达建瓯，补拍封面故事、航拍两溪交汇等。（宿建瓯）
2015年6月11日：漂流组建瓯补拍"闽江"连载内容。（宿建瓯）
2015年6月12日：漂流组前往武夷山自然保护区，下午试漂流，试航拍桐木源头、
　　　　　　　分水关、黄岗山、桐木村、桐木溪漂流等。（宿保护区）
2015年6月13日：漂流组由桐木漂至星村，航拍星村镇、九曲竹筏码头。（宿武夷山）
2015年6月14日：漂流组由星村漂至三姑，航拍晒布岩、玉女、大王、三姑。（宿
　　　　　　　武夷山）
2015年6月15日：漂流组武夷山，航拍武夷山各点。（宿武夷山）
2015年6月16日：漂流组武夷山，航拍武夷山各点。（宿武夷山）
2015年6月17日：漂流组前往城村，航拍城村地形及古越城。（宿兴田）
2015年6月18日：
　　1、漂流组全天漂至建阳，航拍建阳城关及建溪南浦溪交汇处（宿建阳）。
　　2、闽江组、专号组福州出发，中午到达政和，专号组下午谈专号或者
　　　　航拍政和城关，闽江组拍摄政和廊桥等"闽江"内容。（宿政和）
2015年6月19日：
　　1、漂流组一早出发由建阳到达屏南长桥镇，下午航拍长桥（万安桥），
　　　　准备20号拍摄走桥。（宿屏南）

2、上午闽江组赖总、政委、焦社拍摄政和"闽江"内容，下午前往花
　　桥拍摄新娘茶，准备拍摄走桥。
3、专号组上午航拍城关，或者洽谈专号。下午拍摄"闽江"内容。（宿
　　政和）

2015年6月20日：
　　1、漂流组拍摄屏南长桥走桥，下午返回松溪与专号组汇合，阿苏返回
　　　　福州。
　　2、闽江组赖副、政委等拍摄政和花桥走桥。政委、焦社、伟凯下午前
　　　　往武夷山自然保护区。（宿保护区）
　　3、专号组上午拍摄花桥走桥，下午前往松溪（含赖总）。松溪航拍，
　　　　拍摄松溪"闽江"内容。（宿松溪）

2015年6月21日：
　　1、闽江组政委、焦社采访桐木村。
　　2、伟凯采访梁骏德，然后与政委焦社一起傍晚出保护区。（宿武夷山）
　　3、专号组、漂流组航拍松溪城关，拍摄松溪"闽江"内容。（宿松溪）
　　4、李老师到达武夷山（机场）与闽江组汇合，小陈到达松溪与漂流组
　　　　汇合。

2015年6月22日：
　　1、闽江组政委焦社李老师上午大安村、黄连坑村采访，下午樟村村采
　　　　访，李老师吴屯、岚谷一线拍摄民间信仰。（宿武夷山）
　　2、伟凯武夷山采访陈德华等。（宿武夷山）
　　3、专号组、漂流组前往浦城，上午专号组洽谈专号，下午航拍浦城城
　　　　关等。漂流组航拍临江桥，由临江漂流至观前村，航拍观前村。（宿
　　　　浦城）

2015年6月23日：
　　1、闽江组政委焦社伟凯李老师前往建阳，下午政委焦社补拍坳头村，
　　　　李老师拍摄麻阳溪一线，伟凯拍摄手工艺建盏三兄弟。（宿建阳）
　　2、专号组上午浦城谈专号方案或航拍城关，补拍城市河流。下午前往
　　　　建阳。（宿建阳）
　　3、漂流组由观前漂流至水吉。（宿水吉）

2015年6月24日：
　　1、闽江组政委焦社建阳修整或者返回福州，李老师拍摄城关民间信仰。
　　2、闽江组伟凯下午采访手工艺。（宿建阳）
　　3、专号组建阳航拍或洽谈专号。（宿建阳）
　　4、漂流组漂流至建阳。（宿建阳）

2015年6月25日：
　　1、专号组前往建瓯，航拍建瓯及洽谈专号。（宿建瓯）
　　2、漂流组漂流至建瓯。（宿建瓯）
　　3、闽江组伟凯采访手工艺或返回厦门，李老师拍摄建瓯民间信仰。

2015年6月26日：
　　1、专号组建瓯航拍或洽谈专号，下午前往顺昌。（宿顺昌）
　　2、漂流组漂流至南平。（宿南平）
　　3、李老师返回厦门。

2015年6月27日：
　　1、专号组航拍顺昌，谈专号。（宿顺昌）
　　2、漂流组到达顺昌，航拍顺昌。（宿顺昌）

2015年6月28日：专号组崔、寿华拍摄元坑关帝文化节，漂流组上宝山拍摄。
2015年6月29日：全体返回。

Teams:

The canoeing team: Xiaoruan, Ashu

Mingjiang team: political commissar, Chief Jiao, Weikai, Li Shixiong, Zheng Wei

Special issue team: Chief Lai, Wu Shouhua

June 10, 2015: the canoeing team set off to Jian'ou; aerial photograph river convergence; stay in Jian'ou for the night

June 11, 2015: the canoeing team photograph in Jian'ou and stay there for the night

June 12, 2015: the canoeing team go to Wuyishan Nature Reserve and trial canoeing in the afternoon; trial aerial photograph the source of the Tongmuxi River, Guangganshan Mountain, Tongmu Village, etc; stay in the Reserve for the night

June 13, 2015: the canoeing team drift from Tongmu to Xincun Town; aerial photograph Xincun Town and Jiuqu bamboo raft dock; stay in Wuyishan for the night

June 14, 2015: the canoeing team drift from Xincun to Sangu; aerial photograph Shaibuyan, Yunv, Dawang, Sangu; stay in Wuyishan for the night

June 15, 2015: the canoeing team: Wuyishan; the aerial photo team: Wuyishan; stay in Wuyishan for the night

June 16, 2015: the canoeing team: Wuyishan; the aerial photo team: Wuyishan; stay in Wuyishan for the night

June 17, 2015: the canoeing team go to Chengcun Village; the aerial team photograph Chengcun Village and ancient Yue town; stay in Xingtian for the night

June 18, 2015: 1. The canoeing team drift to Jianyang; the aerial team photograph Jianyang and the convergence of the Jianxi River and Nanpuxi River; stay in Jianyang for the nigh

2. the Minjiang team and special issue team set off from Fuzhou and arrive in Zhenghe at noon; photograph Zhenghe city gate and covered bridge; stay in Zhenghe for the night

June 19, 2015: 1. The canoeing team set off from Jianyang to Changqiao Town; aerial photograph Wan'an Bridge in the afternoon; stay in Pingnan for the night;

2. the Minjing team photograph the River Min in Zhenghe in the morning and bride's tea in the afternoon;

3. the special issue team photograph city gate in the morning and the River Min in the afternoon; Stay in Zhenghe for the night

June 20, 2015: 1. The canoeing team photograph Zou Bridge in Changqiao; return to Songxi and meet the special issue team

2. the Minjiang team photograph Zou Bridge and Hua Bridge; go to Wuyishan Nature Reserve in the afternoon;

3. the special issue team photograph Zou Bridge and Hua Bridge in the morning; go to Songxi in the afternoon; photograph the River Min in Songxi; stay in Songxi for the night

June 21, 2015: 1. the Minjiang team interview in Tongmu Village;

2. Weikai interview Liang Junde and go to the Reserve in the evening; stay in Wuyishan for the night;

3. The special issue team and the canoeing team photgraph Songxi city gate and the River Min in Songxi; stay in Songxi for the night;

4. Mr. Li arrive in Wuyishan and meet the Minjiang team; Xiaochen arrive in Songsi and meet the canoeing team

June 22, 2015: 1.The Minjiang team interview in Da'an Village and Huangliankeng Village in the morning; interview in Zhangcun Village in the afternoon; Mr. Li photograph folk beliefs in Wutun and Ganggu; stay in Wuyishan for the night;

2. Weikai interview Chen Dehua in Wuyishan; stay in Wuyishan for the night;

3. The special issue team and the canoeing team go to Pucheng; the canoeing team photograph Linjiang Bridge and drift to Guanqian Village; stay in Pucheng for the night

June 23, 2015: 1. The Minjiang team go to Jianyang; photograph Aotou Village, the Mayangxi River and Tea Cup brothers; stay in Jianyang for the night;

2. The special issue team discuss in Pucheng in the morning and go to Jianyang in the afternoon; stay in Jianyang for the night;

3. The canoeing team drift to Shuiji from Guangqian; stay in Shuiji for the night

June 24, 2015: 1. The Minjiang team rest in Jianyang or return to Fuzhou; Mr. Li photograph folk beliefs;

2. Weikai interview craftsman in the afternoon; stay in Jianyang for the night;

3. The special issue team aerial photograph Jianyang; stay in Jianyang for the night;

4. The canoeing team drift to Jianyang and stay there for the night

June 25, 2015: 1. The special issue team go to Jian'ou and stay there for the night;

2. The canoeing team drift to Jian'ou and stay there for the night;

3. Weikai interview craftsman or return to Xiamen; Mr. Li photograph folk belief in Jian'ou

June 26, 2015: 1. The special issue team aerial photograph Jian'ou; go to Shunchang in the afternoon; stay in Shunchang for the night;

2. The canoeing team drift Nanping and stay there for the night;

3. Mr. Li return to Xiamen

June 27, 2015: 1. The special issue team aerial photograph Shunchang and stay there for the night;

2. The canoeing team arrive in Shunchang and stay there for the night

June 28, 2015: the special issue team photograph Guandi cultural festival in Yuankeng; the canoeing team go to Baoshan

June 29, 2015: all return

闽江
大型影像文化创作工程

行走拍摄记录 / 第七次闽江行走拍摄线路
The photographing itinerary - The seventh journey:

2015 年 11 月 21 日：明溪
　　福州出发经三明到达明溪，下午明溪采访，明溪住宿。
　　下午航拍组拍摄明溪城关，全国体育先进县，闽西最大体育中心。
　　一组拍摄南山塔洞穴遗址（城关溪边）和坪埠万春桥、一组拍摄夏阳紫云岩画（东面夏阳乡）。一组拍摄玉虚洞、杨时故里。

2015 年 11 月 22 日：明溪
　　上午一组拍摄盖洋镇翠竹洋村宝石，一组拍摄夏坊乡苎畲村回龙桥，夏坊乡高洋村徐家古宅。
　　下午一组拍摄夏阳乡御帘村（廊桥书院等），一组拍摄聚龙禅寺（西面较远和夏坊临近）。

2015 年 11 月 23 日：明溪，往将乐
　　上午一组采访明溪美食肉脯干、淮山，一组采访红豆杉。一组拍摄胡坊镇胡坊村下街"古民居一条街"。
　　一组拍摄侯继美明溪县宝石加工厂、宝剑（孙丙祥）、宝扇等。

下午（傍晚）航拍组拍摄将乐城关，其他成员拍摄城市景观、金溪两岸、擂茶广场等。宿将乐。

2015 年 11 月 24 日：将乐
　　上午一组采访玉华洞、天阶山森林公园、杨时墓等，一组前往中国历史文化名村良地村拍摄。
　　下午一组拍摄将乐南词、擂茶，一组前往万全乡常口村的太平山麓证觉寺。宿将乐。

2015 年 11 月 25 日：将乐
　　上午一组拍摄龙栖山（云海观景、水杉小径、余家坪、鹿园、龙潭）。一组前往美丽乡村光明际下村、并拍摄将乐龙池砚。

2015 年 11 月 26 日：泰宁
　　一早前往泰宁。泰宁尚书巷前全体人员合影留念，随后拍摄尚书第、泰宁老街。

下午一组拍摄民俗鱼灯（赖、伟凯），一组拍摄城关水边活动。
晚上一组拍摄泰宁热气球嘉年华彩排，一组拍摄梅林戏演出。

2015 年 11 月 27 日：泰宁
　　上午航拍大赤壁，航拍大金湖全景。下午航拍城关。
　　上午其他人员漂流九龙潭并拍摄。
　　下午采访泰宁历史文化：闽越王无诸行宫、甘露岩寺、李家岩。

2015 年 11 月 28 日：泰宁，福州
　　上午拍摄泰宁城关内容。
　　下午厦门老师返回厦门，福州老师返回福州。

Nov 21, 2015: Mingxi

Set off from Fuzhou; go to Mingxi via Sanming; interview in Mingxi in the afternoon; stay in Mingxi for the night;

Aerial photograph Mingxi city gate in the afternoon, sports center;

One team photograph Nanshan Cave site, Wanchun Bridge; one team photograph Ziyunyan rock carving; one team photograph Yuxu Cave, Yangshi home village

Nov 22, 2015: Mingxi

In the morning, one team photograph gems in Cuizuyang Village, Gaiyang Town; one team photograph Huilong Bridge in Zhushe Village, Xu's old mansion in Gaoyang Village;

In the afternoon, one team photograph Yulian Village, Xiayang Town; one team photograph Julong Temple

Nov 23, 2015: Mingxi, Jiangle

In the morning, one team interview about the food in Mingxi; one team interview about Chinese yew; one team photograph the ancient street in Hufang Village; one team photograph gem processing factory of Mingxi County;

In the afternoon, aerial photo team photograph Jiangle city gate; the other members photograph urban landscape, banks of the Jinxi River, Leisha Square

Nov 24, 2015: Jiangle

In the morning, one team go to Yuhua Cave, Tianjieshang Forest Park, Yangshi Tomb; one team go to Liangdi Village;

In the afternoon, one team photograph Jiangle Nanci Opera, Lei Tea; one team go to Zhengjue Temple in Changkou Village

Nov 25, 2015: Jiangele

In the morning, one team photograph Longqi Mountain; one team go to Jixia Village and photograph Longchi inkstone

Nov 26, 2015: Taining

Go to Taining in the morning; group photo for all members at Shangshuxiang; photograph Shangshudi and ancient streets;

In the afternoon, one team photograph folk fish lantern; one team photograph activities at the river;

In the evening, one team photograph the rehearsal of hot balloon carnival; one team photograph Meilin opera performance

Nov 27, 2015: Taining

Aerial photo Red Cliff, Great Jinhu Lake in the morning and city gate in the afternoon;

The rest drift to Jiulongtan in the morning;

Interview about the history and culture of Taining in the afternoon; Ganluyuan Temple, Lijiayan

Nov 28, 2015: Taining, Fuzhou

Photograph city gate of Taining in the morning;

Return Xiamen or Fuzhou in the afternoon

福建文艺发展基金资助项目
Supported by Fujian Arts Development Fund

总 顾 问：刘瑞州　林 彬

总 策 划：崔建楠

学术顾问：徐希景

主　编：崔建楠

责任编辑：辛丽霞　薛瑜婷

摄　影：曾 璜　焦红辉　李世雄　弗兰克（美）

那兴海　曲利明　赖小兵　吴寿华

周跃东　郭晓丹　王鹭佳　陈伟凯

陈勇鹏　吴 军　阮任艺　崔建楠

撰　文：崔建楠

出 版 人：林 彬（女）

出版发行：海峡书局

出　品：福建画报社

学术支持：中国画报协会学术研究部

图片后期：大扬影像

Chief consultant: Liu Ruizhou Lin Bin

Producer: Cui Jiannan

Academic advisor: Xu Xijing

Editor-in-chief: Cui Jiannan

Editor: Xin Lixia Xue Yuting

Photographer: Zeng Huang　Jiao Honghui　Li Shixiong
Frank (US)　Na Xinghai　Qu Liming
Lai Xiaobing　Wu Shouhua　Zhou Yuedong
Guo Xiaodan　Wang Lujia　Chen Weikai
Chen Yongpeng　Wu Jun　Ruan Renyi
Cui Jiannan

Copy Writer: Cui Jiannan

Publisher: Lin Bin (female)

Publication and Distribution: The Straits Publishing House

Production: Fujian Pictorial

Academic Support: Academic Section of China Association
of Pictorials

post-production: Dayang Image

鸣 谢：
Acknowlegements:

福建省委宣传部　　海峡出版发行集团

福建省旅游局　　　福州市人民政府

南平市人民政府　　三明市人民政府

Publicity department of Fujian Provincial Party Committee

The Straits Publishing and Distributing Group

Fujian Tourist Administration

People's Government of Fuzhou City

People's Government of Nanping City

People's Government of Sanming City

鸣 谢:

Acknowlegements:

南平市委宣传部　　三明市委宣传部　　福州市委宣传部

光泽县委宣传部　　邵武市委宣传部　　顺昌县委宣传部

武夷山市委宣传部　浦城县委宣传部　　松溪县委宣传部

政和县委宣传部　　建阳市委宣传部　　建瓯县委宣传部

延平区委宣传部　　建宁县委宣传部　　宁化县委宣传部

清流县委宣传部　　永安市委宣传部　　沙县县委宣传部

尤溪县委宣传部　　闽清县委宣传部　　古田县委宣传部

闽侯县委宣传部　　永泰县委宣传部

The Publicity Department of Nanping Municipal Party Committee
The Publicity Department of Sanming Municipal Party Committee
The Publicity Department of Fuzhou Municipal Party Committee

The Publicity Department of Guangze County Party Committee / The Publicity Department of Shaowu Municipal Party Committee / The Publicity Department of Shunchang Municipal Party Committee / The Publicity Department of Wuyishan Municipal Party Committee / The Publicity Department of Pucheng County Party Committee / The Publicity Department of Songxi County Party Committee / The Publicity Department of Zhenghe County Party Committee / The Publicity Department of Jianyang Municipal Party Committee / The Publicity Department of Jian' ou County Party Committee / The Publicity Department of Yanping District Party Committee / The Publicity Department of Jianning County Party Committee / The Publicity Department of Ninghua County Party Committee / The Publicity Department of Qingliu County Party Committee / The Publicity Department of Yong' an Municipal Party Committee / The Publicity Department of Shaxian County Party Committee / The Publicity Department of Youxi County Party Committee / The Publicity Department of Minqing County Party Committee / The Publicity Department of Gutian County Party Committee / The Publicity Department of Minhou County Party Committee / The Publicity Department of Yongtai County Party Committee

图书在版编目（ C I P ）数据

闽江 / 崔建楠主编 . -- 福州 ：海峡书局，2016.3
ISBN 978-7-5567-0184-1

Ⅰ．①闽… Ⅱ．①崔… Ⅲ．①闽江－画册 Ⅳ．
① K928.42 － 64

中国版本图书馆 CIP 数据核字（2015）第 321210 号

责任编辑：辛丽霞　薛瑜婷

书　　名：闽江	
主　　编：崔建楠	
出版发行：海峡出版发行集团 海峡书局	
地　　址：福州市东水路 76 号出版中心 12 层	
网　　址：www.hcsy.net.cn	
邮　　编：350001	
设　　计：深圳市佳正航设计印刷有限公司	
印　　刷：雅昌文化（集团）有限公司	
开　　本：787×1092 毫米 1/8	
印　　张：64	
版　　次：2016 年 3 月第 1 版	
印　　次：2016 年 3 月第 1 次印刷	
ISBN 978-7-5567-0184-1	
定　　价：2380.00 元	

CIP Data

The River Min/ Cui Jiannan --Fuzhou: The Straits Publishing House. Mar. 2016
ISBN 978-7-5567-0184-1

I. ① Min… Ⅱ. ① Cui… Ⅲ. ① The River Min - picture album Ⅳ. .
① K928.42 - 64

China Archives of Publications (2015) No. 321210

Editor: Xin Lixia Xue Yuting

Title: the River Min
Editor-in-chief: Cui Jiannan
Publisher: The Straits Publishing House. The Straits Publishing and Distributing Group.
Address: Floor 12. Publishing Center. 76 Dongshui Road. Fuzhou City
Website: www.hcsy.net.cn
Postcode: 350001
Designed by: Jiazhenghang Designing and Printing Ltd. Company
Printed by: Artron Art (Group) Co.. Ltd.
Format: 787×1092 mm 1/8
Pringting Sheets: 64
Edition: first published in Mar 2016
Impression: first print
ISBN 978-7-5567-0184-1
Price: RMB 2380.00